JAMES

PREACHING THE WORD
Edited by R. Kent Hughes

Genesis | R. Kent Hughes

Exodus | Philip Graham Ryken

Leviticus | Kenneth A. Mathews

Numbers | Iain M. Duguid

Deuteronomy | Ajith Fernando

Joshua | David Jackman

Judges and Ruth | Barry G. Webb

1 Samuel | John Woodhouse

2 Samuel | John Woodhouse

1 Kings | John Woodhouse

Job | Christopher Ash

Psalms, vol. 1 | James Johnston

Proverbs | Raymond C. Ortlund Jr.

Ecclesiastes | Philip Graham Ryken

Song of Solomon | Douglas Sean O'Donnell

Isaiah | Raymond C. Ortlund Jr.

Jeremiah and Lamentations | R. Kent Hughes

Daniel | Rodney D. Stortz

Matthew | Douglas Sean O'Donnell

Mark | R. Kent Hughes

Luke | R. Kent Hughes

John | R. Kent Hughes

Acts | R. Kent Hughes

Romans | R. Kent Hughes

1 Corinthians | Stephen T. Um

2 Corinthians | R. Kent Hughes

Galatians | Todd Wilson

Ephesians | R. Kent Hughes

Philippians, Colossians, and Philemon | R. Kent Hughes

1–2 Thessalonians | James H. Grant Jr.

1–2 Timothy and Titus | R. Kent Hughes and Bryan Chapell

Hebrews | R. Kent Hughes

James | R. Kent Hughes

1–2 Peter and Jude | David R. Helm

1–3 John | David L. Allen

Revelation | James M. Hamilton Jr.

The Sermon on the Mount | R. Kent Hughes

(((PREACHING *the* WORD)))

JAMES

FAITH THAT WORKS

R. KENT HUGHES

:: CROSSWAY®

WHEATON, ILLINOIS

James

Copyright © 1991 by R. Kent Hughes

Published by Crossway
       1300 Crescent Street
       Wheaton, Illinois 60187

Cover design: Jon McGrath, Simplicated Studio

Cover image: Adam Greene, illustrator

First printing 1991

ESV edition 2015

Printed in China

Hardcover ISBN: 978-1-4335-3846-9
ePub ISBN: 978-1-4335-3849-0
PDF ISBN: 978-1-4335-3848-3
Mobipocket ISBN: 978-1-4335-3847-6

Library of Congress Cataloging-in-Publication Data

Hughes, R. Kent.
  James : faith that works / R. Kent Hughes
  ISBN 13: 978-0-89107-627-8
  ISBN 10: 0-89107-627-1
    p. cm.—(Preaching the word)
  Includes bibliographical references and indexes.
    1. Bible. N.T. James—Commentaries. I. Title. II. Series:
Hughes, R. Kent. Preaching the word.
BS2785.3.H84   1991
227'.9107—dc20   91–3298

Crossway is a publishing ministry of Good News Publishers.

RRDS		31	30	29	28	27	26	25	24	23	22	21
16	15	14	13	12	11	10	9	8	7	6	5	4

For my brother
Robert Steven Hughes,
a practical book
for a practical man

For as the body apart from the spirit is dead,
so also faith apart from works is dead.

JAMES 2:26

Contents

Acknowledgments		9
A Word to Those Who Preach the Word		11
1	Count It All Joy (1:1–4)	15
2	If Any of You Lacks Wisdom (1:5–8)	23
3	Wisdom for the Humble and the High (1:9–12)	31
4	The Source and Course of Temptation (1:13–15)	39
5	The Goodness of God (1:16–18)	47
6	Accepting the Word (1:19–21)	55
7	Doing the Word (1:22–25)	63
8	Acceptable Religion (1:26, 27)	71
9	The Folly of Favoritism (2:1–7)	79
10	The Perils of Favoritism (2:8–13)	89
11	Real Faith, Part 1 (2:14–19)	97
12	Real Faith, Part 2 (2:20–26)	105
13	The Peril of Teaching (3:1, 2)	115
14	The Mighty Tongue (3:3–12)	123
15	Wisdom from Below (3:13–16)	131
16	Wisdom from Above (3:17, 18)	139
17	Troubles' Source (4:1–3)	147
18	He Gives Us More Grace (4:4–6)	155
19	The Gravity of Grace (4:7–10)	163
20	Watch What You Say (4:11, 12)	171
21	*Deo Volente* (4:13–17)	179
22	Riches That Corrode (5:1–6)	189
23	Patient Till He Comes (5:7–9)	199
24	The Perseverance of Job (5:10, 11)	207
25	Straight Talk (5:12)	219

26   The Divine Prescription for Healing (5:13–16)   229

27   The Prayer of the Righteous (5:16–18)   237

28   Spiritual Reclamation (5:19, 20)   245

Notes   253

Scripture Index   275

General Index   285

Index of Sermon Illustrations   291

Acknowledgments

I must express appreciation to my secretary, Mrs. Sharon Fritz, for her professional expertise and care in typing the manuscript of these studies; also to Mr. Herbert Carlburg for his cheerful, weekly proofreading, and to Mr. Ted Griffin, Managing Editor of Crossway Books, for his painstaking editing.

A Word to Those Who Preach the Word

There are times when I am preaching that I have especially sensed the pleasure of God. I usually become aware of it through the unnatural silence. The ever-present coughing ceases and the pews stop creaking, bringing an almost physical quiet to the sanctuary—through which my words sail like arrows. I experience a heightened eloquence, so that the cadence and volume of my voice intensify the truth I am preaching.

There is nothing quite like it—the Holy Spirit filling one's sails, the sense of his pleasure, and the awareness that something is happening among one's hearers. This experience is, of course, not unique, for thousands of preachers have similar experiences, even greater ones.

What has happened when this takes place? How do we account for this sense of his smile? The answer for me has come from the ancient rhetorical categories of *logos*, *ethos*, and *pathos*.

The first reason for his smile is the *logos*—in terms of preaching, God's Word. This means that as we stand before God's people to proclaim his Word, we have done our homework. We have exegeted the passage, mined the significance of its words in their context, and applied sound hermeneutical principles in interpreting the text so that we understand what its words meant to its hearers. And it means that we have labored long until we can express in a sentence what the theme of the text is—so that our outline springs from the text. Then our preparation will be such that as we preach, we will not be preaching our own thoughts about God's Word, but God's actual Word, his *logos*. This is fundamental to pleasing him in preaching.

The second element in knowing God's smile in preaching is *ethos*—what you are as a person. There is a danger endemic to preaching, which is having your hands and heart cauterized by holy things. Phillips Brooks illustrated it by the analogy of a train conductor who comes to believe that he has been to the places he announces because of his long and loud heralding of them. And that is why Brooks insisted that preaching must be "the bringing of truth through personality." Though we can never *perfectly* embody the truth we preach, we must be subject to it, long for it, and make it as much a part of our ethos as possible. As the Puritan William Ames said, "Next to the Scriptures, nothing makes a sermon more to pierce, than when it comes out of the inward affection of the heart without any affectation." When a preacher's *ethos* backs up his *logos*, there will be the pleasure of God.

Last, there is *pathos*—personal passion and conviction. David Hume, the Scottish philosopher and skeptic, was once challenged as he was seen going to hear George Whitefield preach: "I thought you do not believe in the gospel." Hume replied, "I don't, but *he does*." Just so! When a preacher believes what he preaches, there will be passion. And this belief and requisite passion will know the smile of God.

The pleasure of God is a matter of *logos* (the Word), *ethos* (what you are), and *pathos* (your passion). As you *preach the Word* may you experience his smile—the Holy Spirit in your sails!

R. Kent Hughes
Wheaton, Illinois

James, a servant of God and of the Lord Jesus Christ, To the twelve tribes in the Dispersion: Greetings. Count it all joy, my brothers, when you meet trials of various kinds, for you know that the testing of your faith produces steadfastness. And let steadfastness have its full effect, that you may be perfect and complete, lacking in nothing.

1:1–4

1

Count It All Joy

THE PROSPECT OF STUDYING the book of James is inviting for several reasons. To begin with, it was apparently written before the famous Council of Jerusalem in AD 49, which means it is probably the oldest of the twenty-seven books of the New Testament, and thus reflects Jewish-Christian teaching in its initial stages of development.[1] Next, because it was composed before Paul's writings, James discusses the subject of faith and works independently from Paul's teaching. James and Paul do not contradict each other, but rather supplement each other. James approaches faith *subjectively*—in the sense of trust or confidence in the Lord, while Paul explains it *objectively*—as the instrument by which a believer is justified before God.[2]

The Epistle of James enlarges our practical understanding of faith. To be sure, Paul is practical, but normally he begins with an imposing theological argument (for example, Romans 1—11 or Ephesians 1—3) and then gives practical exhortation (for example, Romans 12—16, Ephesians 4—6). James, however, begins right off with a series of practical admonitions and continues on nonstop to the end. E. J. Goodspeed has called James' discussion "just a handful of pearls, dropped one by one into the hearers' mind."[3] Some see twenty-five major divisions, others twelve, some four, and some as few as two. One thing is clear—the dominant theme is, *faith that is real works practically in one's life. That is, true faith is a faith that works.*

James shows us how to have a living, visible, productive faith in a fallen world. In this respect, it is significant that this brief book has fifty-four imperatives.[4] James is a "Do this! Do that!" book that, taken to heart, will dynamically affect our lives on every level. We will not be the same at the end of this study if we prayerfully ask the Spirit to apply what we learn.

James' brief greeting in verse 1—"James, a servant of God and of the Lord Jesus Christ, To the twelve tribes in the Dispersion: Greetings"—serves as an excellent introduction to his letter, introducing us to the author, his self-perception, and his pastoral focus.

James the Man

James was none other than a blood-brother, a half-brother, of the Lord Jesus Christ. The Gospels mention this fact (see Matthew 13:55; Mark 6:3). Apparently he was at first an unbeliever—"For not even his brothers believed in him" (John 7:5). However, during the forty-day period between Jesus' resurrection and his ascension, Jesus "appeared to James, then to all the apostles"—and James believed (1 Corinthians 15:7). James is mentioned as being in the upper room in Jerusalem, praying with his mother and the rest of the disciples (Acts 1:13) and was presumably present when the Holy Spirit descended at Pentecost. He had become the leader of the Jerusalem church when Peter was released from prison (Acts 12:17), and eventually he chaired the Council of Jerusalem (Acts 15:13ff.; 21:18; Galatians 1:19; 2:9, 12).

James was a late bloomer, but he flowered well! James knew Christ as only a few could. For years he had eaten at the same table, shared the same house, played in the same places, and watched the development of his amazing older brother. And when he truly came to *know* Christ, his boyhood privilege was not wasted, for he became known as James the Just, a man of immense piety. The historian Eusebius records the testimony of Hegesippus that James "used to enter alone into the temple and be found kneeling and praying for forgiveness for the people, so that his knees grew hard like a camel's because of his constant worship of God, kneeling and asking forgiveness for the people. So from his excessive righteousness he was called the Just."[5]

James' Self-Perception

James had so much going for him, yet merely viewed himself as "a *servant* of God and of the Lord Jesus Christ." This is remarkable in a world that then, and now, parades its heredity, for James had immense ground on which to pull rank. He could have begun his letter, "James the Just, from the sacred womb of Mary, congenital sibling of Christ his brother, confidant of the Messiah." But James did not even allude to this status, being content with "servant" (cf. Mark 10:45; Philippians 2:5–8; Romans 12:7). James the Just was also James the Humble and so was eminently qualified to author Holy Scripture.

James' Pastoral Focus

Humble James writes pastorally to "the twelve tribes in the Dispersion." The Jews' scattering, known as the *Diaspora*, began in 722 B.C. when the Assyrians deported the ten northern tribes. Later the southern tribes suffered the same fate when the Babylonians took them captive in 586. Because of this, Jews were spread all over Mesopotamia, around the Mediterranean, and into Asia Minor and Europe (cf. Acts 2:5, 9–11). Some of the major cities of the world—Alexandria, for example—had large populations of expatriate Jews. Also, when Jewish Christians were first persecuted in Jerusalem after the death of Stephen, they fled first to Judea and Samaria (Acts 8:1) and then to Jewish communities around the Mediterranean (Acts 11:19, 20). Tragically these Jewish Christians were not taken in by their expatriate Jewish kinsmen, but rather were rejected and persecuted.

Further, refused protection by the Jewish community, these Jewish Christians were exploited by the Gentiles. Homeless and disenfranchised, they were robbed of what possessions they had, hauled into court, and subjected to the Gentile elite. They had less standing than slaves. They became religious, social, and economic pariahs. A good way to get a feel for their position is to read modern post-Holocaust Jewish writers such as Elie Wiesel. It is to these Jewish Christian brothers, mistreated ex-parishioners of James' church, that Pastor James sends his letter.

James' "Irrational" Call (v. 2)

James wastes no time getting to his imperatives: "Count it all joy, my brothers, when you meet trials of various kinds" (v. 2). Has James lost his senses? He is writing to beat-up brothers and sisters and he says, "Count it all joy," or as the NEB says, "count yourselves supremely happy." How nice . . . a letter of encouragement from Pastor Whacko! "Don't worry . . . be happy!" Then and now James' command to "Count it all joy . . . when you meet trials of various kinds" sounds irrational! Put this verse on a sign next to the expressway and it would appear to be the work of a crazed fanatic. Indeed, to any culture (including ours) determined to insulate itself from trials, even from discomforts, this sounds crazy. Tragically, it even seems irrational to many who identify with Christianity.

What does James' command really mean? In answer, we must first understand what it does *not* mean. James is not ordering *all-encompassing joyful emotion* during severe trials; nor is he demanding that his readers must *enjoy* their trials, or that trials are *joy*. He knew, as did the writer of Hebrews, that "For the moment all discipline seems painful rather than pleasant" (Hebrews 12:11).

James was not commanding that we exult upon hearing that our career position has been given to our secretary, or that the neighbor's children have leukemia, or that one's spouse is adulterous. Rather, James is commending the conscious embrace of a Christian understanding of life that brings joy into the trials that come because of our Christianity. James says, "*Count* it all joy," which means to make a deliberate and careful decision to experience joy even in times of trouble. Is this possible? Yes. Paul told the Corinthian church, "In all our affliction, I am overflowing with joy" (2 Corinthians 7:4). Luke reports that when the Sanhedrin "called in the apostles, they beat them and charged them not to speak in the name of Jesus, and let them go. Then they left the presence of the council, rejoicing that they were counted worthy to suffer dishonor for the name" (Acts 5:40, 41). Later, Luke tells us, Paul and Silas, having been severely flogged and being in intense pain, were in prison, and "About midnight Paul and Silas were praying and singing hymns to God, and the prisoners were listening to them" (Acts 16:25). Their concert so pleased God that he brought down the house! This apostolic experience is still the experience of the church today.

Several years ago the Presbyterian pastor Lloyd John Ogilvie underwent the worst year of his life. His wife had undergone five major surgeries, plus radiation and chemotherapy, several of his staff members had departed, large problems loomed, and discouragement assaulted his feelings. But he wrote,

> The greatest discovery that I have made in the midst of all the difficulties is that I can have joy when I can't feel like it—artesian joy. When I had every reason to feel beaten, I felt joy. In spite of everything, [God] gave me the conviction of being loved and the certainty that nothing could separate me from him. It was not happiness, gush, or jolliness but a constant flow of the Spirit through me. At no time did he give me the easy confidence that everything would work out as I wanted it on my timetable, but that he was in charge and would give me and my family enough courage for each day: grace. Joy is always the result of that.[6]

James did not say, "Count it all joy, my brothers, *if* you meet trials" but "*when*." Such trials are a part of every believer's life. We are to thoughtfully find joy in our own *diaspora* experiences—when we feel alienated, disenfranchised, unpopular, even when difficulty and tragedy come our way that have no apparent connection with our Christianity. Such joy may seem irrational, but in Christ it is perfectly rational.

The Rationale for the Irrational Call (vv. 3, 4)

The rationale for such joy comes from knowing that the various trials we face have spiritual value. James says there is a two-step process through which our trials elevate us.

The first step is to understand that "*the testing of your faith produces steadfastness*" (v. 3) Elaboration on what is meant by "steadfastness" will unlock rich truth. J. H. Ropes renders this "staying power."[7] Martin Dibelius calls it "heroic endurance."[8] And the NEB translates this as "fortitude." James is talking about toughness—"the testing of your faith produces *toughness*."

Here is how this works: we develop toughness or fortitude by repeatedly being tested and *prevailing*. The more tests we pass, the tougher we become. As a boxer engages in bout after bout, he toughens and becomes wiser and stronger. After a time he develops such fortitude, perseverance, and staying power that he can take on the best. There is no way a fighter, or any of us, can develop toughness without testing! The endurance and fortitude of the Apostle Paul or William Carey or Corrie ten Boom did not come overnight and did not come apart from trials. Paul, in Romans 5:3, confirms this truth: "but we rejoice in our sufferings, knowing that suffering produces endurance."

My experience in raising children has helped me understand how God views our testing. When my wife and I were young parents and our oldest child was in the first grade, we bought her a winter coat. We had intentionally bought a size too large, but it was a marvelous blue, fluffy, mock-fur coat with gold buttons down the front. The day after we bought it, a most unusual thing happened in California. It rained! It was a perfect day to wear her coat.

I never will forget how she looked as she went out the door—dressed in red boots, her blue coat with gold buttons, a little white knit hat, yellow yarn around her pigtails, and a red umbrella. We were so proud of her. It did not matter that her coat was a little long at the sleeves and at the hem. She was so happy as she walked out the door and down the driveway. Barbara and I stood behind the foggy windowpanes, watching her go.

Two little friends approached from down the street. Although I could not hear them, I saw one of them point at our daughter's hair, and I knew she was saying something like, "Your hair looks dumb!" Then she pointed to the hem of my daughter's coat, and my temperature went up. The little girls marched off to school. Holly trudged slowly behind.

I really wanted to set those little girls straight! But I knew that if I continued to step in whenever she experienced such difficulties, she might not develop fortitude and staying power—qualities she now has in abundance!

Nature teaches us the same principle. Free a butterfly from its chrysalis, and thus from the struggle of liberating itself, and you destroy its life, for it will never develop the strength to soar as it should. When fortitude is lacking in one of God's children, he has a time-tested remedy—"the testing of your faith." With this in mind, James' irrational call—"Count it all joy, my brothers, when you meet trials of various kinds"—becomes brilliant.

The rationale becomes even clearer when we observe the second step: *perseverance produces maturity.* "And let steadfastness have its full effect, that you may be perfect and complete, lacking in nothing" (v. 4). Spiritual perseverance or toughness produces a *dynamic maturity.* "Perfect" refers to a personality that has reached its full development. Regarding the corresponding synonym "complete," Peter Davids explains: "Perfection is not just a maturing of character, but a rounding out as more and more 'parts' of the righteous character are added."[9] Thus, maturity is a dynamic state in which a thousand parts of us are honed, shaped, tempered, and brought together, making a dynamic wholeness.

It is commonly taught that trials bring maturity, but it is not so. Rather, fortitude and perseverance in times of testings produce maturity. In troubled times we must practice spiritual toughness. As we endure "trials of various kinds"—economic stress, disappointments, criticisms, domestic pressures, persecution for our faith, illnesses—the multiple facets of our being are touched with grace. Dick Seume wrote beautifully about this:

> Life on earth would not be worth much if every source of irritation were removed. Yet most of us rebel against the things that irritate us, and count as heavy loss what ought to be rich gain. We are told that the oyster is wiser; that when an irritating object, like a bit of sand, gets under the "mantle" of his shell, he simply covers it with the most precious part of his being and makes of it a pearl. The irritation that it was causing is stopped by encrusting it with the pearly formation. A true pearl is therefore simply a victory over irritation. Every irritation that gets into our lives today is an opportunity for pearl culture. The more irritations the devil flings at us, the more pearls we may have. We need only to welcome them and cover them completely with love, that most precious part of us, and the irritation will be smothered out as the pearl comes into being. What a store of pearls we may have, if we will![10]

The key to a graced life, pearl-tipped facets of personality, and thus full maturity is constancy, tenacity, perseverance. *Spiritual toughness is the key to saintliness!*

The idea that when we "get it all together" our trials will lessen is a falsehood. Paul told Timothy the truth: "Indeed, all who desire to live a godly life in Christ Jesus will be persecuted" (2 Timothy 3:12). Life will always be full of testings for the true Christian. We must not imagine they will lessen with time—say, fewer trials at thirty-five than twenty-five, or at forty-five than thirty-five, or at fifty-five than forty-five, or at sixty-five than fifty-five, or at seventy-five than sixty-five. Trials are not a sign of God's displeasure but are opportunities to persevere in the Lord.

James commands the irrational: "Count it all joy, my brothers, when you meet trials of various kinds." Is this crazy talk—pious prattle? Not when we embrace the double rationale:

1) Testing brings spiritual toughness—"for you know that the testing of your faith produces steadfastness" (v. 3). When we, by God's grace, tough it out, our entire person becomes pearly.
2) Toughness brings a dynamic maturity—"And let steadfastness have its full effect, that you may be perfect and complete, lacking in nothing" (v. 4).

When God wants to drill a man
And thrill a man
And skill a man,
When God wants to mold a man
To play the noblest part;
When He yearns with all His heart
To create so great and bold a man
That all the world shall be amazed,
Watch His methods, watch His ways!
How He ruthlessly perfects
Whom He royally elects!
How He hammers him and hurts him,
And with mighty blows converts him
Into trial shapes of clay which
Only God understands;
While his tortured heart is crying
And he lifts beseeching hands!
How He bends but never breaks
When his good He undertakes;
How He uses whom He chooses
And with every purpose fuses him;
By every act induces him
To try His splendor out—
God knows what He's about![11]

Such logic makes the command rational and supremely sane: "Count it all joy, my brothers, when you meet trials of various kinds." James calls for a decisive act—to consider our troubles opportunities for joy and endurance. May we in prayer so acknowledge today and in days to come!

If any of you lacks wisdom, let him ask God, who gives generously to all without reproach, and it will be given him. But let him ask in faith, with no doubting, for the one who doubts is like a wave of the sea that is driven and tossed by the wind. For that person must not suppose that he will receive anything from the Lord; he is a double-minded man, unstable in all his ways.

1:5–8

2

If Any of You Lacks Wisdom

JAMES 1:5–8

AN UNKNOWN AUTHOR of another century wrote this timeless poem:

My life is but a weaving,
between my Lord and me;
I cannot choose the colours.
He worketh steadily.
Ofttimes He weaveth sorrow
and I in foolish pride,
Forget He sees the upper
and I the under side.
Not till the loom is silent
and the shuttles cease to fly,
Shall God unroll the canvas
and explain the reason why,
The dark threads are as needful
in the Weaver's skillful hand,
As the threads of gold and silver,
in the pattern He has planned.

This old poem correctly expresses the truth that in this life we will never fully understand the particular blending of joys and woes in our lives because we see only the underside of the tapestry. Only when death stills the loom and we stand before God will he turn the canvas over and allow us, to our eternal delight, to see what he has done.

However, we must not think we cannot understand anything of what God is doing or that the mixture of trials and joys in our lives is totally inscrutable, for it is not so. In James' opening words (1:1–4) he informs the suffering church that testing develops perseverance (spiritual fortitude) and that as they tough it out they will develop a dynamic maturity, becoming "perfect and complete, lacking in nothing" (1:4b). We can understand something of the process, and this is why he has called the suffering church to "Count it all joy" (1:2a).

The problem immediately apparent to any who have experienced the various trials of life is that while you are in the midst of them it is hard to understand what is going on and to believe they are for your benefit. It is easy to be the wise pastor assuring the hurting that they are being matured and to "hang tough." But it is another thing when *I* am the one being tested! It's much easier to say to someone else, "Count it all joy . . . when you meet trials of various kinds" than to joyfully embrace my own *angst*.

James, who was no armchair general, understood this, and in the closely connected verses that follow (vv. 5–8),[1] he instructs those who are suffering on how to get the wisdom necessary to plow victoriously through life's many trials. James, brother of one whose life was filled with trials and who died at the hands of murderers, is telling us how to lasso the bucking, uncontrollable trials of life and ride them to wisdom and triumphant spirituality. What he says ought to command our undivided attention.

Wisdom for the Asking (v. 5)

When we are in the midst of trials, we may reflexively cry out, "God, why me? There is nothing redemptive in my trial! Why does it go on?" Or, "Lord, get me out of this." But how many of us say, while being tested, "Lord, I need *wisdom*—please use this trial to increase my wisdom and understanding of you, your people, and life"? But that is exactly what James commands: "If any of you lacks wisdom, let him ask God" (v. 5a). What is this wisdom for which we are to ask? The idea becomes clear when we see what it is *not*.

It is *not* knowledge. Wisdom is far more than the accumulation of information and intellectual perception. The fact is, man, through his vast accumulation of knowledge, has learned to travel faster than sound, but displays his need of wisdom by going faster and faster in the wrong direction! Man has amassed a huge store of information about the world, but shows his abysmal lack of wisdom by failing to live any better in the world.[2]

Professor Allan Bloom touched on this in his best-selling book *The Closing of the American Mind*:

> My grandparents were ignorant people by our standards, and my grandfather held only lowly jobs. But their home was spiritually rich because all the things done in it, not only what was specifically ritual, found their

origin in the Bible's commandments, and their explanation in the Bible's stories and the commentaries on them, and had their imaginative counter-parts in the deeds of the myriad of exemplary heroes. My grandparents found reasons for the existence of their family and the fulfillment of their duties in serious writings, and they interpreted their special sufferings with respect to a great and ennobling past . . . [and then comes the punch] I do not believe that my generation, my cousins who have been educated in the American way, all of whom are M.D.s or Ph.D.s, have any comparable learning. When they talk about heaven and earth, the relations between men and women, parents and children, the human condition, I hear nothing but clichés, superficialities, the material of satire.[3]

Wisdom, therefore, in distinction to knowledge, is understanding for liv-ing. And *Biblical wisdom* is understanding for living that surpasses earthly wisdom. It is temporally and eternally practical. A. T. Robertson, the towering genius of Greek grammar, calls wisdom "the practical use of knowledge."[4] F. J. A. Hort, in his painstaking commentary, terms it "that endowment of heart and mind which is needed for right conduct in life."[5] J. H. Ropes de-scribes it as "the supreme and divine quality of the soul which man knows and practical righteousness."[6] And Ralph Martin in his study states, "For the Jewish mind wisdom meant practical righteousness in everyday living."[7]

The Scriptures teach that this practical wisdom is rooted in the fear/rev-erence of God. Job asked the question, "But where shall wisdom be found? And where is the place of understanding?" (Job 28:12). Then, as he variously discussed its whereabouts, he said in verse 15, "It cannot be bought for gold, and silver cannot be weighed as its price," and similarly in verse 18b, "the price of wisdom is above pearls." Further, he said in verses 23, 24, "God understands the way to it, and he knows its place. For he looks to the ends of the earth and sees everything under the heavens." And finally he concluded in verse 28, "And [God] said to man, 'Behold, the fear of the Lord, that is wisdom.'" That proclamation is a persistent motif in the Old Testament. Con-sider the following Scriptures:

> The fear of the LORD is the beginning of wisdom;
>> all those who practice it have a good understanding.
>> His praise endures forever! (Psalms 111:10)

> The fear of the LORD is the beginning of knowledge;
>> fools despise wisdom and instruction. (Proverbs 1:7)

> The fear of the LORD is the beginning of wisdom,
>> and the knowledge of the Holy One is insight. (Proverbs 9:10)

Because of this we must understand that Einstein may have been a genius in atomic theory, but if he had no fear of God he was a man without wisdom—which at one point in his life he indeed was. During a conference attended by outstanding churchmen and scientists, Albert Einstein read a paper in which he said: "In their struggle for the ethical good, teachers of religion must have the stature to give up the doctrine of a personal god."[8] God's Word says, "The fool says in his heart, 'There is no God'" (Psalm 14:1).

Wisdom begins with a healthy reverence for God. For the Christian, this is personally connected with Christ, "who became to us wisdom from God" (1 Corinthians 1:30). Jesus Christ is the perfect expression of the wisdom of God, and if we know him, we receive and are changed by his wisdom.

This practical knowledge for living is a gift from God. While we have its beginning in our reverence for God and a further endowment as we come alive in Christ, he has even more wisdom to give us—practical wisdom that will enable us to ride the trials of life to new spiritual heights.

The thrust of James' language in verse 5 is that God is just waiting for us to ask: "If any of you lacks wisdom, *let him ask God, who gives generously to all without reproach*, and it will be given him." In the original the phrase "God, who gives" graphically emphasizes giving as a grand characteristic of God. It reads literally, "let him ask the constantly giving God."[9] The Scriptures are replete with this facet of the character of God. "He himself *gives* to all mankind life and breath and everything" (Acts 17:25). "He *gave* his only Son, that whoever believes in him should not perish but have eternal life" (John 3:16). "He who did not spare his own Son but *gave* him up for us all, how will he not also with him graciously *give* us all things?" (Romans 8:32). God is like a pitcher tilted toward his children, just waiting to pour wisdom over the trial-parched landscape of their lives, if they will but ask.

Notice how James says God gives—"who gives generously to all without reproach." God will pour wisdom over us without putting us down or demeaning us. It is easy to wear out our human benefactors after they have repeatedly given to us, but not so with God. We will never encounter divine irritation, like "I gave you a head, why don't you use it?" or "What did you do with what I most recently gave you? Have you ever been thankful?" Rather, his response is, "I'm so glad you asked. Here it comes!"

The "trials of various kinds" (1:2) which come to us all are nothing less than gigantic opportunities to become wise. The geniuses among us have no head start on wisdom. If anyone has an edge, it is those who are undergoing testings with fortitude.

You and I will become wise if we are open to the wisdom God offers us.

"And this is the confidence that we have toward him, that if we ask anything according to his will he hears us" (1 John 5:14). We need to learn to ask for wisdom instead of getting angry and saying, "Why me?" By God's grace let us covenant to ask God for a large measure of that which he has promised.

Wisdom for the Believing (vv. 6–8)

Is there any condition we must meet in order to receive wisdom in our trials? Our text reveals the affirmative: *faith.* "But let him ask in faith, with no doubting, for the one who doubts is like a wave of the sea that is driven and tossed by the wind. For that person must not suppose that he will receive anything from the Lord; he is a double-minded man, unstable in all his ways" (vv. 6–8).

James' seafaring simile dramatically drives home the futility of doubt. I have only been seasick twice in my life. Once was as a junior-higher in a sixty-foot fishing boat off California's Coronado Islands, when the sea was so high that our boat disappeared in the trough of the waves while other boats rode the crests several stories above us, only to have the situation reverse a few seconds later. The other experience of *mal de mer* was on Lake Michigan. Lake Michigan has no wave pattern. When it gets rough, the surface goes up, down, sideways, even whirling. This is what James describes here (perhaps because his experience was the freshwater Sea of Galilee).

The eminent Greek scholar Marvin Vincent says, "The emphasis falls on *tossing*; moving before the impulse of the wind, but not even moving in regular lines; tossed into rising and falling peaks." Says another commentator, this created a "vivid picture of four dimensional instability."[10] The doubter is completely out of control. He is on a wild ride to nowhere.

James caps the description in verse 8: "he is a double-minded man, unstable in all his ways." He is literally a "two-souled" man. He has one soul that believes and one that does not. Bunyan called him "Mr. Facing-both-ways."[11]

Truly, and tragically, James' graphic description of a man bobbing like a cork on a raging sea, torn within by two souls, describes many in the church. And James' warning in verse 7 is all too applicable and appropriate: "For that person must not suppose that he will receive anything from the Lord." "That person" is a believer. He has received eternal life. He is indwelt by the Spirit. But his doubting, unstable, vacillating life means he will get no wisdom to help handle his troubles. He will not ride his trials onward and upward to spiritual maturity. What a tragic waste!

James has said, "But let him ask in faith, with no doubting" (v. 6) Like the writer of Hebrews, he sees faith as the essence of spiritual life: "And without faith it is impossible to please him, for whoever would draw near to God must believe that he exists and that he rewards those who seek him" (Hebrews 11:6). We must believe in the immense, omnipotent, holy God of Scripture and that he is equitable in giving to his own. In terms of our present passage, if we are in trials and *ask* for wisdom, truly believing, God will give it to us. It is as simple as that!

Is the Lord demanding perfect faith? Is he insisting that we never waver? I do not think so. If our faith had to be perfect, few would ever receive anything, for we are all doubters. Abraham and Moses were great men of God, but they were not perfect in their faith. Jesus honored the stumbling faith of the distraught father in the midst of testing—"I believe; help my unbelief" (Mark 9:24). Moreover, faith is a gift of God (Ephesians 2:8).

In mentioning the double-minded man, James is not referring to one who is wrestling with doubt, but one who has two minds. He looks to God; he says he has no need. We must ask wholeheartedly for the wisdom we need.

To be sure, we must wait until the loom is silent to see the tapestry God has woven from the bright and dark threads of our lives. Nevertheless, we can be given wisdom to understand something of what he is doing and embrace the process.

The testings of our lives
Make it possible for us
To become immensely wise.

God's pitcher, brimming with wisdom, is tilted over us. He is *the God who continuously gives*. And he is waiting for us to ask.

Long ago Solomon prayed for wisdom, asking God for "an understanding mind to govern your people, that I may discern between good and evil" (1 Kings 3:9). The Lord was so pleased that he said to him:

Because you have asked this, and have not asked for yourself long life or riches or the life of your enemies, but have asked for yourself understanding to discern what is right, behold, I now do according to your word. Behold, I give you a wise and discerning mind, so that none like you has been before you and none like you shall arise after you. (1 Kings 3:11b, 12)

The Lord is pleased to give wisdom and "gives generously to all without reproach" (v. 5).

Are we going through some testings now? If so, do we want to ride those wild things, so beyond our control, up to God? If we do, then let us *ask* him for wisdom *believing* and we will receive it, as the Apostle John has promised: "if we ask anything according to his will he hears us" (1 John 5:14).

> Wisdom has built her house;
>   she has hewn her seven pillars.
> She has slaughtered her beasts; she has mixed her wine;
>   she has also set her table.
> She has sent out her young women to call
>   from the highest places in the town,
> "Whoever is simple, let him turn in here!"
>   To him who lacks sense she says,
> "Come, eat of my bread
>   and drink of the wine I have mixed.
> Leave your simple ways, and live,
>   and walk in the way of insight." (Proverbs 9:1–6)

Let the lowly brother boast in his exaltation, and the rich in his humiliation, because like a flower of the grass he will pass away. For the sun rises with its scorching heat and withers the grass; its flower falls, and its beauty perishes. So also will the rich man fade away in the midst of his pursuits. Blessed is the man who remains steadfast under trial, for when he has stood the test he will receive the crown of life, which God has promised to those who love him.

1:9–12

3

Wisdom for the Humble and the High

JAMES 1:9–12

WEBSTER DEFINES A PARADOX AS "a statement that is seemingly contradictory or opposed to common sense and yet is perhaps true." An example of this is the statement, "giving is receiving." The Scriptures contain many paradoxes, telling us that the weak are strong, the empty are full, the slave is free, the cursed are blessed, and death brings life—all statements that first strike the ear as contradictory, but become increasingly true to us as we meditate on them. G. K. Chesterton gave this magnificent definition of a paradox: "a paradox is truth standing on its head shouting for attention." In my mind's eye I see truths lined up like ridiculous people on their heads, feet waving in the air, calling, "Hey, look at me! Up is down! Down is up! Think about it." Paradox is a powerful vehicle for truth, because it makes people think.

James, concerned that his pressured readers not succumb to instability, resorted to paradoxes in verses 9, 10 to convey stabilizing wisdom. First: "Let the lowly brother boast in his exaltation"—the paradox of the *rich poor*. And second: ". . . and the rich in his humiliation"—the paradox of the *poor rich*. Together these powerful paradoxes shouted with poignancy and effect to James' persecuted, scattered brethren, and they do the same for all today who feel out of sync with the prevailing culture, and especially to those suffering for their faith socially and economically.

The Rich Poor (v. 9)

The initial paradox of the *rich poor*—"Let the lowly brother boast in his exaltation"—powerfully emphasizes that *the low are high* because the first part of the verse reads literally, "the brother, the lowly,"[1] and "his exaltation" correspondingly reads, "in his height." So we can translate it, "The lowly brother ought to boast in his height!" The low are high!

Who are the low? The context demands that we understand them as poverty-stricken Jewish Christians who were poor because of their faith. And because they were economically low, they were low in the eyes of the world and, no doubt, in most instances low in their own eyes. Their poverty produced a lowliness of mind.

But James paradoxically says such a person ought to "boast in his exaltation." James' reasoning for this is implicit in the words of this verse: the man is a "brother." He is part of God's family, one of God's children. "And if [we are] children, then heirs—heirs of God and fellow heirs with Christ" (Romans 8:17a). This lowly brother is in fellowship with God, his people, and even his angels, as the writer of Hebrews explains: "But you have come to Mount Zion and to the city of the living God, the heavenly Jerusalem, and to innumerable angels in festal gathering, and to the assembly of the firstborn who are enrolled in heaven, and to God, the judge of all, and to the spirits of the righteous made perfect, and to Jesus, the mediator of a new covenant . . ." (Hebrews 12:22–24a). Moreover, as Peter says, "But you are a chosen race, a royal priesthood, a holy nation, a people for his own possession . . ." (1 Peter 2:9). If this man could but grab these stupendous realities and hang on, he would realize his height. The low are truly high!

The lowly must not only grasp this, but must also see that a mighty reversal is coming in which the low will be made high and the high low. A general once sat at a table in a royal court, seated beside the court chaplain. In the course of the meal the general turned to the chaplain and, to make conversation, asked, "Pastor, in this moment together here, could you tell me something about Heaven?" The court chaplain looked at him carefully and said, "Well, yes, I could. The first thing I would tell you, general, is that in Heaven you will not be a general."[2]

James is so sure of the grand reversal, and so sure that the low will become high, that he encourages the humble brother to "boast" in it. This is to be a joyous boasting. Paul uses the same word in Romans 5:2 speaking of rejoicing in the hope of glory and in Romans 5:11 to refer to rejoicing in reconciliation. Here James orders the lowly to paradoxically and cheerfully boast in their height.

Why does this great exaltation come to the poor man? It is not simply that he is economically poor, but that his poverty has produced in him a lowliness of spirit that keeps him open to God. Jesus' very first words of public ministry were a quotation from Isaiah 61:1—"The Spirit of the Lord is upon me, because he has anointed me to proclaim good news to the poor . . ." (Luke 4:18). This is why the Incarnation came through Mary, for as she affirmed in her Magnificat, "he has looked on the humble estate of his servant" (Luke 1:48). Luke quotes the first Beatitude this way: "Blessed are you who are poor, for yours is the kingdom of God" (Luke 6:20). Their economic poverty inclined them to spiritual poverty, as Matthew made clear in his record of the first Beatitude: "Blessed are the poor in spirit, for theirs is the kingdom of heaven" (Matthew 5:3). James did not pity his poor brethren or encourage their commiseration. Rather, he saw them as spiritually advantaged.

Here is wisdom for Christians of every age, all of whom live in a world that equates prosperity with happiness/God's blessing and humble circumstances with misery/God's displeasure. The lowly who are in the midst of hard times are tempted to doubt. No Christian who has been oppressed either economically or socially or both has not at some time doubted. Unamuno, the Spanish philosopher, said, "Those who believe that they believe in God, but without passion in their hearts, without anguish in mind, without uncertainty, without doubt, without an element of despair even in their consolation, believe only in the God idea, not God Himself."[3]

A living faith has its ups and downs because it is the faith of a living being who is imperfect and in process. But to the doubting, James stands deep spiritual truth on its head and shouts that Christians are the *rich poor*, the *low high*, and paradoxically commands that "the lowly brother [ought to] boast in his exaltation." This truth shouts for attention in our upside-down world! Perhaps no one needs to hear it more than rich Christians, the people to whom James aims the second paradox, to which we now turn.

The Poor Rich (vv. 10, 11)

We tend to think of the rich as overprivileged, but Jesus taught that they are underprivileged—spiritually. That is the indisputable point of the story of the rich young man who came to Jesus asking what he must do to inherit eternal life (Mark 10:17). Thus, after Jesus told him to sell all, he "went away sorrowful, for he had great possessions" (Mark 10:22). Jesus' resulting pronouncement—"Children, how difficult it is to enter the kingdom of God! It is easier for a camel to go through the eye of a needle than for a rich person to enter the kingdom of God" (Mark 10:24b, 25)—teaches categorically that it is impossible for a man or woman who *trusts* in riches to get into Heaven. Riches steel the unregenerate against the primary requirement for entering the kingdom of God: *helpless dependence* (see Matthew 5:3). It is difficult for the rich to present themselves as naked, humble beggars before God. Our rich culture is, therefore, disadvantaged and underprivileged.

But what about rich Christians, the small minority who in James' day had not suffered deprivation of wealth—at least not yet? Did their wealth present a problem? Of course it did, just as it does for rich Christians today. Material wealth lures the possessor to focus his or her attention on things. Jesus warned against "the deceitfulness of riches," which strangles spiritual life (Matthew 13:22). The greater one's possessions, the greater the likelihood of delusion. Jesus also categorically said, "You cannot serve God and money" (Matthew 6:24). In the Revelation the Lord warned against pride and independence: "For you say, I am rich, I have prospered, and I need nothing, not realizing that you are wretched, pitiable, poor, blind, and naked" (Revelation 3:17). Following this wisdom, Paul tells Timothy, "As for the rich in this present age, charge them not to be haughty, nor to set their hopes on the uncertainty of riches, but on God, who richly provides us with everything to enjoy" (1 Timothy 6:17). Those with great wealth tend to regard what they have as eternal. This is why some people want more and more and more. So many live under the illusion that their houses will go on forever.

The entire New Testament, as well as what we see in people's lives, suggests that riches are a potential danger to spiritual life. Jesus views them as a spiritual liability rather than an asset. His beatitude goes to the poor, not the rich. "You are blessed because your poverty directs your soul to me."

Realizing this, James' paradox of the poor rich makes good sense: "And the rich [should boast] in his humiliation" (v.10a).The last part can be rendered "lowliness" (it is the same word just used to describe the position of the poor). Calvin has it right: "He tells them to glory in their lowliness, their smallness, to restrain those lofty motives that swell out of prosperity."[4] In other words, the rich Christian is to cultivate the poverty of spirit he experienced when he came to Christ. He is to work at this lowliness, focus on it, and make it his boast.[5]

This has monumental implications for Christians today who live in western affluence. *For a believer, an immortal soul, to build his or her life on perishable riches is a debasement beyond description!* It is nothing less than spiritual prostitution (cf. 4:4). Furthermore, those who focus on their riches progressively diminish the measure of their eternal reward. If they are saved, it will be "only as through fire" (1 Corinthians 3:15). It is a delusion to suppose that once we become Christians we are to outgrow the initial salvific poverty of spirit. Never! Rather, this ought to become more and more pronounced. We, like Paul, must honestly and progressively see ourselves as "the foremost" of sinners (1 Timothy 1:15). Truth is standing on its head, crying out to us, "And the rich [should boast] in his humiliation" (v. 10). *This is wisdom!*

James' brilliant paradox can stand on its own, but he adds an illustration that drives it home with unforgettable force. He reaches back to the rich treasure of Old Testament illustration, especially Isaiah 40:6–8, and says, ". . . because like a flower of the grass he will pass away. For the sun rises with its scorching heat and withers the grass; its flower falls, and its beauty perishes. So also will the rich man fade away in the midst of his pursuits" (vv. 10b, 11).

Having lived in the arid climate of Southern California, I know what James is describing. In Palestine it is called a *sirocco*, and in the Los Angeles basin it is called a *Santa Ana*. Hot winds rush relentlessly off the desert for a period of several days so that even at midday the bare ground becomes so hot one cannot walk barefoot on it. The heat is so intense that plants must be watered at night or they will burn. I have seen this kind of desert wind turn a spring lawn and flowers into a parched brown patch in only a few days. The sun rises like a ball of fire bringing a furnace of heat, the flower hangs its head, and the petals fall from the calyx. As the original literally says, "the beauty of its face is destroyed."

This is the way it is for the rich, who bloom so ostentatiously in life. It is also true for the poor man, but James applies it especially to the rich because that man is more apt to think his flower is eternal. "So also will the rich man fade away in the midst of his pursuits" (v. 11b; cf. 4:14). His life will be like a parched dandelion in a sudden gust of wind. Poof! "That's all, folks!"

> Man is like a tender flower,
> And his days are like the grass,
> Withered where it lately flourished,
> By the blighting winds that pass.
>
> The Psalter Hymnal[6]

Life is transitory and ephemeral for us all. A mayfly, sometimes called an *ephemeron* (from the Greek word for day, *hemera*), has its lifetime in one day. What obvious folly if it were to spend that entire day weighing itself down with supposed "treasures" that must be dropped at sundown when it is no more. Likewise, how foolish for us mortal flowers of the field to glory in our riches, especially when there is an eternity beyond. Wise John Wesley (perhaps thinking of the mayfly) once wrote:

I am a creature of a day, passing through life as an arrow through the air. I am a spirit, coming from God, and returning to God; just hovering over the great gulf; a few months hence I am no more seen; I drop into an unchangeable eternity! I want to know one thing—the way to heaven . . .

Here the prayer of Joseph Bayly says it all: "Lord, burn eternity into my eyeballs!"

The Eternally Rich (v. 12)

James crowns his discussion with a beatitude promising eternal life: "Blessed is the man who remains steadfast under trial, for when he has stood the test he will receive the crown of life, which God has promised to those who love him" (v. 12). Perseverance, fortitude, toughing it out through the various trials of life that come to both the low and the high brings the divine compliment and prophecy "Blessed." Oh, the bliss of the man or woman who so perseveres. "He will receive the crown of life." Because this person is a believer, he already has eternal life, just as Jesus promised: "whoever hears my word and believes him who sent me *has* eternal life" (John 5:24; cf. 17:3). Therefore when he receives the crown of life he receives the final full endowment of life—*life indeed!*

The wise will choose what is best for the long run. The fool looks ahead five years, ten years, perhaps even twenty years and plans what he thinks will benefit him best. The wise fixes his sight beyond the grave, for he knows the high will be made low and the low high.

Wisdom cries aloud in the street,
    in the markets she raises her voice;
at the head of the noisy streets she cries out;
    at the entrance of the city gates she speaks:
"How long, O simple ones, will you love being simple?
How long will scoffers delight in their scoffing
    and fools hate knowledge?
If you turn at my reproof,
behold, I will pour out my spirit to you;
    I will make my words known to you." (Proverbs 1:20–23)

The beginning of wisdom is this: Get wisdom,
    and whatever you get, get insight.
Prize her highly, and she will exalt you;
    she will honor you if you embrace her.
She will place on your head a graceful garland;
    she will bestow on you a beautiful crown. (Proverbs 4:7–9)

Let no one say when he is tempted, "I am being tempted by God," for God cannot be tempted with evil, and he himself tempts no one. But each person is tempted when he is lured and enticed by his own desire. Then desire when it has conceived gives birth to sin, and sin when it is fully grown brings forth death.

1:13–15

4

The Source and Course
of Temptation

JAMES 1:13–15

A YOUNG WOMAN came to Christ in a marvelous way. Her conversion was, from a human perspective, partly due to the fact that she had come to a very low place in her marriage, making her intensely aware of her spiritual need. But having met Christ in her extremity, her life immediately took on an attractive buoyancy. She was truly a new person—and it was beautiful to behold. Sadly, her troubled husband did not follow suit as she had so dearly hoped. After a year of continuing marital disappointment, she sought help from a counselor. Instead of receiving help, she became the victim of a professional seduction. It began with extravagant sympathy, compliments about her attractiveness (ostensibly to shore up her fractured ego), then subtly suggestive comments. The next appointment, she dressed and scented herself with the palpitating self-attention of a first date. She was seduced, and there followed the inevitable history of liaisons and further damage to her fragile self-esteem.

When she came to my wife and me, she was a ruined person seething with bitterness and rage. To be sure, she was a victim of an unprincipled male in professional sheep's clothing, but she was also a victim of self. But amazingly it was neither to him nor herself that she placed ultimate blame. Rather, she said through clenched teeth, "I asked God to lead me to the right person, and he led me to this man. It is God's fault! He is to blame for what happened!"

This was the beginning of years of bitterness and estrangement from her Lord, ironically, the only one who loved her with an everlasting love. Most stories like this do not end well. Happily, I can say in this case she did repent, and after more than a decade her husband came to Christ. All this after the needless miseries of those terrible years!

This woman's absurd accusation was nothing new. In fact, we find the same thing at the beginning of human history when ridiculous Adam said to God, "The woman whom you gave to be with me, she gave me fruit of the tree, and I ate" (Genesis 3:12). Way to go, Adam! "And, yea, verily Adam and Eve did have 930 years more of marital bliss!" We may say, shame on Adam. But the truth is, none of Adam's children like to take the blame for sin, and we will do almost anything to escape it—blame others, blame our loved ones, even blame God.

Blaming the gods was typical of the pagan mind-set in Biblical times because their gods were capricious, vengeful, soap-opera deities who taunted and tantalized humanity. We read over and over again of Zeus and his pantheon in classical Greek writings like *The Odyssey*. Jewish believers, dispersed in various pagan cities by persecution, were not immune to this mind-set. Evidently in their misery certain of their people were saying God was tempting them to fall, that he had lost patience with them and was deliberately bringing them down.[1] This being so, God was to blame for their sin.[2]

Putting the blame elsewhere is popular in our culture. Will Rogers once remarked that there are two eras in American history—"the passing of the buffalo and the passing of the buck." Someone else has said, "To err is human; to blame it on the divine is even more human." How true this is of all of us!

Ordained. A common Christian delusion is to say that since God ordains everything, he has ordained that we succumb to sin. We may smile at this, but some have actually believed and practiced it. Some even carried it a step further—for example, the demonic monk Rasputin who controlled the Romanov family. Rasputin argued that those who sin more require more forgiveness and that those who sin with abandon will experience even greater forgiveness and joy. Therefore, it is the believer's holy duty to sin greatly! This is, of course, totally out of accord with the Scriptures, which teach us that God abhors sin with a perfect hatred. God never ordains or approves sin.[3]

Circumstances. Others fault God for placing them in circumstances that are simply too much for them. We see this in the student who cheats, rationalizing that God is to blame for giving him such a difficult professor and such a weak mind, or the thief who steals, blaming God for his poverty, or the drunkard who blames his partying friends. This thinking was also true of the young woman who was seduced by her counselor.

Disposition. The commonest delusion is that "God has given me passions

and appetites so strong, I can do nothing but yield to them." The Scottish poet
Robert Burns put it like this:

Thou know'st that Thou has formed me
With passions wild and strong;
And list'ning to their witching voice
Has often led me wrong.[4]

Burns blamed God for his sensual disposition. He made God responsible
for his sins. It was similar thinking that Nikos Kazantzakis celebrated in
Zorba the Greek, whom he presented as a kind of peasant superman whose
strength was displayed in his will to live out his appetites. In doing so, living
out his *elan vital*, he was following God, according to this view. Nonsense!

Today our culture celebrates this kind of man—an Ernest Hemingway
whose life of sensual indulgence is seen as "art." For him there is a right
way to drink a Margarita, to shoot an antelope, to eat a shrimp, to commit
adultery. A man or woman who fulfills his or her lusts with artistic style is
"authentic"—which means good.[5] But the truth is, however we rationalize
our behavior, yielding to our appetites is not divine but demonic.

The conclusion James comes to in the opening sentence of verse 13 is,
"Let no one say when he is tempted, 'I am being tempted by God.'" No one
can blame God by mouthing uninformed rationalizations about divine ordina-
tion or circumstances or disposition. The perverse intellectualizing of poets
and writers is not true. Adam's pathetic attempt, no matter how deceptively
rephrased by us, will not suffice. God's Word stands: we must never say, or
even *imagine*, that God is tempting us. He never has, and he never will!

James gives us the reason for this in the rest of verse 13: "for God cannot
be tempted with evil, and he himself tempts no one." This assertion that God
cannot be tempted is stressed by a rare verbal adjective that means that he
is "unable to be tempted"[6]—he is "untemptable."[7] The sense is that "God is
unsusceptible to evil; evil has never had any appeal for Him. It is repugnant
and abhorrent to Him."[8] Evil cannot promote even the slightest appealing tug
in the heart of God. Because he cannot be tempted to sin, James' conclusion
follows: "he himself tempts no one" to sin. God has never tempted us to sin
because he cannot! It is a moral impossibility. This is extremely important
because the human inclination from the Garden of Eden to this day is to
consciously, or at least subconsciously, blame God and thus try to palliate
our own feelings of guilt.

It is true, of course, that while God does not *tempt* us, he does *test* us
in order to prove and improve our character. The refrain from the Lord's

Prayer—"And lead us not into temptation, but deliver us from evil" (Matthew 6:13)—means, "Don't allow us to come under the sway of temptation that will overpower us and cause us to sin." This is a prayer that Jesus taught and that he certainly answers. As Paul says, "No temptation has overtaken you that is not common to man. God is faithful, and he will not let you be tempted beyond your ability, but with the temptation he will also provide the way of escape, that you may be able to endure it" (1 Corinthians 10:13).

The Source of Temptation (v. 14)

Having made a powerful defense of the character of God, James now describes the *source* of temptation in no uncertain words: "But each person is tempted when he is lured and enticed by his own desire" (v. 14). James well knew that Satan is busy tempting believers to sin (see 4:7), but he also knew that the root of the problem is our own evil. We should never be surprised by this, as was the young priest who served in the confessional for the first time, accompanied by an older senior priest. At the end of the day the older priest took him aside and said, "My boy, when a person finishes with confession, you have got to learn to say something other than, 'Wow!'"[9] We are all sinners and are frequently guilty of sins of commission and omission. (Regarding omission, I chuckle at the answer a little boy gave his Sunday school teacher: "Omission? They're the sins we should have committed but didn't get around to.")

Romans 5:12 tells us that we all "sinned" in Adam (aorist tense), which means that we share such solidarity with him that we actually sinned when he sinned. And, of course, we have verified this in our own lives a million times over. But the point is, having sinned in him, we share the same pathology to sin as Adam and Eve who fell to "the lust of the *flesh*" ("the woman saw that the tree was good for food"), "the lust of the *eyes*" ("a delight to the eyes"), and "the *pride of life*" ("to be desired to make one wise")—so that each one of us, as James says, is "tempted when he is lured and enticed by his own desire" (v. 14; cf. Genesis 3:6 and 1 John 2:16, KJV). This verse in James is one I have a good feel for, not only because of the pathology of my own heart, but because the language "lured and enticed" is the language of the fisherman, which is something I imagine myself to be.

One summer my wife, Barbara, and I and our boys spent a week fishing in northern Maine. In the final hour of the final day my boys caught the biggest smallmouth bass I have ever seen—five pounds, one ounce! Those are cosmic dimensions for a smallmouth bass! That old bass, the best I can tell, was over ten years old. For 3,650 days he had resisted every ploy known to man around Grand Lake Stream, Maine—until August 1989.

On that fateful afternoon my boys were slowly trolling a salmon-colored, soft plastic, spinner-bladed jig, innocuously named "Little Fishy," when it passed by the lair of the monster bass. The combination of the speed of the lure, its depth, the slant of the sun, and the refraction of the light ineluctably dragged the old bronze-backed bass away from his lair, just as the Greek word "lured" in our text describes. Then he began to follow the lure, "enticed," as our text has it, by its peculiar wiggle and the delicate fibrillations, so that he opened his mouth wide and in a sudden burst engulfed the jig. My boys' shouts echoed across the lake, and today that fish's grand, painted, mummified form graces my sons' wall. It was a remarkable experience, but not unique, for it is universal among fishermen. The ancient Greek Oppian used these same words to describe drawing a fish from its original retreat under a rock, so that it succumbs to the bait.[10]

James, in using these words, has graphically painted a picture of how we are tempted by our own illicit desires (lusts). When the temptation passes by, we are drawn away from the things that keep us safe. Soon they are far behind us as we are lured by the bright, delicious temptation, and in a moment we forget who and what we are and throw caution to the wind and bite. So it was for Eve and Adam and Samson and David and Demas and . . .

Bonhoeffer, in his book entitled *Temptation*, describes how this works:

> With irresistible power desire seizes mastery over the flesh. . . . It makes no difference whether it is sexual desire, or ambition, or vanity, or desire for revenge, or love of fame and power, or greed for money. . . . Joy in God is . . . extinguished in us and we seek all our joy in the creature. At this moment God is quite unreal to us, he loses all reality, and only desire for the creature is real . . . Satan does not here fill us with hatred of God, but with forgetfulness of God. . . . The lust thus aroused envelops the mind and will of man in deepest darkness. The powers of clear discrimination and of decision are taken from us. The questions present themselves: "Is what the flesh desires really sin in this case?" "Is it really not permitted to me, yes—expected of me, now, here, in my particular situation, to appease desire?" . . . It is here that everything within me rises up against the Word of God.[11]

This is so true! When we are in the grip of lust, God is never more distant. We forget who we are, who God is, and discount his Word. Is God at that time truly distant? Was he once real, but now only a faint mirage? If we think so, it is because we are fish-eyed over a lust, either material or immaterial—perhaps ambition or revenge or power or sex or fame. There is only one thing to do—turn tail and head for home and the safety of Christ. Do you need to turn around? Do I?

James could not be more explicit—the *source* of temptation is not God, or even the devil, but man's own sinful heart. Man is drawn away and then lured to the hook by his own lusts. He is accountable, and no one else! If we are in the grip of lust, the fault is ours and ours alone.

The Course of Temptation (v. 15)

Now, in no less explicit terms, James turns us from the *source* to the *course* of temptation: "Then desire when it has conceived gives birth to sin, and sin when it is fully grown brings forth death" (v. 15). This is the familiar language of childbirth. There are two births here. First, evil desire gives birth to sin. And second, sin gives birth to death. This second birth in the course of temptation ("and sin when it is fully grown brings forth death") is particularly chilling. The root idea of "brings forth" is, "ceases to be pregnant," emphasizing the inevitability of the process running its course. The idea is that sin grows rapidly, just as an embryo grows to maturity, and when it is full-grown, the state of pregnancy must end. But the horror here is, sin does not give birth to life, as would normally be expected, but to death![12] There are three mutant generations here: the mother is evil desire, the daughter is sin, and the granddaughter is death.[13] This death is spiritual and eternal—forever and forever.

In summary, we must never say, "I am being tempted by God." God's nature makes that a moral impossibility. The source of our sin is our "own desire" (v. 14). Temptations would not be tempting if it were not for our own evil desires. We must never say, "The devil made me do it" or "My friends made me do it" or "Circumstances made me do it" or "God made me do it." *We are responsible!*

Once the hook is in, there is a dreaded three-generational course: evil desire—sin—death (v. 15). But the cycle can be broken through solidarity with and submission to the second Adam, the Lord Jesus Christ. "For as by the one man's disobedience the many were made sinners, so by the one man's obedience the many will be made righteous" (Romans 5:19). Jesus is the *source* of victory over sin and temptation! And Jesus is the *course* of a life that triumphs over temptation: "I have been crucified with Christ. It is no longer I who live, but Christ who lives in me. And the life I now live in the flesh I live by faith in the Son of God, who loved me and gave himself for me" (Galatians 2:20).

This is the glory of the gospel. It breaks the power of sin and halts its inevitable train. If you are in the grip of temptation, take the eternally healthy step of admitting that you are to blame and no one else. Then, having confessed your responsibility fully to God, thank him for forgiveness and appropriate to yourself the life-giving solidarity you have in Christ.

Do not be deceived, my beloved brothers. Every good gift and every perfect gift is from above, coming down from the Father of lights with whom there is no variation or shadow due to change. Of his own will he brought us forth by the word of truth, that we should be a kind of firstfruits of his creatures.

1:16–18

5

The Goodness of God

JAMES 1:16–18

I HAVE GONE THROUGH much harder times in the ministry than what I am about to describe. In fact, anyone who has several years of Christian living under his or her belt has gone through much more difficult trials. But the significance of my experience is not in its degree of difficulty, but that it almost made me renounce my divine calling.

In retrospect my problem was rooted in, to borrow Charles Dickens's phrase, "great expectations." They began when, as a twelve-year old, I came to know Christ and felt called to preach, which meant to my inexperienced, preadolescent mind that only great things awaited me. The positive side of this was that my teenage years were full and focused on ministry, despite some notable ups and downs.

My expectations were further increased when at age sixteen I preached my first sermon on Jonah and the whale. It was a sermon of doubtful quality and dubious wit, full of one-liners like "God has a whale of a plan for your life," fleeing Jonah was "the chicken of the sea," etc. I even announced that when the whale swallowed Jonah that prophet was "down in the mouth." It definitely was not a good sermon! But when you are sixteen and willing to preach, almost everyone will tell you that you did "a good job" or will give the inevitable well-meaning cliché "God has great things in mind for you," which of course was music to my ears. As a result I devoted myself whole-heartedly to ministry: my church, Youth for Christ, Open Air Campaigners, Campus Crusade, and other opportunities.

In my twenties, when I met and married Barbara, my ministry-minded, outgoing wife, my expectations further increased. And when I finally got to seminary I felt as if I had died and gone to Heaven. I was studying theology, the "Queen of Sciences," and I loved my studies. I grew to so relish opening a critical commentary that I experienced an almost sensual thrill as I breathed its aroma and ran my fingers down the pages feeling the print. All of this, along with the many lifelong friendships I made in seminary, served to increase my expectations that great things were ahead.

During seminary I began ten years of youth ministry—a decade that almost perfectly coincided with the turbulent "up for grabs" sixties. As terrible as the sixties were culturally, they were great days of evangelism. During one banner year I recall there was hardly a Wednesday Bible study that someone of the nearly one hundred beaded, tie-dyed, bell-bottomed crowd did not come to Christ. When the seventies came, I felt it was time to begin preaching. So with the full, enthusiastic support of our church, I began a spin-off church. And expectations ran high! We prayed long and hard. We did everything scientifically, with aerial photographs, demographic studies, ethnographic surveys—you name it. And we worked hard. Everyone told me it would not be long until our church outsized the mother church.

But that is not how it went at all. In fact, after considerable time and immense effort we had fewer attenders than in the initial months—the church was shrinking. My bright prospects were melting around me, and I descended into the deepest, darkest depression of my life.

One hot late-summer night in 1975, I felt a midnight of the soul and poured out all my dark, pent-up thoughts to my wife. Without being specific, I must say they were mean and ugly—and shameful. But I reached bottom when I said to my poor wife, "God has called me to do something he hasn't given me the gifts to accomplish. Therefore, God is not good." I felt as though I was the butt of a cruel joke, and I wanted to quit. In desperation I said, "What am I to do?" As long as I live, I will never forget her kind and confident response: "I don't know what you're going to do. But for right now, for tonight, hang on to my faith . . . because *I* believe. I believe God is good. I believe he loves us and is going to work through this experience. So hang on to my faith. I have enough for both of us." And with that, being the fearless, gallant man that I am, I went off to bed. That dark night marked the inception of a process through which Barbara and I began to think through what the ministry is all about—a story that is chronicled in our book *Liberating Ministry from the Success Syndrome*.[1]

I have told this story here to underscore from my own wretched experience the human tendency to imagine when things go wrong that God is not good, and even sometimes to say it! Perhaps all of us have had such thoughts at one time or another. Let's face it—we sometimes think evil of God when tragedy comes to those we love, when we have been fired or have undergone a divorce, or as we observe the dominating presence of evil in human life. Honesty with ourselves reveals that questioning God's goodness is endemic to the human condition.

Blasphemous moments may come and go to the believer's soul, but if they lodge themselves in one's thinking, they can neutralize and even destroy spiritual life. It is impossible to walk with God if we question his goodness. Further, if such thinking becomes part of one's mind-set, the result can be disbelief and apostasy—like that of Thomas Hardy, who concluded his novel *Tess* by saying, "'Justice' was done, and the President of the Immortals (in Aeschylean phrase) had ended his sport with Tess."[2] Or consider Stephen Crane who blasphemously repeated in stanza after stanza in one of his poems, "God is cold."[3]

Some of the readers of James' letter were in similar peril. Their miserable flight from Jerusalem and the ongoing persecution as Christians at the hands of fellow Jews had left them not only saying, "I am being tempted by God" (1:13), but mouthing the parallel logic that God is not good. James begins to respond to them in verse 16: "Do not be deceived, my beloved brothers." This is a command that rings down the centuries to us: "For your soul's sake, brothers and sisters, stop being deceived!" This command forms a bridge to James' defense of the goodness of God.

In light of my questioning of God's goodness, it is ironic that the very Scripture my wife and I announced our engagement with is the opening sentence of James' defense of God's benevolence: "Every good gift and every perfect gift is from above, coming down from the Father of lights with whom there is no variation or shadow due to change" (v. 17). How badly I later needed to be refreshed by this great Scripture!

God's Goodness: The Gifts (v. 17a)

The opening phrase, "Every good gift and every perfect gift is from above," asserts that all goodness comes from God. The sense is even stronger in the literal reading—"All good giving and every perfect gift is from above"— because it emphasizes that the *action* of giving is good and that all his *gifts* are *telion* (perfect/complete).[4] Thus God's giving is intrinsically and comprehensively good—totally good! The logical, implied sense is that nothing evil can possibly come from above.

Further, since his gifts are perfect, they, unlike those that come from human hands, manifest their perfection the more they are examined and experienced. This, of course, has been the experience of the saints down through the centuries. "This God—his way is perfect; the word of the LORD proves true" (Psalm 18:30). "The law of the LORD is perfect, reviving the soul" (Psalm 19:7).

God's Goodness: The Giver (v. 17b)

Every gift from above is perfect because of *the perfect goodness of God the giver*, who is beautifully described in the phrase "the Father of lights with whom there is no variation or shadow due to change" (v. 17). This means that God fathered the lights of the universe, giving birth to each of its ten octillion stars in their individual brightnesses, ordering them in their distinctive constellations, and framing the physical laws that keep them on their courses, as well as ordering and sustaining the suns and planets and moons of the solar systems—all of which exist in such perfection that he pronounced them "good" (Genesis 1:18). The Jews daily celebrated this before repeating their *Shema*, by saying:

> The following are the "benedictions" before the *Shema*, in their original form: I. "Blessed be Thou, O Lord, King of the world, Who formest the light and createst the darkness, Who makest peace and createst everything; Who in mercy, givest light to the earth and to those who dwell upon it, and in Thy goodness day by day and every day renewest the works of creation. Blessed be the Lord our God for the glory of His handiwork and for the light-giving lights which He has made for His praise, Selah! Blessed be the Lord our God, Who hath formed the lights."[5]

Going deeper, God's being called "the Father of lights" points to his essential nature as light and to his moral goodness. Paul tells us that God's "invisible attributes, namely, his eternal power and divine nature, have been clearly perceived, ever since the creation of the world, in the things that have been made" (Romans 1:20). God's goodness is at the center of what we see in God's handiwork.[6] When on a clear night we look out past the moon and the spinning planets of our solar system to the relentless blanket of stars and the luminous backdrop of the Milky Way, a message dazzles our eyes from a zillion points of light: God is not only powerful, he is perfect and good! "God is light," said John, "and in him is no darkness at all" (1 John 1:5). There is only goodness in God, and no evil at all.

Understanding that the term "the Father of lights" proclaims God's goodness, we are prepared for the stupendous truth of the next phrase: "with whom there is no variation or shadow due to change." We earthlings, with our feet planted here on earth, are subjected to constantly changing light.

The sun rises, and our shadows fall long to the west; it stands high at noon, brightening all; and as it sets, our shadows are to the east, until they fade to nothingness. Day and night light perpetually change. The moon waxes full and wanes to a crescent. Light is reflected and refracted differently moment by moment.

But it is not so with the goodness of God. With God "there is no variation or shadow due to change." God's goodness is always at high noon.

Process theology falsely portrays a changing, relativistic God. Evangelicals properly debate the exact meaning of some of the attributes of God, such as his omniscience or omnipotence. But no committed Christian can debate or doubt the unchangeable goodness of God.

An old music teacher was once asked in greeting, "What's the good news today?" The old man, without saying a word, walked across the room, picked up a tuning fork, and struck it. As the note sounded, he said, "That is A. It is A today, it was A five thousand years ago, and it will be A ten thousand years from now. The soprano upstairs sings off-key, the tenor across the hall is out of tune." He struck the note again and said, "That is A, my friend, and that's the good news today!"[7]

The good news today and for all eternity is this: God is *infinitely* good. He has never had and will never have more goodness than he has now. He is unchangeably good. He stands like an eternal sun in a cloudless sky radiating unbroken goodness upon us. God will always—*eternally*—be good to us.

In his final column in *Eternity* magazine, a column he authored for over twenty years, Joe Bayly said, "Since I've shared the severity of God with my readers [speaking of the deaths of three of his children], I want to share the goodness of God in this final column." And then he recounted God's grace in the lives of each of his four living children. What is especially significant in relation to the truth of the text we are expounding are his final words:

> Mary Lou and I are aware that all this represents the grace of God, but also that for ourselves and our children the road hasn't ended. Yet we know that both by his severity and by his goodness God has shown consistent faithfulness. God is good. He is worthy of all trust and all glory.
> Amen.[8]

Brothers and sisters, we live in constant change, to which our bodies bear inescapable testimony. For example, suppose you pinch the skin on the back of your index finger. If you are six years old, it will snap back into place. If you are twenty-six, it will take a few seconds to smooth out. If you are forty-six, it may return to its place by the end of this chapter. If you are over seventy, do not even try it! We are constantly changing, and our world too is in constant change. But our text urges us on to one immutable fact: God is good, and he rains goodness upon us.

The present participle in verse 17, "coming down," describes an unending succession of good gifts: "Every good gift and every perfect gift is from above [all good comes from above], coming down [in unending succession] from the Father of lights [the good framer of the universe] with whom there is no variation or shadow due to change [his goodness stays at unchanging, eternal high noon]." That is the good news! *God is good!*

God's Goodness: The Gift (v. 18)

To further drive home the point of God's goodness, James now takes his readers from the macrocosm of the universe in explaining the divine goodness to the microcosm of their own experience in becoming Christians. God's goodness is personally experienced in that "Of his own will he brought us forth by the word of truth, that we should be a kind of firstfruits of his creatures" (v. 18).

Just as God acted freely in his goodness when he created the universe, he freely chose to bring the believers to whom James was writing (and us) to himself (cf. Ephesians 1:4, 5). Everything in salvation was, and is, of God. We are God's people because of a total act of grace rooted in God's unprompted goodness.

They experienced salvation "by the word of truth." All of them had the Word come alive to them, just as we have if we know Christ. My own experience was that the gospel message began to have an appeal to me, though I did not understand it. Next, though my understanding was imperfect, certain parts of the Word began to convict me. And when I came to Christ, it was like an explosion of understanding! I still have the delicate India paper Bible with the enlightened markings I made in it by flashlight in my sleeping bag the night I came to Christ. James appeals to this common experience of God's goodness, for he knew that all true believers would respond to it with praise and commitment. "So faith comes from hearing, and hearing through the word of Christ" (Romans 10:17). "You have been born again, not of perishable seed but of imperishable, through the living and abiding word of God" (1 Peter 1:23).

Finally, the results can only be called good as well—"that we should be a kind of firstfruits of his creatures." These Jewish Christians were the first sheaves of a harvest that has been continuing for two thousand years. They were the original, privileged *sample* of what was to come, a *pledge* of the full harvest. God's unmitigated goodness will ultimately be worked out when all creation will be transformed (Romans 8:18–22).[9]

I sometimes wonder what would have happened if my wife had not had such an awareness of the goodness of God. What if she had said, "You're echoing my thoughts. I used to think God is good, but living with you is changing my mind. Let's chuck the whole thing!" I was in big trouble. But God met me through his Word and the saintly sanity of my wife.

Are you doubting his goodness? Then hear God's Word. "Do not be deceived, my beloved brothers," and let me give you four reasons why: (1) *Only good comes from God*—"Every good gift and every perfect gift is from above." (2) *Our Gift-giver is the good Father of creation*, "the Father of lights." What he gives is in spiritual accord with the goodness we see in the stars. (3) *His goodness will never change*—"with whom there is no variation or shadow due to change." And (4) If this is not enough, *his goodness is in accord with, and an extension of, the goodness we experienced in salvation* when "Of his own will he brought us forth by the word of truth, that we should be a kind of firstfruits of his creatures" (vv. 16–18).

The goodness of God is the key to spiritual sanity. God is good! Since this is so, let us embrace Joe Bayly's ultimate logic: "He is worthy of all trust and all glory. Amen."

Know this, my beloved brothers: let every person be quick to hear, slow to speak, slow to anger; for the anger of man does not produce the righteousness of God. Therefore put away all filthiness and rampant wickedness and receive with meekness the implanted word, which is able to save your souls.

1:19–21

6

Accepting the Word

JAMES 1:19–21

IT WAS SUNDAY, THE LORD'S DAY, the day of the Resurrection. It wasn't the Sabbath, so the congregation had worked a full day, but now had come together in the evening for a common meal and commemoration of the death of Jesus. It was a larger gathering than usual, because the Apostle Paul's presence, coupled with his intended departure at sunrise, had brought out everyone who was able to attend. The room was packed.

Paul was an experienced and effective communicator. He knew how to keep the cookies on the bottom shelf—he fed the sheep as well as the giraffes! He also knew that the mind can absorb no more than the seat, or as John Newton more properly said, "When weariness begins, edification ends." But Paul couldn't help himself! This was the first contact with the infant church of Troas, and very possibly his last. With the rising of the morning sun he would be off to Jerusalem. He had so much he wanted to say. Each thought brought ten more to his scintillating mind—all of equal importance. He just couldn't seem to close. And besides, no one was complaining. Indeed, it was a welcome treat for the church at Troas. They hoped it would never end.

There were many torches in the room, creating a stuffy atmosphere in the third-story chamber. The Mediterranean heat, the grimy press of the weary crowd just returned from work, the lack of oxygen all made for drowsiness. Finally the warm room and the hypnotic flickering of the flames did their work, and a young man named Eutychus, sitting on the windowsill, nodded off into a "deep" sleep (Acts 20:9—we derived our word *hypnosis* from this Greek word). He relaxed just a bit too much, and he went headlong to the pavement three floors below. The congregation gave a horrified gasp and immediately poured down the outside stairs to the broken form. Eutychus was quite dead! Some began to wail.

But not for long! Dr. Luke tells us, "Paul went down and bent over him, and taking him in his arms, said, 'Do not be alarmed, for his life is in him'" (Acts 20:10). The old apostle had prostrated himself across the boy's lifeless form, much as did the prophets Elijah and Elisha with others, and the young man was revived. No one was sleeping now! Up the stairs and back into the building they all marched, and "[Paul] conversed with them a long while, until daybreak, and so departed. And they took the youth away alive, and were not a little comforted" (Acts 20:11, 12).

I feel sorry for poor Eutychus. First, because he fell asleep on the Apostle Paul. That was a no-no. Second, because he was unfortunately sitting in a third-story window. And third, because Luke was there, pen in hand, to record the whole thing! This is the first record ever of someone falling asleep in church. There have been thousands, alas millions, of successors, but Eutychus is the one everyone remembers. I think he got a bum deal!

After twenty-seven years in the ministry I know that on any given Sunday many are in danger of falling asleep in church. I have seen people fall asleep and bump their heads on the pew in front of them. I have been sitting on the platform when one of my associates dozed off and dropped his hymnal! I have heard people awaken with a snort. In our congregation there was a young man who sat in the front row and slept *every* Sunday. As soon as I was through with the introduction, his eyes invariably lowered to half-mast and his head tilted. The most memorable of his "sleeps" came on a Sunday when both he and his wife fell asleep with their heads propped one against the other. I have heard a preacher tell of an elder who fell asleep, and when his wife nudged him during the service, he stood and pronounced the benediction.

Actually I have great sympathy for those who have trouble staying awake in church. Some work such trying schedules that when they sit down in church motionless, it is the first time they have relaxed all week. Others take medication that puts them in dreamland. Sometimes it's just so warm and comfortable and . . . The truth is, some of the best saints have fallen asleep in church. Also, I suspect that Eutychus was an enthusiastic new Christian who though he was tired wouldn't miss church for anything! He could not have died in church if he had not wanted to be there.

Falling asleep in church really doesn't concern me. It can happen for any number of reasons, both good and bad. What does concern me is that God's people need to have hearts that are receptive to the Word and a posture of soul that inclines them to hear the Word and profit from it. This was clearly James' pastoral concern as he wrote to his dispersed Jewish flock. The flow of his thought was this: having defended God's goodness in verses 16–18, he ended by noting God's ultimate goodness in giving them salvation "by the word of truth" (v. 18). This mention of the *Word* in their regeneration now turns his thoughts, in verses 19–27, to urging them to *live* according to the Word. This study will cover verses 19–21, "Accepting the Word," and the next chapter will cover verses 22–27, "Doing the Word."

Instructions on Accepting the Word (v. 19)

James begins by using Hebrew parallelism to inform his people of their triple duty in responding to the Word: "Know this, my beloved brothers: let every person be quick to hear, slow to speak, slow to anger" (v. 19).

The first duty is to be "quick to hear." This was particularly important to the Jewish church because, apart from the Old Testament, there were no canonical Scriptures at this early date. Virtually all communication of the gospel was oral, when they met together in their house churches. Thus listening was imperative. Those who were not disciplined in listening ran the risk of spiritual impoverishment. It is not too dramatic to say that ready listeners gained for themselves a life-giving spiritual advantage.

In so challenging his first-century flock, James has put his finger on a great need in the church today, for many of us today are non-listeners. Celebrated psychologist Paul Tournier has memorably said, "Listen to the conversations of our world, between nations as well as between couples. They are, for the most part, *dialogues of the deaf.*"[1] Billions and billions of words are produced every second, but only a fraction is truly heard. All of us regularly have "conversations" in which we are speaking, but the vacant eyes of our "hearers" and their body language indicate that they do not hear. Sometimes our listeners are "on another planet," sometimes they are so self-consumed they cannot listen, other times they are so intent on what they want to say next that they are not catching a word we are saying. And to be honest, we are often like this ourselves.

Why these dialogues of the deaf? Why are we such poor listeners? Today one of the major reasons is that we are so busy. Our busyness substitutes frenzy for conversation and wrecks our relationships. It fills our calendars and empties our lives of the ability to listen to anything that turns us away from our little gods.

The visual media also feed our inability to concentrate. The networks have learned that Americans' attention span is brief. They, in fact, helped make it that way. Watch a typical cop show or sitcom, and you will discover that few scenes last longer than ten or fifteen seconds. A culture so dependent on visual changes to keep its attention has difficulty concentrating on anything, especially the unadorned Word. Perhaps this is why Adlai Stevenson, when he addressed the students at Princeton, said, "I understand I am here to speak and you are here to listen. Let's hope we both finish at the same time."

This inability to listen has huge implications regarding the hearing of God's Word, the central concern of James text: "be quick to hear." Bible reading, the primary source for God's Word, is in jeopardy, for not only do people have trouble concentrating, but films and videos are the primary way many learn. The written page is too tame to hold their attention. Devotions, likewise, suffer. The devotional prayer of the modern man is, "Lord, speak to me! You have sixty seconds." There is no place in the busy secular desolation to hear God say, "Be still, and know that I am God" (Psalm 46:10). Few moderns have the discipline or time to say:

Speak, Lord, in the stillness,
While I wait on Thee;
Hushed my heart to listen
In expectancy.

E. May Grimes

Lastly, because of this problem preaching becomes a daunting proposition. If our attention can be held for a limited amount of time only by the peacock's unfolding colors and automobiles exploding and commercials that depend on sixty images in twenty seconds, how can we listen to a modest exposition of God's Word?

Obviously, something must be done if we are to maintain and enhance our ability to hear God's Word. Briefly there are at least five things that will help make us "quick to hear."

1) We must work at truly listening to others. Listening requires an intense interest in the other person. As Simon Kistemaker says: "Listening is loving the neighbor as oneself; his concerns and problems are sufficiently important to be heard."[2] This requires eye contact and sensitivity to the other's gestures and moods and silences.
2) We must limit our exposure to the visual media. If we do not control our time, the media will! And if they do, they will impair our ability to hear.
3) We must read God's Word, and that involves more than advancing a bookmark. It means "hearing" as we read.
4) We must slow down and take time to listen, perhaps praying Samuel's eager words, "Speak, for your servant hears" (1 Samuel 3:10).
5) We must prepare for worship and the hearing of God's Word. For many, the time before Sunday church is the most stress-filled time of the week. I

may be wrong, but I suspect there are more fights in Christian households on Sunday mornings than at any other time. We must prepare not to have this happen, beginning the night before. Ever so practical, Pastor James says we must "be quick to hear." This is a continuous command (present act imperative)—that is, we are to keep at it. It is the first duty of those who would profit by the Word.

The second of our triple duties is to be "slow to speak." The churches to which James wrote were unstructured and thus both invited personal participation and created a climate where abuse was possible. The speaker could be easily interrupted, and hasty unthought-through comments could detract from the ministry. James commands those who had such tendencies to be "slow to speak." James is not barring a friendly, fast-paced conversation or repartee. Neither is he suggesting that Christians are to be inarticulate. But he is enjoining the common-sense principle to think before you speak.

The ancient world understood this, though many disregarded it. Zeno, the Stoic philosopher, said, "We have two ears and one mouth, therefore we should listen twice as much as we speak." The rabbis put it even better: "This is the reason why we have two ears and only one mouth, that we may hear more and speak less. The ears are always open, ever ready to receive instruction; but the tongue is surrounded with a double row of teeth to hedge it in, and keep it within proper bounds."[3]

If you've opened your mouth only "to change feet" as much as I have, this advice rings so true! I've never had to take back something I *didn't* say. The tragedy is, even though you take your words back, they never really completely return. Solomon was right: "When words are many, transgression is not lacking, but whoever restrains his lips is prudent" (Proverbs 10:19).

Our natural tendency in respect to God's Word is to be slow to hear and quick to speak. Not fully understanding because of faulty listening, we are quick to jump to wrong conclusions, quick to judge, quick to say the worst, quick to offer advice. We so naturally pronounce opinions and verdicts on every situation and person. But we must keep in mind that "slow to speak" is an ongoing command from the Holy Spirit himself.

The third of the triple duties for those who hope to benefit from the Word is to be "slow to anger." James knew that often people do not really listen to the Word as it is taught. They foolishly speak out without thinking; one gets angry, another gets angry, and the church is no longer a lighthouse but a towering inferno! We jump to our feet and shout, "I'm not angry!"—our faces flushed with rage, veins popping—and then stomp from the room, slamming the door behind us, proving how un-angry we are!

We rationalize our anger, calling it frankness or attributing it to our up-bringing or the pressure we are under—but anger like this is *sin* (Ephesians 4:31; Colossians 3:8; Titus 1:7). Here wise Solomon again gives advice: "A fool gives full vent to his spirit, but a wise man quietly holds it back" (Proverbs 29:11). And, "Whoever is slow to anger is better than the mighty, and he who rules his spirit than he who takes a city" (Proverbs 16:32).

The bottom line regarding anger in respect to James' desire that we profit from the Word is this: *an angry spirit is never a listening, teachable spirit.* Those who live the reverse of the triple duty and are slow to hear, quick to speak, and quick to become angry will not grow in the Word. Have you reached a sticking point in your spiritual life? Perhaps it is because you are hung up on one of your triple duties.

Reason for Accepting the Word (v. 20)

The rationale for being "quick to hear, slow to speak, slow to anger" is given in verse 20: "for the anger of man does not produce the righteousness of God." Anger produces an ugly, unrighteous life. Few people in literary history were more self-centered or had a more grotesque personality than Henrik Ibsen. He was a preening, pompous, insufferable man who took two hours to dress and place his literary medals on his coat. Though he wrote *The Doll House*, he was an inveterate misogynist. In a terrifying letter he wrote to a fellow writer whose daughter was to marry Ibsen's son, he said:

> Anger increases my strength. If there is to be war, then let there be war! . . . I shall not spare the child in its mother's womb, nor any thought nor feeling that may have motivated the actions of any man who shall merit the honor of being my victim. Do you know that all my life I have turned my back on my parents, on my whole family.[4]

When we feed on anger and bitterness, the feast is us.

> In the desert
> I saw a creature, naked, bestial.
> Who, squatting upon the ground,
> Held his heart in his hands,
> And ate of it.
> I said, "Is it good, friend?"
> "It is bitter—bitter," he answered;
> "But I like it
> Because it is bitter,
> And because it is my heart."[5]

Jesus says, "But I say to you that everyone who is angry with his brother will be liable to judgment; whoever insults his brother will be liable to the council; and whoever says, 'You fool!' will be liable to the hell of fire" (Matthew 5:22). It is eternally true that "the anger of man does not produce the righteousness of God." This is why we need to cultivate the triple duty and listen with all we have to God's Word however it comes, to think well before we speak in response, and to be very slow to anger.

Command to Accept the Word (v. 21)

James completes his thought with a two-part command regarding receiving the Word. The first is negative and the second positive.

The negative is, "Therefore put away all filthiness and rampant wickedness . . ." (v. 21a). It is important that we not miss what James is saying here: an unwillingness to listen, a sinful tongue, and unrighteous anger are *moral evils*. If we are slow to hear God's Word, quick to speak, and quick to anger, moral filth is not only our lot but our destiny. Thus, if we wish to receive and benefit from the Word, we must get rid of the sins it has revealed to us. If the Word is not active and alive to us, we must do a spiritual house-cleaning. Is the Bible relevant? Do you thrill to read it? Is it sweet to your soul? Do you find that it is always unfolding more riches? If not, toss out the sins James has highlighted and open yourself to God's Word.

Once we have done this, we are ready for the positive command: ". . . and receive with meekness the implanted word, which is able to save your souls" (v. 21b). God's Word was not native to our hearts, but it has been implanted in us. However, if we have been unhearing, our tongues out of control, building up anger and moral filth, the Word has not been flourishing as it was meant to do. But it will again prosper if, having cast out the sin, we "receive with meekness the implanted word." By *humble* acceptance James means the opposite of self-assertiveness—teachableness[6]—welcoming the Word with open arms.

Eutychus fell asleep in church, but he was not asleep to God's Word. He did what he could to place himself in a position to hear and respond. What about us? We hear the Word of God at church, on Christian radio and TV, but are we alive to it? James' words are for the church of every age: "Know this, my beloved brothers: let every person be quick to hear, slow to speak, slow to anger; for the anger of man does not produce the righteousness of God. Therefore put away all filthiness and rampant wickedness and receive with meekness the implanted word, which is able to save your souls" (vv. 19–21). If we have accepted the word planted in us, there is only one thing to do— *listen!* Read it, and *listen*. Be still, and *listen*. Worship, and *listen*.

But be doers of the word, and not hearers only, deceiving yourselves. For if anyone is a hearer of the word and not a doer, he is like a man who looks intently at his natural face in a mirror. For he looks at himself and goes away and at once forgets what he was like. But the one who looks into the perfect law, the law of liberty, and perseveres, being no hearer who forgets but a doer who acts, he will be blessed in his doing.

1:22–25

7

Doing the Word

JAMES 1:22–25

WE HAVE DISCUSSED ACCEPTING THE WORD. Now we will consider *doing the Word*. Together these two topics express the spiritual logic of James' flow of thought: the *hearing* of the Word must be followed by *obedience*; truly *accepting* God's Word logically means *doing* it.

This spiritual logic was given memorable illustration by Chuck Swindoll in his book *Improving Your Serve*:

> Let's pretend that you work for me. In fact, you are my executive assistant in a company that is growing rapidly. I'm the owner and I'm interested in expanding overseas. To pull this off, I make plans to travel abroad and stay there until the new branch office gets established. I make all the arrangements to take my family in the move to Europe for six to eight months, and I leave you in charge of the busy stateside organization. I tell you that I will write you regularly and give you direction and instructions.
>
> I leave and you stay. Months pass. A flow of letters are mailed from Europe and received by you at the national headquarters. I spell out all my expectations. Finally, I return. Soon after my arrival I drive down to the office. I am stunned! Grass and weeds have grown up high. A few windows along the street are broken. I walk into the receptionist's room and she is doing her nails, chewing gum, and listening to her favorite disco station. I look around and notice the waste baskets are overflowing, the carpet hasn't been vacuumed for weeks, and nobody seems concerned that the owner has returned. I ask about your whereabouts and someone in the crowded lounge area points down the hall and yells, "I think he's down there." Disturbed, I move in that direction and bump into you as you are finishing a chess game with our sales manager. I ask you to step into my office (which has been temporarily turned into a television room for watching afternoon soap operas).

"What in the world is going on, man?"

"What do ya' mean . . . ?"

"Well, look at this place! Didn't you get any of my letters?"

"Letters? Oh, yeah—sure, got every one of them. As a matter of fact . . . we have had *letter study* every Friday night since you left. We have even divided all the personnel into small groups and discussed many of the things you wrote. Some of those things were really interesting. You'll be pleased to know that a few of us have actually committed to memory some of your sentences and paragraphs. One or two memorized an entire letter or two! Great stuff in those letters!"

"Okay, okay—you got my letters, you studied them and meditated on them, discussed and even memorized them. BUT WHAT DID YOU DO ABOUT THEM?"

"Do? Uh—we didn't *do* anything about them."[1]

Such behavior is professionally absurd. It is, in fact, professional suicide! But how much less absurd are we when we hear God's Word without the slightest inclination to obey it? At the very least we are self-deceived. This is why James follows his call to be hearers with the command of verse 22: "But be doers of the word, and not hearers only, deceiving yourselves." If we are going to profit from God's Word, we must accept and do it.

To enforce the importance of this, James employs two examples, based on the rich simile of a mirror—again one positive and one negative.

The Wrong Example/Way (vv. 23, 24)

James explains the wrong approach by saying, "For if anyone is a hearer of the word and not a doer, he is like a man who looks intently at his natural face in a mirror. For he looks at himself and goes away and at once forgets what he was like" (vv. 23, 24).

This hypothetical man begins well enough. As James indicates, he is "a hearer of the word." This is good. After all, there are multitudes who simply do not listen, especially in our visually-oriented, post-literate society that is not only unwilling to listen but has often lost the ability to hear.

James' man listens, and his listening has some positive effect—he "is like a man who looks intently at his natural face in a mirror" (v. 23b). Ancient mirrors were not like today's glass mirrors, but were polished metal—bronze or even silver and gold. But they did enable someone to get a good look at himself. What the man sees here is literally "the face of his birth," or as James Ropes has it, "the face that nature gave him."[2] He sees his nose, eyes, whiskers, wrinkles, blemishes—everything. And the longer he looks, the more he sees. The mirror, like the proverbial camera, does not lie. Yes, the wicked witch's mirror kept telling her she was "the fairest of them all"—until Snow White came on the scene, and then it had to tell the truth.

A story from the last century tells how a missionary out in the bush had hung a small mirror on a tree in order to shave. The local witch doctor happened by and curiously looked into the strange glass—and seeing her hideously painted features she jumped back! Immediately she began to bargain with the missionary for the mirror. The man demurred, but to no effect. Finally, realizing that the witch doctor would not be put off, he let her have the mirror—whereupon she threw it to the ground, breaking it to pieces, shouting, "There . . . it won't be making ugly faces at me anymore!" We too have ways to deal with a mirror's truth, and our false ways don't work, either.

In James the "mirror" is God's Word, and when we look into God's Word we see the *heart of our birth*—ourselves as we really are—our very souls. We not only see that we are sinners, but we begin to see the awful depth of our sin. Previously our conscience showed us part of the picture, but now we see there is no part of us that is not tainted with sin. Though I had an active conscience before coming to God's Word, I only saw dimly what I was. But the mirror of God's Word revealed the truth and continues to do the same. It is also true that God's Word is a mirror in which "God allows us to gaze upon Himself."[3] These two reflections of self and of God pave the way to seeing the necessity and way of salvation.

The mirror ministry of God's Word, which is rooted in showing us what we are, is essential. But there is also a danger here, because we can be deluded into thinking we have accomplished all God requires by hearing his Word. It is natural to imagine that the accumulation of Biblical knowledge is not just the main thing, but the *only* thing. Being the kind of person who thrills to open a book, who gets a sensual thrill from turning the pages and enjoys the esoteric language of theology, it is so easy to imagine that by reading books on spiritual subjects great virtue will course through my soul—like the primitives who thought they could imbibe others' powers by drinking their blood.

Don't misunderstand me—I believe we should read the mirror of God's Word, to be "beavers for the Bible," to use J. I. Packer's term.[4] We ought to read it daily. We should put ourselves under adequate preaching and listen well. Bible studies, tapes, and radio broadcasts can be tremendous sources of help. Scripture memorization is a must. But in doing these very "Christian" things we must never simply imagine that we have arrived. "But be doers of the word, and not hearers only, deceiving yourselves" (v. 22a).

James's first mirror viewer began well. The verb "looks" in verse 23 suggests "attentive scrutiny of an object."[5] He has truly seen himself as he is and has also glimpsed God and salvation, but he ends tragically: "For he looks at himself and goes away and at once forgets what he was like" (v. 24). Admittedly, looking in the mirror at oneself is not always a pleasant experience. As someone once said to me, "Whenever I forget what I look like, I count it a blessing!" But spiritually it is catastrophic whenever we stop looking. The man here sees his reflection in the mirror, contemplates his appearance, and goes on his way. There is no real effect on his life. He has failed to respond to God's Word. He has gotten no more lasting benefit from God's Word than a passing look.

The solemn truth is, unless the Word has made a change in our lives, it has not really entered our lives. God's Word becomes a millstone if we do not make it a milestone.

> Lord, deliver us from the delusion that accumulating knowledge, even if it is directly from your Word, is enough!

The Right Example (v. 25)

Turning from the folly of the first man, James now treats us to the wisdom of the second: "But the one who looks into the perfect law, the law of liberty, and perseveres, being no hearer who forgets but a doer who acts, he will be blessed in his doing" (v. 25).

This man is a superior listener. In describing him as one who "looks" into God's Word, James uses a word that pictures the man as bending over a mirror on a table and looking with a studied, penetrating look. The first man's look involved some laudable scrutiny, but this second man is gripped by what he sees and *keeps on looking.*[6] This word is used twice in John 20:5, 11 to first describe Peter as he bent over and looked into the empty tomb and then Mary Magdalene when she wept and likewise bent over to look in the tomb. This is an absorbing look.

"The perfect law, the law of liberty" is a fuller designation of "the word of truth" (1:18), "the implanted word" (1:21), and "the word" (v. 22). It encompasses the Old Testament Scriptures, but since it is "perfect" it includes the teaching of Christ—the gospel—for Jesus fulfilled the Law (Matthew 5:17).[7]

This Word radiates liberating power, for it is "the perfect law, the law of liberty." As this man bends over it in soul-absorbing study, he sees more deeply than the first viewer the mirror image of his soul. His imperfect spiritual features are forever impressed upon him. He thus becomes truly poor in spirit, for he knows what he is. He does not outgrow this, but rather his self-knowledge grows deeper. He knows that in his natural self, apart from God, there dwells no good thing. He recognizes, "Wretched man that I am! Who will deliver me from this body of death?" (Romans 7:24).

This understanding of self from the mirror of God's Word is enhanced as he also sees the reflection of a totally holy, transcendent, awesome God who makes demands on his soul. And, finally, this double-mirrored knowledge of self and God enables him to understand the necessity of atoning forgiveness from God. In his reception of the free grace of God he experiences the full work of "the perfect law, the law of liberty." He is free to do as he ought.

This brings us to the apex of James' argument in our text where the man is described as "doing" the Word. He lives in profound obedience. He keeps looking and doing, looking and doing, looking and doing. He has become part of a God-created process in which knowledge followed by obedience brings more knowledge.

Biblically, true knowledge demands action. They cannot be separated. But here we must face an ominous related truth: when we have been given spiritual instruction from the mirror of God's Word and do not act upon it, we imperil our spiritual health. Jesus expounded this same principle in Matthew 13 when his disciples asked why he spoke in parables. His answer was, in effect, that it was because the religious establishment had not responded to his earlier revelations given to them by God. He said,

> To you it has been given to know the secrets of the kingdom of heaven, but to them it has not been given. For to the one who has, more will be given, and he will have an abundance, but from the one who has not, even what he has will be taken away. This is why I speak to them in parables, because seeing they do not see, and hearing they do not hear, nor do they under-stand. (Matthew 13:11–13)

Truth acted on brings more truth, but failure to respond to truth will ultimately result in the loss of truth. The same principle is showcased in the servant who did nothing with his talent in the Parable of the Talents in Matthew 25: "So take the talent from him and give it to him who has the ten talents. For to everyone who has will more be given, and he will have an abundance. But from the one who has not, even what he has will be taken away" (Matthew 25:28, 29).

For our souls' health we must apply what we hear. For example, when our conscience is moved by a sermon, or in daily devotional reading, we should commit ourselves to do *something*, be it ever so small, and then do it! When we do this, more truth will be given. There is a world of difference between reading a menu and eating a meal.

James closes with a beatitude: "he will be blessed in his doing." Listen again to the divine logic that culminates with this blessing:

> But be doers of the word, and not hearers only, deceiving yourselves. For if anyone is a hearer of the word and not a doer, he is like a man who looks intently at his natural face in a mirror. For he looks at himself and goes away and at once forgets what he was like. But the one who looks into the perfect law, the law of liberty, and perseveres, being no hearer who forgets but a doer who acts, he will be blessed in his doing. (vv. 22–25)

Doing God's Word is the key to blessing and happiness. "If you know these things, blessed are you if you do them" (John 13:17).

"Letters, Lord? Oh, yeah—sure, got every one of them. As a matter of fact, Lord, we have had *letter study* every Friday night. We have even divided all the congregation into small groups and discussed many of the things you wrote. Some of the things were really interesting. You'll be pleased to know that a few of us have actually committed to memory some of your sentences and paragraphs. One or two memorized an entire letter or two! Great stuff in those letters!"

"Okay, you got my letters, you studied them and meditated on them, discussed and even memorized them. BUT WHAT DID YOU DO ABOUT THEM?"

If anyone thinks he is religious and does not bridle his tongue but deceives his heart, this person's religion is worthless. Religion that is pure and undefiled before God, the Father, is this: to visit orphans and widows in their affliction, and to keep oneself unstained from the world.

1:26, 27

8

Acceptable Religion

JAMES 1:26, 27

JAMES HAS POWERFULLY DRIVEN HOME the point that if we are merely *hearers* of the Word, we have deluded ourselves, for we must also be *doers* of the Word. Now he issues a further warning against the danger of deceiving ourselves with false religious doings. The doings are not bad in themselves, but the practice of them can delude believers with a deceptively comfortable sense of religiosity.

Vocabulary. Primary among these deceptive doings is the appropriation of religious terminology. The Old Testament records that during a war the Gileadites developed a password in order to detect Ephraimites who pretended to be Gileadites when captured. The word was *Shibboleth*, which the Ephraimites (who had trouble with the *sh* sound) could only pronounce *Sibboleth*. This worked perfectly on the unsuspecting enemy (Judges 12:4–6). We Christians have our Shibboleths, but they are much easier to pick up. They are words like "fellowship" and "brother" and "born again." Use these passwords with the right inflection and you will be considered *Christian*.

Social conventions. In the same way, if you show the "right" socioreligious attitudes toward alcohol and tobacco, social issues, and modesty and style, you will be thought religious or pious. The ease with which one can adopt the behavioral mores of evangelical Christianity has been sadly made easier by the gradual alignment of many Christians with the materialism and hedonism of our secular culture.

Worship. The words "religious" and "religion" in our text denote *outward worship*.[1] If we carry a Bible and are somewhat familiar with it, if we read the "right" books, if we attend church regularly, sing the hymns, apparently listen, and especially if we give, we can easily deceive ourselves into thinking we are properly and adequately religious. Our doing can produce a deadly religious delusion!

To combat this real danger, James puts forth three penetrating dimensions of "religion" that is acceptable to God. These challenge those who think themselves safely religious.

Dimension 1: Control of the Tongue (v. 26)

The first dimension cuts like a hot knife through warm butter, dissecting all the cant and piety of the self-satisfied religious: "If anyone thinks he is religious and does not bridle his tongue but deceives his heart, this person's religion is worthless" (v. 26).

James compares the tongue to a powerful, rearing horse that will take off on a wild ride if the reins are not kept taut. If you've ever sat on 1,500 pounds of restless bone and muscle and then hung on at full gallop, you have the idea. There are actually people who consider themselves "religious" (they are very proper in their worship) but who have galloping tongues and thus are in a state of perpetual self-deception. In fact, all their religious worship is "worthless"—an exercise in futility.[2]

This is a spiritually terrifying statement, to say the least! An out-of-control tongue suggests bogus religious devotion, no matter how well one's devotion is carried out. "A true test of a man's religion is not his ability to speak," as we are so apt to think, "but rather his ability to bridle his tongue."[3]

The Lord Jesus himself explained this in no uncertain terms in a heated exchange with the Pharisees: "Either make the tree good and its fruit good, or make the tree bad and its fruit bad, for the tree is known by its fruit. You brood of vipers! How can you speak good, when you are evil? For out of the abundance of the heart the mouth speaks" (Matthew 12:33, 34). *The tongue will inevitably reveal what is on the inside.* That which is within will ultimately come forth. This is especially true under stress, when the tongue is compulsively revealing.

A preacher with hammer in hand, doing some work on a church workday, noticed that one of the men seemed to be following him around. Finally the preacher asked why. The man answered, "I'm just listening to hear what you say when you hit your thumb." His curious parishioner understood that would be the existential moment of truth. The same could be said of the domestic stresses of the home, where the mouth unfailingly trumpets one's essence.

The tongue comes out with many things, often with *filth*. This is why Paul says, "Let no corrupting talk come out of your mouths" (Ephesians

4:29). There is also *lying*: "Therefore, having put away falsehood, let each one of you speak the truth with his neighbor" (Ephesians 4:25). *Gossip* is another by-product. It isn't so much the things that go in one ear and out the other that hurt as the things that go in one ear, get all mixed up, and then slip out of the mouth.

All these sins spew from the unbridled tongue, but what James' metaphor points to most is the uncontrolled slanderous tongue—carping, critical, judgmental. The outwardly religious person characteristically avoids filth and lying, but falls easily to slander. John Calvin, himself often the victim of such speech, wrote:

> When people shed their grosser sins, they are extremely vulnerable to contract this complaint. A man will steer clear of adultery, of stealing, of drunkenness, in fact he will be a shining light of outward religious observance—and yet will revel in destroying the character of others; under the pretext of zeal . . . but it is a lust for vilification. This explains . . . the bloated pharisaical pride that feeds indulgently on a general diet of smear and censure.[4]

Sometimes the slander is whispered, sometimes inferred, and sometimes shouted, but it always has a perverted religious base. It is a "religious" sin!

James does not mean that those who *sometimes* fall into this sin have a worthless religion, for all are guilty at times. But he is saying that if anyone's tongue is *habitually* unbridled, though his church attendance be impeccable, his Bible knowledge envied, his prayers many, his tithes exemplary, and though he "thinks he is religious . . . [he] deceives his heart, [and] this person's religion is worthless."

Ever practical, James has cut through all the religious decorum, but it is not butter that glistens under his knife, but the marrow of our souls. True religion controls the tongue.

Once while John Wesley was preaching, he noticed a lady in the audience who was known for her critical attitude. All through the service she sat and stared at his new tie. When the meeting ended, she came up to him and said very sharply, "Mr. Wesley, the strings on your bow tie are much too long. It's an offense to me!" He asked if any of the ladies present happened to have a pair of scissors in her purse. When the scissors were handed to him, he gave them to his critic and asked her to trim the streamers to her liking. After she clipped them off near the collar, he said, "Are you sure they're all right now?" "Yes, that's much better." "Then let me have those shears a moment," said Wesley. "I'm sure you wouldn't mind if I also gave you a bit of correction.

I must tell you, madam, that your tongue is an offense to me—it's too long! Please stick it out . . . I'd like to take some off." On another occasion someone said to Wesley, "My talent is to speak my mind." Wesley replied, "That's one talent God wouldn't care a bit if you buried!"

How's your religion? Is it true or worthless? The wise *hear* and *do* God's Word. That is the first dimension of acceptable religion.

> "The boneless tongue, so small and weak,
> Can crush and kill," declares the Greek.
> "The tongue destroys a greater horde,"
> The Turk asserts, "than does the sword."
> The Persian proverb wisely saith,
> "A lengthy tongue—an early death!"
> Or sometimes takes this form instead,
> "Don't let your tongue cut off your head."
> "The tongue can speak a word whose speed,"
> Say the Chinese, "outstrips the steed."
> The Arab sages said in part,
> "The tongue's great storehouse is the heart."
> From Hebrew was the maxim sprung.
> "Thy feet should slip, but ne'er the tongue."
> The sacred writer crowns the whole,
> "Who keeps the tongue doth keep his soul."[5]

Dimension 2: Care for the Unfortunate (v. 27a)

If those so smug in their excellence of worship were shaken by James' first dimension of acceptable religion, they undoubtedly were sent reeling by the second: "Religion that is pure and undefiled before God, the Father, is this: to visit orphans and widows in their affliction . . ." (v. 27a).

"Orphans and widows" were the most helpless people in Jewish society, their "affliction" (literally "pressure") coming from their desperate need of food and clothing. James uses them as representative of all who are in need. Religious observances, no matter how perfectly observed and appropriately reverent, are empty if there is no concern for the needy. We may participate in an elegant call to worship and prayer, heartily sing the *Gloria Patri*, solemnly repeat the Apostles' Creed, join together on a grand hymn, reverently pray the Lord's Prayer, and listen attentively to the Word preached, but if we ignore the needy our worship is ashes on the altar! The Old Testament contains repeated reproofs along this line, as Isaiah records in this oracle:

> What to me is the multitude of your sacrifices?
>   says the LORD;

I have had enough of burnt offerings of rams
　　and the fat of well-fed beasts;
I do not delight in the blood of bulls,
　　or of lambs, or of goats. . . .

Bring no more vain offerings;
　　incense is an abomination to me. . . .

When you spread out your hands,
　　I will hide my eyes from you;
even though you make many prayers,
　　I will not listen;
　　your hands are full of blood.
Wash yourselves; make yourselves clean;
　　remove the evil of your deeds from before my eyes;
cease to do evil,
　　learn to do good;
seek justice,
　　correct oppression;
bring justice to the fatherless,
　　plead the widow's cause. (Isaiah 1:11–17)

God's people have had to relearn this lesson over and over. Today in the center of Picadilly Circus there stands the statue of Eros (in the form of Cupid with bow and arrow in hand). Most people think it is a monument to romantic human love, but they are wrong. It is actually a statue honoring the great Christian social reformer Lord Shaftesbury and his *Christian Eros*—love for mankind. Shaftesbury awakened his land, if only momentarily and partially, to its Christian responsibility regarding a number of social/moral issues. True religion, religion God accepts, cannot exist apart from caring for orphans and widows in their distress.

James would have agreed with D. L. Moody who when he encountered a man who said, "I have been on the Mount of Transfiguration for five years" shot back, "How many souls have you led to Christ?" "Well, I don't know," was the reply. "Have you led any?" persisted Mr. Moody. "I don't know that I have," answered the man. "Well," said Moody, "sit down, we don't want that kind of mountaintop experience. When a man gets so high that he can't reach down and save others there is something wrong."

The Apostle John put this truth in unforgettable words: "But if anyone has the world's goods and sees his brother in need, yet closes his heart against him, how does God's love abide in him? Little children, let us not love in word or talk but in deed and in truth" (1 John 3:17, 18). James is telling us that our care for the needy must not just be by supporting social programs or through the hands of others—but *personally*. We are to be involved in their "affliction"—the pressures that squeeze them in their circumstances—pressures due to illness or fractured relationships or unemployment or family tensions. James insists that *acceptable religion* reaches out to people in their needs.

The finest worship we can offer to God is the giving of our "bodies as a living sacrifice, holy and acceptable to God, which is your spiritual worship" (Romans 12:1). Worship that pleases God involves throwing ourselves on the altar and before the needy world in service. We may plead a lack of time, but if we have time for recreation and social visits we have the time![6]

Dimension 3: An Unsoiled Life (v. 27b)

The third dimension of acceptable religion is ". . . to keep oneself unstained from the world."

Today's world is increasingly polluted. Much contemporary thought evacuates words of moral meaning: perversion is "gay," the murder of unborn children is "reproductive choice," Marxism in the church is "liberation theology."[7] Today Isaiah's lament is being lived out: evil is called good and good evil, and light is darkness and darkness is light (Isaiah 5:20).

A story told by Frank Gaebelein, beloved headmaster of Stony Brook School, emphasizes the point, though it may seem puritanical and overly fastidious to our jaded eyes.

> Early in his ministry Dr. Maltbie Babcock, who was the distinguished pastor of the Brick Presbyterian Church in New York, was approached by a physician who was a member of his congregation. The physician, a good friend of Dr. Babcock, was concerned about the health of his pastor, who had been working very hard and clearly needed relaxation. Handing Dr. Babcock some theatre tickets, he said: "Take these, you need the recreation of going to this play."
>
> His pastor looked at them, and seeing that they were tickets to a play of a kind he could not conscientiously attend, said kindly: "Thank you, but I can't take them. I can't go."
>
> "Why not?" the physician asked. "You're tired and need the entertainment."
>
> Then Dr. Babcock replied somewhat in this way: "Yes, I am tired, and I do need recreation. But, doctor, it's this way. You are a physician, a surgeon, in fact. When you operate you scrub your hands meticulously until you are antiseptically clean. You wouldn't dare operate with dirty hands. Well, I am a servant of Christ; I deal with precious human souls. And I wouldn't dare do my work with a dirty life."[8]

How much more necessary do we need today "to keep [ourselves] un-stained from the world," for example, by television programs that would probably make the tickets offered to Dr. Babcock seem as harmless as *Leave it to Beaver*! James is deadly serious, and if we will take him seriously we will change our television viewing. God may even be telling some to toss the TV in the trash! The same is true, no doubt, of some of our reading habits. For others there are places they must never set foot in again. If appropriate, tell God right now that you are quitting whatever destructive pattern you need to renounce.

It is so easy to become self-deceived by our religiosity. But James shows us that acceptable religion is three-dimensional.

First, it means keeping a tight rein on the tongue. We must be free from gossip and slander or our religion is worthless.

Second, true religion means hands-on caring for the victims of the pressures of life.

Third, acceptable religion is a pure life.

The three dimensions of acceptable religion involve our *words*, our *hands*, and our *hearts*. May we live life in all its dimensions Christianly.

My brothers, show no partiality as you hold the faith in our Lord Jesus Christ, the Lord of glory. For if a man wearing a gold ring and fine clothing comes into your assembly, and a poor man in shabby clothing also comes in, and if you pay attention to the one who wears the fine clothing and say, "You sit here in a good place," while you say to the poor man, "You stand over there," or, "Sit down at my feet," have you not then made distinctions among yourselves and become judges with evil thoughts? Listen, my beloved brothers, has not God chosen those who are poor in the world to be rich in faith and heirs of the kingdom, which he has promised to those who love him? But you have dishonored the poor man. Are not the rich the ones who oppress you, and the ones who drag you into court? Are they not the ones who blaspheme the honorable name by which you were called?

2:1–7

9

The Folly of Favoritism

JAMES 2:1–7

SOMEWHERE, SOMETIME CHURCH IS ABOUT TO BEGIN. All the usual faces of our Christian brothers and sisters and their children are there. Suddenly two unfamiliar profiles darken the door. The first is regal, to say the least! His hands are, as we say in Greek, *chrusodaktulios*—that is, "gold-fingered." Some of his fingers even have more than two rings, and that big Rolex is not just any Rolex! This chic display is of Roman origin and is the culture's way of indicating one's wealth. I have been told that in Rome they have shops where rings can be rented for special occasions.[1] The Roman philosopher Seneca has written, "we adorn our fingers with rings; a gem is fitted to every joint."[2] This visitor, though a Jew, clearly likes the Roman custom and is obviously into "big bucks"! And his clothing is something else! It is *lampra*—"bright" or "shining." He is decked out totally in white, as our wealthy countrymen like to do.[3] The man almost glows! (Cf. Acts 10:30.) How great he looks with his Caribbean tan and the white linen Gatsbyesque suit and the panama. We are impressed!

Oh yes . . . the other man's robe is *rhupara*—"shabby." It apparently is the only thing he has to wear because it is so tattered and grimy. But frankly, no one really notices him because all eyes are fixed on the dazzle of the first visitor.

One of the brothers rises quickly to his feet and, nodding deferentially to the rich man, says, "You sit here in a good place." As the man settles himself, the brother brusquely gestures to the shabby visitor, "You stand over there," or, "Sit down at my feet." Soon the worship service begins—or does it?

How could any group that calls itself "Christian" do such a thing? Yet well-respected scholars such as Ralph Martin say that the language of verses

2, 3, as well as the context, indicates an actual happening in the early church. James probably witnessed this tragic event himself.[4] But even if the event were hypothetical, subsequent church history has documented that this sin repeats itself in the church. We do not even have to look back to the so-called Dark Ages to find it. Because the eighteenth-century Church of England had become so elitist and inhospitable to the common man, in 1739 John Wesley had to take to graveyards and fields to preach the gospel. And thus we have poignant accounts of his preaching to thirty thousand coal miners at dawn in the fields, and the resulting saving power of the gospel evidenced by tears streaming white trails down their coal-darkened faces. Wesley was no schismatic, but because there was no room in the established church for common people, he reluctantly founded the Methodist-Episcopal Church.

Tragically, the irony went on (unbelievably, in Methodism itself!) so that one hundred years later Methodist William Booth noticed that the poorest and most degraded were never in church. Richard Collier in his history of the Salvation Army, *The General Next to God*, describes Booth's experience:

> Those who made part of Broad Street congregation never forgot that electric Sunday in 1846: the gas jets, dancing on whitewashed wall, the Minister, the Rev. Samuel Dunn, seated comfortably on his red plush throne, a concord of voices swelling into the evening's fourth hymn:
>
> > Foul I to the fountain fly;
> > Wash me, Savior, or I die.
>
> The chapel's outer door suddenly shattered open, engulfing a white scarf of fog. In its wake came a shuffling shabby contingent of men and women, wilting nervously under the stony stares of mill-manager, shopkeepers and their well-dressed wives. In their rear, afire with zeal, marched "Wilful Will" Booth, cannily blocking the efforts of the more reluctant to turn back. To his dismay the Rev. Dunn saw that young Booth was actually ushering his charges, none of whose clothes would have raised five shillings in his own pawnshop, into the very best seats; pewholders' seats, facing the pulpit, whose occupants piled the collection-plate with glinting silver.
>
> This was unprecedented, for the poor, if they came to chapel, entered by another door, to be segregated on benches without backs or cushions, behind a partition which screened off the pulpit. Here, though the service was audible, they could not see—nor could they be seen.
>
> Oblivious of the mounting atmosphere, Booth joined full-throatedly in the service—even, he later admitted, hoping this devotion to duty might rate special commendation. All too soon he learned the unpalatable truth: since Wesley's day, Methodism had become "respectable."[5]

This experience, followed by many more similar catastrophes, led to William and Catherine Booth's expulsion by the Methodists and fourteen years of poverty before founding the Salvation Army.

The use of these stories is not meant to impugn our great denominations, because at one time or another the same can be said of virtually every denomination, large or small, every Christian movement, each independent church. Christian bodies all tend to succeed, calcify, and become elitist, as a woman who lived across the tracks and wanted to join a very fashionable church found out. She talked to the pastor about it, and he suggested she go home and think about it carefully for a week. At the end of the week she came back. He said, "Now, let's not be hasty. Go home and read your Bible for an hour every day this week. Then come back and tell me if you feel you should join." Although she wasn't happy about this, she agreed to do it. The next week she was back, assuring the pastor she wanted to become a member of the church. In exasperation he said, "I have one more suggestion. You pray every day this week and ask the Lord if he wants you to come into our fellowship." The pastor did not see the woman for six months. He met her on the street one day and asked her what she had decided. She said, "I did what you asked me to do. I went home and prayed. One day while I was praying, the Lord said to me, 'Don't worry about not getting into that church. I've been trying to get into it myself for the last twenty years!'"[6]

James' word picture, church history, and our own experiences chronicle the inconsistent tendency of vibrant Christianity to become discriminatory and given to favoritism. Money—economics—is the principal medium for discrimination. Christians tend to listen more intently to the prosperous man, to defer to his wishes, to place him in positions of leadership. "If he can run the bank," we think, "he can lead the church."

But money is not the only factor of favoritism. We also make too much of education. A man or a woman may not be rich, but if they are academically pedigreed they are told, "Welcome to the church board." Similarly, if the person is well-connected within the Christian pantheon and has some evangelical nobility in his blood, there will come a knowing glint in the church's eye and a favored place.

Lane Adams, who served many years with the Billy Graham Evangelistic Association, has told how when first pastoring a large church, his wife sat anonymously in the services for several weeks next to a woman who would not even acknowledge her presence. But then came a Sunday when Mrs. Adams signed the registration—and suddenly found herself the object of the woman's fawning attention.

No "social register" mentality ought to be found in the church. The problem in James' time was that God's Word did not triumph over culture. That was also the problem in the eighteenth- and nineteenth-century church we have described. Likewise, in today's church when the poor/uneducated and the rich are not welcomed with equal enthusiasm, it is precisely because the Bible has not triumphed over culture.

Listen to James' illustration and the question with which it ends:

> For if a man wearing a gold ring and fine clothing comes into your assembly, and a poor man in shabby clothing also comes in, and if you pay attention to the one who wears the fine clothing and say, "You sit here in a good place," while you say to the poor man, "You stand over there," or, "Sit down at my feet," have you not then made distinctions among yourselves and become judges with evil thoughts [literally, "evil reasonings"]? (vv. 2–4)

Those who discriminate are possessed of wicked thoughts! They place more value on the soul of the rich man. The cavalier disregard for the poor man was an implicit devaluation of his soul. Perhaps the reasoning here was, "What a coup this rich man would be. Think what he could do for the church! But the poor man? It would take years to get him up to speed, if indeed it could be done at all." These are evil thoughts!

The evident assumption in this favoritism was that the rich man was considered to be morally superior, or obviously smarter, more disciplined, more hard-working, and thus a "better man"—more fit for the kingdom.

James detests such thinking. In fact, he sees this matter of partiality as a test of real faith. Favoritism is an indication of a heart that at best is in need of spiritual help and at worst is a heart without grace.

James introduces the rich man/poor man illustration with a command that may now be seen with its proper force: "My brothers, show no partiality as you hold the faith in our Lord Jesus Christ, the Lord of glory" (v. 1). Literally this reads, "don't receive the face," referring to receiving someone with biased judgment based on externals. The Bible repeatedly and categorically condemns such behavior.

> To show partiality is not good. (Proverbs 28:21)

> You shall do no injustice in court. You shall not be partial to the poor or defer to the great, but in righteousness shall you judge your neighbor. (Leviticus 19:15)

So I make you despised and abased before all the people, inasmuch as you do not keep my ways but show partiality in your instruction. (Malachi 2:9)

The rich and the poor meet together; the Lord is the maker of them all. (Proverbs 22:2)

Simon Peter's vision of the large sheet crawling with unclean things and God's command to eat them taught Peter this lesson in a most impressive way, so that Peter would say, "Truly I understand that God shows no partiality"—God does not *receive the face* (Acts 10:34).

The motivational power of James' command not to show favoritism lies in the fact that he calls them believers "in our Lord Jesus Christ, the Lord of glory" (v. 1). The gist of this is, "My brothers, as believers in our glorious Lord Jesus Christ, *who so lowered himself in poverty and humility*, don't show favoritism to the rich." They undoubtedly knew, as Paul would later say, "that though [Jesus] was rich, yet for your sake he became poor, so that you by his poverty might become rich" (2 Corinthians 8:9). They knew that while on earth their Lord said, "Foxes have holes, and birds of the air have nests, but the Son of Man has nowhere to lay his head" (Luke 9:58). They knew that he performed a miracle to get the money to pay his taxes (Matthew 17:27). They knew that though he was God, he had humbled himself and became obedient to death. "Therefore God has highly exalted him and bestowed on him the name that is above every name, so that at the name of Jesus every knee should bow, in heaven and on earth and under the earth, and every tongue confess that Jesus Christ is Lord, to the glory of God the Father" (Philippians 2:9–11). Seeing that the glory of Christ sprang from his downward mobility, James' readers knew that favoritism to the upwardly mobile rich, the proud and self-sufficient, was wrong.

Charles Colson, in his book *Kingdoms in Conflict*, tells how he influenced diverse interest groups through White House visits to ensure Nixon's reelection. When his guests arrived, he would escort his guests past saluting guards, down a long corridor lined with dramatic photographs of the President in action. Then he would pause at the executive dining room door, point to the door on the right, and say in hushed tones, "That's the situation room"—the legendary super-secret national security nerve center. (Actually it was just a crowded office. The real command center had been moved to the Pentagon.)

Next came dinner in the richly paneled executive dining room, lined with red-jacketed Navy stewards, the tables filled with Cabinet members and senior staff. Here Colson's "clients" began to melt. Even avowed enemies sometimes offered their help. If they needed more work, he treated them to a walk upstairs and a reverent walk through the Oval Office. If the President was there, Colson would ask (always by prearrangement) if the visitor would like to see the President.

Nixon was master at the game. He always gave his dazzled visitor gold-plated cuff links with the presidential seal. The person would be overwhelmed as he left, almost bowing, not more than sixty seconds later. It's not easy to resist the allure of the Oval Office. . . . Invariably, the lions of the waiting room became the lambs of the Oval Office. No one ever showed outward hostility. Most, except the labor leaders, forgot their best-rehearsed lines. They nodded when the President spoke, and in those rare instances when they disagreed, they did so apologetically, assuring the President that they personally respected his opinion. Ironically, none were more compliant than the religious leaders. Of all people, they should have been the most aware of the sinful nature of man and the least overwhelmed by pomp and protocol. But theological knowledge sometimes wilts in the face of worldly power.[7]

Does our theology make a difference? Does the unified call of Scripture and the example of Christ not to show partiality have an effect on us?

The Reasoning against Favoritism (vv. 5–7)

In case his hearers were not yet convinced, James now presents them with some formidable logic in the form of spiritual paradox: "Listen, my beloved brothers, has not God chosen those who are poor in the world to be rich in faith and heirs of the kingdom, which he has promised to those who love him?" (v. 5). James, contrary to some liberation theologians, does *not* say only the poor are saved.[8] Sadly, there are many poor who are spiritually poor, though there are also rich who are spiritually rich.

James' point is that in general the poor are spiritually advantaged. Our Lord chose to be born to a poor woman in an obscure town in a provincial backwoods. When he began his ministry in the synagogue in Nazareth, he took up the scroll of Isaiah and read these inaugural words: "The Spirit of the Lord is upon me, because he has anointed me to proclaim good news to the poor. He has sent me to proclaim liberty to the captives and recovering of sight to the blind, to set at liberty those who are oppressed, to proclaim the year of the Lord's favor" (Luke 4:18, 19 quoting Isaiah 61:1, 2). At the beginning of the Sermon on the Mount, the greatest sermon ever preached, the declaration of the character of those in the kingdom, he said, "Blessed are the poor in spirit, for theirs is the kingdom of heaven" (Matthew 5:3). Luke's version is the unadorned, "Blessed are you who are poor, for yours is the kingdom of God" (Luke 6:20) and the negative, "But woe to you who are rich, for you have received your consolation" (Luke 6:24).

The fact is, the materially poor are so much more likely to truly realize their spiritual need—and to entrust themselves to the grace of God. This is why Paul would write:

> For consider your calling, brothers: not many of you were wise according to worldly standards, not many were powerful, not many were of noble birth. But God chose what is foolish in the world to shame the wise; God chose what is weak in the world to shame the strong; God chose what is low and despised in the world, even things that are not, to bring to nothing things that are, so that no human being might boast in the presence of God. (1 Corinthians 1:26–29)

As James drives home the poor rich/rich poor paradox, he is powerfully asserting that the *ground is level at the foot of the cross.* This being so, it is absurd to be partial toward anyone. All should be treated equally—as beings created in the image of God. Rich and poor should be accorded equal honor and cordiality. Discrimination or favoritism is spiritually irrational.

Finally James argues that showing favoritism to the rich is socially irrational: "But you have dishonored the poor man. Are not the rich the ones who oppress you, and the ones who drag you into court? Are they not the ones who blaspheme the honorable name by which you were called?" (vv. 6, 7). James is not saying that *all* the rich oppressed them, for some did not, but this was the general *historic* experience of the Jews, as well as their *present* experience in the Jewish-Christian dispersion. The Jewish Christians of James' day were disenfranchised by both Jews and Gentiles. And being debtor-poor, they were further exploited by those rich entrepreneurial classes. Calvin expressed the folly of showing deference to rich persecutors, commenting, "There is no reason . . . for men zealously to pay respect to their own executioners, and at the same time to hurt men who are on their side."[9] To fawn over one's oppressors is strangely irrational.

In regard to our situation today, materialism perverts the human soul. How else do we explain how a man who steals a ham goes to jail and a man who steals an airline goes to the Senate? How else do we account for the adulation we give to selfish celebrities who spend their lives exploiting us? The answer can only be that a materialistic focus fosters spiritual derangement.

Jesus saw everyone as they really are. Gold fingers and flowing garments meant nothing to him. Neither did the shabby attire of the poor. He noted the heart, not the wardrobe.

In observing people perform acts of worship in the temple, Jesus watched the Jerusalem elite parade by as they dropped their offerings into the treasury—and he was not impressed. But then he saw something that made his heart thrill: a poor widow bearing only a fraction of a penny approached the coffers quietly, head bowed, hoping to draw no attention to herself. Though she did not know Jesus was watching, she knew that God was. Silently her tiny coins fell upon the shekels of the rich. But she had given *all*. That day Jesus had seen little to impress him, but when the widow passed by, though he remained seated, he was inwardly giving her a standing ovation (Mark 12:41–44).

To see like Jesus, to stand on the level plain at the foot of the cross and live out our varied relationships to God's glory—that is our call and our privilege.

If you really fulfill the royal law according to the Scripture, "You shall love your neighbor as yourself," you are doing well. But if you show partiality, you are committing sin and are convicted by the law as transgressors. For whoever keeps the whole law but fails in one point has become guilty of all of it. For he who said, "Do not commit adultery," also said, "Do not murder." If you do not commit adultery but do murder, you have become a transgressor of the law. So speak and so act as those who are to be judged under the law of liberty. For judgment is without mercy to one who has shown no mercy. Mercy triumphs over judgment.

2:8–13

10

The Perils of Favoritism

JAMES 2:8–13

DURING SABBATICAL STUDY IN CAMBRIDGE, England, Barbara and I became good coffee-drinking friends with a clergyman and a theology professor who teaches at a theological college in Sydney, Australia. Late one evening as the four of us were sipping our coffees at a Cambridge cafe, the professor told a revealing story.

He was friends, he said, with a don of one of Cambridge's most prestigious colleges, and his friend had recently invited him to one of the college's great annual feasts so he could see "the other England." So my friend dutifully showed up for the event properly attired in his formal ecclesiastical gown. But as he was greeted he noticed that his host, and most of the others, were also wearing their academic hoods. He quietly apologized to his host for his omission. But his host replied with an apologetic smile that it was quite all right—his hood would have been unacceptable, for they only recognized doctorates from Cambridge or Oxford. My friend coolly disguised his shock with a whimsical shrug. Even doctorates from Heidelberg and Harvard and the equally ancient Sorbonne would not be good enough for this snobbish elite!

That was only the beginning of my friend's peek at "the other England." Next they were ushered into a large sixteenth-century dining room and seated at tables illuminated by high candelabra. A boys' choir entered, sang a Latin grace, and exited, and the feast began. Each plate was surrounded by eight goblets to sample the separate vintages that were passed—the first bottle was a forty-year-old port! The two hundred men (no women please!) who attended the feast drank 20,000 pounds sterling ($40,000) worth of rare wines that night.

This was an academic banquet, not a church feast. Nevertheless, the ecclesiastical architecture, the soaring Gothic spires of the college's magnificent chapel, and the fact that this feast was rooted in a tradition extending back to when the college was dominated by a Christian establishment underscores the tragic irony. There could scarcely be an event more elitist and more alien from Christ and Biblical Christianity than this!

As we shall see, James views such snobbery as not being at all Christian. James is preeminently a moral theologian. For him, what we do says far more about the authenticity of our faith than what we say we believe. A heart that practices favoritism toward the privileged and ignores the poor is imperiled, to say the least. James now shows how partiality relates to God's Law.

The Peril of Transgression (vv. 8–11)

James begins positively: "If you really fulfill the royal law according to the Scripture, 'You shall love your neighbor as yourself,' you are doing well" (v. 8). To catch the force of what James is saying here, we need to understand that the Ten Commandments—in fact, the entire Law—was summarized in two commandments, the first being *vertical* (Deuteronomy 6:4, 5): to love God with all that you are, and the second *horizontal* (Leviticus 19:18): to love your neighbor as yourself.

James' readers knew that if they truly loved God they would fulfill the first four of the Ten Commandments: (1) they would put no other gods before him, (2) they would not make an idol, (3) they would not misuse the name of the Lord, and (4) they would remember to keep the Sabbath holy. Following this, if they loved their neighbors as themselves they would keep the last six of the Ten Commandments: (5) they would honor their fathers and mothers, (6) they would not murder, (7) they would not commit adultery, (8) they would not steal, (9) they would not give false testimony against their neighbors, and (10) they would not covet (cf. Exodus 20:1–17).

Christ himself affirmed the comprehensiveness of the two commandments that summarize all this when a legal expert asked which is the greatest commandment in the Law. Jesus answered, "You shall love the Lord your God with all your heart and with all your soul and with all your mind. This is the great and first commandment. And a second is like it: You shall love your neighbor as yourself. On these two commandments depend all the Law and the Prophets" (Matthew 22:37–40). Elsewhere, in the Parable of the Good Samaritan, Jesus expanded the definition of "neighbor" to mean any needy human whom God gives us an opportunity to help (cf. Leviticus 19:18; Luke 10:25–37, esp. vv. 29, 36).

So we have it from the very lips of Jesus that if we love God and our neighbor, we fulfill the whole Law. The problem is, no one has ever perfectly fulfilled this except Jesus! Thus we understand that the Law is meant to bring us to the end of ourselves, to prepare us to humbly receive the gift of Christ's righteousness by faith. Then, as Christians indwelt by the Spirit, we can begin to love God and love people as we ought and thus fulfill the Law of God.

This is why James says in verse 8, "If you really fulfill the royal law according to the Scripture, 'You shall love your neighbor as yourself,' you are doing *well*"—you are living out the royal law of love that came from Heaven and was lived out by King Jesus!

When the royal law is lived, marvelous things happen *horizontally* and *vertically*. Ernest Gordon, in his book *Through the Valley of the Kwai*, tells of the miraculous transformation that took place among the allied prisoners in a Japanese concentration camp in 1943. In 1942 the camp was a sea of mud and filth, the scene of grueling labor and brutal treatment by Japanese guards. There was hardly any food, and the law that pervaded the whole camp was the law of the jungle: every man for himself. Twelve months later the ground of the camp was cleared and clean. The bamboo bed slats had been debugged. Green boughs had been used to rebuild the huts, and on Christmas morning two thousand men were at worship. What had happened? During the year a prisoner had shared his last crumb of food with another man who was also in desperate need. Then he died. Among his belongings they found a Bible. Some who witnessed his ultimate act of love wondered, could that Bible be the secret of willingness to give sacrificially to others? One by one the prisoners began to read it. Soon the Spirit of God began to grip their hearts and change their lives, and in a period of less than twelve months there was a spiritual and moral revolution within that camp.[1] The royal law lived out had done its work.

As we further trace James' argument, we see that he abruptly moves from the upside of keeping the royal law to the downside of breaking it: "But if you show partiality, you are committing sin and are convicted by the law as transgressors" (v. 9). Showing favoritism to the elite and privileged is a flagrant violation of loving your neighbor (those in need) as yourself. And such sin is no small thing. Peter Davids says, "The expression ["you . . . sin"] is stark and clear in its accusative force."[2] James views such an action as deliberate and ugly. It is not merely an excusable lack of courtesy, but a scandalous breach of God's love. When James saw the gold-fingered rich man politely seated, and the poor man treated brusquely, he knew Heaven was deeply offended. The literati of Cambridge at their exclusive bacchanal feast were committing a serious moral offense, notwithstanding the innocence of some in the crowd. Likewise, our more subtle ways of discrimination do not escape our Lord's notice and condemnation.

James underlines the seriousness of this sin in the following sentence: "For whoever keeps the whole law but fails in one point has become accountable for all of it" (v. 10). James sees the Law as a seamless garment that, when ripped in one place, tears the whole garment. Early Jewish writings said similar things, and later writings such as the *Talmud* were explicit: "If he do all, but omit one, he is guilty of all severally" (Shabbath 70, 2). Jesus himself alluded to the Law's unity (cf. Matthew 5:18, 19; 23:23), and Paul would say, "For all who rely on works of the law are under a curse; for it is written, 'Cursed be everyone who does not abide by all things written in the Book of the Law, and do them'" (Galatians 3:10; cf. 5:3).[3]

James illustrates the seamless garment principle in verse 11: "For he who said, 'Do not commit adultery,' also said, 'Do not murder.' If you do not commit adultery but do murder, you have become a transgressor of the law." It takes but one lie to make a liar, one adulterous act to make an adulterer, one theft to make a thief, one murder to make a murderer, and only one broken law to make a lawbreaker. This does not mean you and I have committed every individual sin mentioned in the Law, but that we have broken the seamless garment of the whole Law—and thus are guilty of breaking all of it! "The law is a transcript of divine character,"[4] and any violation of it is a violation of the character of God. The same evil that causes us to break one of God's laws will, in different circumstances, cause us to break the others.

It may seem like James is making a "big deal" out of the rather common sin of favoritism—"everyone does it." But he isn't, for favoritism indicates the tilt of one's soul. Christians who practice favoritism are flagrant lawbreakers. James has made favoritism a notorious sin, listing it with murder and adultery, perhaps because he sees favoritism as adultery with wealth, or maybe because Scripture associates murder with discrimination against the poor and failure to love one's neighbor (Jeremiah 7:6; 22:3; 1 John 3:15).[5]

Lives of favoritism are lives in jeopardy. What is our attitude in our heart of hearts toward the poor, toward other races, toward the uneducated? Do we favor the privileged? These are the questions of a moral theologian who is concerned that we have a real faith.

The Peril of Judgment (vv. 12, 13)

James' assertion that favoritism is a sin naturally leads to the subject of judgment. "So speak and so act," he advises in verse 12, "as those who are to be judged under the law of liberty." This advice, taken seriously, can radically

change our lives, as it did that of Amy Carmichael, the celebrated missionary to India.

The decisive moment which determined the direction of her life came on
a dull Sunday morning in Belfast as the family was returning from church.
They saw what they had never seen before in Presbyterian Belfast—an old
woman lugging a heavy bundle. Amy and her brothers turned around, took
the bundle, and helped her along by the arms. "This meant facing all the re-
spectable people who were, like ourselves, on their way home. It was a horrid
moment. We were only two boys and a girl, and not at all exalted Christians.
We hated doing it. Crimson all over (at least we felt crimson, soul and body
of us) we plodded on, a wet wind blowing us about, and blowing, too, the
rags of that poor old woman, till she seemed like a bundle of feathers and we
unhappily mixed up with them." There was an ornate Victorian fountain in
the street, and just as they passed it, "this mighty phrase was suddenly flashed
as it were through the grey drizzle: 'Gold, silver, precious stones, wood, hay,
stubble—every man's work shall be made manifest; for the day shall declare
it, because it shall be declared by fire; and the fire shall try every man's work
of what sort it is. If any man's work abide—'" Amy turned to see who had
spoken. There was nothing but the fountain, the muddy street, the people
with their politely surprised faces. The children plodded on with the bundle
of feathers, but something had happened to the girl which changed forever
life's values.[6]

The knowledge that God was her judge and that judgment was coming
gave Amy Carmichael the strength of character to ignore the pressures of a
class-driven society and forever identify with the poor, which she did in her
legendary ministry. She no longer courted the favor of the privileged.

The unchangeable fact for all of us is that we will undergo a final judgment by the Law that gives freedom. All nonbelievers will be judged by the
Law and will be condemned, receiving eternal equity for all transgressions.
However, no true Christian will be condemned, for as Paul says, "There is
therefore now no condemnation for those who are in Christ Jesus" (Romans
8:1). But this does not mean Christians will not be judged, for Paul also says,
"For we must all appear before the judgment seat of Christ, so that each one
may receive what is due for what he has done in the body, whether good or
evil" (2 Corinthians 5:10; cf. Romans 14:12). God will judge "every idle
word" (Matthew 12:36, 37, KJV). Even more, he will judge every action according to what was in our hearts.

This judgment will be no casual prelude to eternity. It will be a solemn time. True, some believers' works will be seen as "gold, silver, precious

stones," but others will suffer immense shame for their "wood, hay [or] straw." Truly, our "work will become manifest, for the Day will disclose it, because it will be revealed by fire, and the fire will test what sort of work each one has done. If the work that anyone has built on the foundation survives, he will receive a reward. If anyone's work is burned up, he will suffer loss, though he himself will be saved, but only as through fire" (1 Corinthians 3:12–15).

James, the Lord's brother, lived in awareness of this reality and so commands those prone to favoritism to "So speak and so act as those who are to be judged under the law of liberty" (v. 12). "Speak" and "act" are present active imperatives: keep on speaking and keep on acting in the reality of the coming judgment.

This is sobering grist for spiritual meditation. You do not know my heart, and I do not know yours, but God does. And we are going to be relentlessly and perfectly judged.

James now concludes his warning with the insertion of a note of terror, a proverb-like statement: "For judgment is without mercy to one who has shown no mercy" (v. 13a). Jesus taught this in his Parable of the Unmerciful Slave (Matthew 18:21–35). The slave owed his master an immense sum—in today's currency, about twenty million dollars! The debt was impossible to repay, so he pleaded with his master, who in turn had compassion on him and astonishingly forgave him the entire debt. Then incredibly the wicked slave went out, found one of his fellow slaves who owed him about $2,000, and threw him in prison because he could not pay. When the other slaves told the master about this injustice, he summoned the wicked slave and said to him, "You wicked servant! I forgave you all that debt because you pleaded with me. And should not you have had mercy on your fellow servant, as I had mercy on you?" Jesus continues the story, "And in anger his master delivered him to the jailers, until he should pay all his debt. So also my heavenly Father will do to every one of you, if you do not forgive your brother from your heart" (Matthew 18:32–35).

Jesus' parable reveals the spiritual psychology of the soul: an unmerciful spirit reveals a heart that has not received mercy, but the heart that has been the object of divine mercy will be merciful. This is why the fifth beatitude proclaims, "Blessed are the merciful, for they shall receive mercy" (Matthew 5:7). If we are not merciful we have much to fear, for the beatitude becomes a curse parallel to James' words. The unmerciful will not receive mercy. A terrifying thought!

A deeper terror in James' words is this: *favoritism is evidence of an un-*

merciful spirit. The merciful do not ignore the poor in favor of the privileged, but reach out to them. James is saying that a life characterized by discrimination and favoritism indicates a damned soul![7] This is frightening moral theology from the brother of Jesus.

Of course, there is an upside in his final sentence: "Mercy triumphs over judgment" (v. 13b). A heart full of mercy through faith in the mercy of God "triumphs over [literally *boasts against*] judgment." A truly merciful Christian heart looks forward to judgment.

The beauty of James' practical, moral approach to faith is that it cuts through all the religious words and rhetoric. We can fool each other so easily, simply by learning to quote a few Bible verses and slip in some evangelical clichés. We can learn to give a proper Christian testimony and deliver it with apparent conviction, but that does not mean our faith is real.

James is saying that real faith is not indicated only by avoiding the big no-no's like murder and adultery, but by how we treat people, especially the needy.

Personal peril. We must by all means apply James' tests to ourselves, but must *never* apply them to others, for no one can know another's heart. The personal question James demands we ask ourselves is, how is *my* heart in this matter of favoritism? Is it in peril of judgment because I am transgressing the royal law? Or does it wait triumphantly? Each of us must answer for himself or herself.

Corporate peril. There is a particular corporate application for any church that is made up of educated, upwardly mobile people. It is so easy for today's affluent church to practice an urbane, omni-smiling favoritism that offers a brighter fraternal smile to well-dressed professionals and a cordial but less enthusiastic greeting to the less-favored or troubled. Such subtle discrimination may defy human detection, but God always sees it. And if it is practiced long enough it can eviscerate a church even while its walls stand and its spires point symbolically to Heaven.

If a church is strong in worship, missions, evangelism, or youth ministry, that is because it has worked at strengthening those areas. By God's grace, a church can also become strong in caring for the poor, the refugees, the disabled, the disenfranchised, and the broken as believers intentionally submit to God's Word. This is a choice God wants us to make individually and corporately as we follow Christ in his love for all.

Lord, deliver us from the folly of favoritism!

What good is it, my brothers, if someone says he has faith but does not have works? Can that faith save him? If a brother or sister is poorly clothed and lacking in daily food, and one of you says to them, "Go in peace, be warmed and filled," without giving them the things needed for the body, what good is that? So also faith by itself, if it does not have works, is dead. But someone will say, "You have faith and I have works." Show me your faith apart from your works, and I will show you my faith by my works. You believe that God is one; you do well. Even the demons believe—and shudder!

2:14–19

11

Real Faith, Part 1

JAMES 2:14–19

THE FIRST THING PEOPLE DO when they get *The New Yorker* is read the cartoons, because a good cartoon not only entertains, but often humors the truth home in a powerful way. Recently I came across a cartoon in another publication that did just that for me. It pictured a conventional-looking church with a large billboard in the foreground advertising its ministry. The sign read:

> The Lite Church
> 24% FEWER COMMITMENTS,
> HOME OF THE 7.5% TITHE,
> 15-MINUTE SERMONS,
> 45-MINUTE WORSHIP SERVICES.
> WE HAVE ONLY 8 COMMANDMENTS—YOUR CHOICE.
> WE USE JUST 3 SPIRITUAL LAWS.
> EVERYTHING YOU'VE WANTED IN A CHURCH . . . AND LESS![1]

That is the stained-glass experience of so many in the modern church today—no quickening of the conscience, no feeding of the mind, no opening of the heart, no commitment—*no real faith*.

This was James' concern millennia ago, because it was just as likely then as today for church attenders to slide along with a bogus faith that made no real difference in the way they lived. James wants to make crystal-clear what makes faith real faith, and in doing so he sheds eternal wisdom on the relationship of faith and action. James' teaching, taken to heart, will steel the church against a "lite" faith.

Illumination through Rhetorical Questions (v. 14)

James begins his argument with two rhetorical questions that (in the Greek) demand negative answers:[2] "What good is it, my brothers, if someone says he has faith but does not have works? Can that faith save him?" (v. 14). James seems at first glance to be saying that faith alone does not save, a truth he will again express in 2:24: "You see that a person is justified by works and not by faith alone." This puts James in apparent contradiction with the Apostle Paul who argues for *faith alone* in Romans 3:28 — "For we hold that one is justified by faith apart from works of the law" (cf. Romans 4:5; Galatians 3:6–14; Ephesians 2:8–10). Paul says unequivocally that salvation is *sola fide*, by faith alone. Is this a huge contradiction within the New Testament Scriptures? Martin Luther, who was battling for the Reformation doctrine of salvation through faith alone, thought so, and in the preface to his 1522 edition of the New Testament he called James a "right strawy epistle."[3]

However, there is no real contradiction between James and Paul regarding faith, for Paul's teaching about faith and works focuses on the time *before* conversion, and James' focus is *after* conversion. As Douglas Moo has pointed out, "Paul denies any efficacy to pre-conversion works, but James is pleading for the absolute necessity of post-conversion works."[4] Paul was fighting against tradition that promoted a false works salvation. James was fighting against a "lite" faith that minimized the necessity of works after coming to Christ. Paul says works cannot bring us to Christ. James says after we come to Christ they are imperative.

Illumination through Illustration (vv. 15–17)

To further emphasize the importance of a faith that works, James now gives a shocking illustration: "If a brother or sister is poorly clothed and lacking in daily food, and one of you says to them, 'Go in peace, be warmed and filled,' without giving them the things needed for the body, what good is that? So also faith by itself, if it does not have works, is dead" (vv. 15–17). In this illustration a "brother or sister," a fellow believer who sits at the Lord's Table with the rest of the church in worship, is inadequately clad, perhaps in rags or lacking an outer garment, and is so destitute that he or she does not even have food to eat that day. You, feeling full and satisfied in your fashionable wardrobe, see the tattered believer and with a radiant smile say, "Go in peace, be warmed and filled" and without the slightest twinge of conscience go merrily on your way.

If and when this happens, something is radically wrong with one's faith.

So James properly asks, "What good is that?," the only answer being, "None at all." Thus he concludes, "So also faith by itself, if it does not have works, is dead" (v. 17). It is not only outwardly dead but *inwardly* dead[5]—totally lifeless and useless.

The inconsistency between what one claims to be and what one actually is is typical of those outside Christ. Historian Paul Johnson says Rousseau was the first intellectual to repeatedly proclaim himself the friend of all mankind. Rousseau said he was a man born to love and in fact taught the doctrine of love more persistently than most preachers.[6] He once said of himself that whoever "examines with his own eyes my nature, my character, morals, inclinations, pleasures, habits, and can believe me to be a dishonest man, is himself a man who deserves to be strangled."[7] But how did Rousseau actually relate to humanity? His father meant nothing to him but an inheritance. His only concern for his long-lost brother was to certify him dead so he could get the family money. All five of his children were unnamed and were placed immediately after birth in the Hospital des Enfants-trouves where two-thirds of all babies died the first year and only fourteen out of every one hundred lived to the age of seven. It is believed that none survived. Rousseau, the self-proclaimed lover of mankind, did not even record the dates of their births![8]

Rousseau's conduct, horrifying as it is, is at least comprehensible in terms of his antagonism to Christianity and cosmic egoism. But similar conduct in the church, such as the pious disregard for the poor brother James describes, gives the lie to any claims to real faith. The Apostle John affirms this in a different context saying, "If anyone has the world's goods and sees his brother in need, yet closes his heart against him, how does God's love abide in him? Little children, let us not love in word or talk but in deed and in truth" (1 John 3:17, 18).

True faith requires compassion and action. An English preacher happened across a friend whose horse had been accidentally killed. While the crowd of onlookers expressed empty words of sympathy, the preacher stepped forward and said to the loudest sympathizer, "I am sorry five pounds. How much are you sorry?" Then he passed the hat. Profession requires action or it is not real!

If we tend to talk about our faith in Christ and the truth of his Word but do nothing, or very little, we may be in spiritual trouble. If we refuse to get our hands dirty, or if we are cheap and grudging with other people, we must take inventory of our souls. James says "faith by itself, if it does not have works, is *dead*"—*nekros*, an ugly word. If we are "lite" on works, we may be in the clutches of Satan, the *necromancer* of lost souls.

Illumination through an Imaginary Objector (v. 18)

James now brings forth an imaginary objector who has what we call a laissez-faire, "live and let live," "I'm OK, you're OK" attitude regarding faith and works. This objector says, "You have faith and I have works" (v. 18a), or as the NEB has it, "Here is one who claims to have faith and another who points to his deeds." He says in effect, "You like theology and are more theoretical and prefer to talk about faith. On the other hand, I'm of a practical bent. Faith for me is living out Jesus' teaching. We're both Christians, but we have different emphases."[9] James explodes, "Show me your faith apart from your works, and I will show you my faith by my works" (v. 18b). James challenges the pseudo-faith of the "live and let live" objector, believing that faith and works are inseparable.[10]

James' divine brother, the Lord Jesus, agrees. In his Parable of the Sower the first three soils (the hard soil, the rocky soil, and the weed-infested soil) yielded no fruit. But as Jesus concludes, "As for what was sown on good soil, this is the one who hears the word and understands it. He indeed bears fruit and yields, in one case a hundredfold, in another sixty, and in another thirty" (Matthew 13:23). True living faith produces fruit—living action. Similarly, at the end of the Sermon on the Mount Jesus warns, "You will recognize them by their fruits. Are grapes gathered from thornbushes, or figs from thistles? So, every healthy tree bears good fruit, but the diseased tree bears bad fruit. A healthy tree cannot bear bad fruit, nor can a diseased tree bear good fruit. Every tree that does not bear good fruit is cut down and thrown into the fire. Thus you will recognize them by their fruits. Not everyone who says to me, 'Lord, Lord,' will enter the kingdom of heaven, but the one who does the will of my Father who is in heaven" (Matthew 7:16–21). Faith and works are like the wings of a bird. There can be no real life, no flight, with a single wing, whether works or faith. But when the two are pumping together in concert, their owner soars through the heavens. Faith and works—neither is authentic without the other!

Illumination through Absurdity (v. 19)

James concludes this section by taking his hearers to the absurd: "You believe that God is one; you do well. Even the demons believe—and shudder!" (v. 19). There is not a demon in the universe who is an atheist! There are, no doubt, some who are spirits of atheism, demons who have influenced and danced on the graves of the likes of Bertrand Russell. But all are thorough-going *monotheists*, for they believe God is one (cf. Deuteronomy 6:4, 5).

And they are all *Trinitarian*. They know the Apostles' Creed is true: God is the Maker, and Jesus is his virgin-born Son. They know the truth of Christ's death, resurrection, ascension, and coming return. Some, no doubt, can quote the Nicene Creed—that Jesus is

> God of God, Light of Light,
> Very God of Very God,
> Begotten, not made,
> Being of one substance with the Father,
> By whom all things were made.

Some demons are great theologians, having been unseen interlopers at Nicea and Chalcedon and Worms.

In fact, some demons have better theology than we do! But it does them no good. James says they "shudder"—*phrissousin*. Literally they "bristle up" like a frightened cat.

James' point is, *there is a belief that is not true faith*. Simon the sorcerer is another prime example. Luke records in Acts 8:13 that Simon believed and was baptized. But several verses later, after his attempt to buy spiritual power, Luke records Peter as saying to Simon, "You have neither part nor lot in this matter, for your heart is not right before God. Repent, therefore, of this wickedness of yours, and pray to the Lord that, if possible, the intent of your heart may be forgiven you. For I see that you are in the gall of bitterness and in the bond of iniquity" (Acts 8:21–23). Simon the sorcerer's faith did not even benefit him as much as it does the demons, because at least they shudder! Simon foreshadows the multitudes who week after week have said their creedal "I believe," but have neither faith nor fear of God. Tragically Hell will have its share of people who are monotheistic, Trinitarian, orthodox, and *lost*.

Real faith is more than mental assent to truth. It is a belief that involves the heart "because, if you confess with your mouth that Jesus is Lord and believe in your heart that God raised him from the dead, you will be saved. For with the heart one believes and is justified, and with the mouth one confesses and is saved" (Romans 10:9, 10). It is one thing to say, "I believe this airplane will hold me"; it is quite another thing to fly somewhere in it.

When Paul answered the Philippian jailer's cry, "Sirs, what must I do to be saved?" (Acts 16:30) with "Believe *in* the Lord Jesus, and you will be saved" (Acts 16:31), he said it all. The preposition "in" (*epi*) means moving toward and resting upon its object, "the Lord Jesus."[11] This means to rest *everything* on him. Perhaps you are well taught in the Scriptures, but have you truly done this?

What about works? we may ask. The answer was given by Christ to some good-deeds Jews: "This is the work of God, that you believe in him whom he has sent" (John 6:29). The unregenerate heart thinks of works first as it desires salvation. But Jesus says the first "work" is to believe. After this, a true faith works and works and works and works!

This is exactly what happened with John Wesley. Before he was a believer he was a clergyman and a missionary who worked with all he had. He memorized most of the Greek New Testament. He had a disciplined devotional life. As a missionary to the American Indians, he slept on the dirt to increase his merit and hopefully be accepted by God.

But then came that celebrated day when he trusted in *Christ alone* for his salvation. It was then—with his wings of faith and works in place—that he began a works-filled life that warmed the heart of James. The rest of the story is well-known. He preached in Saint Mary's in Oxford, he preached in the churches, he preached in the mines, he preached in the fields and on the streets, and he preached on horseback. He even preached on his father's tombstone. "John Wesley preached 42,000 sermons. He averaged 4,500 miles a year. He rode 60 to 70 miles a day and preached three sermons a day on an average. When he was 83, he wrote in his diary, 'I am a wonder to myself, I am never tired, either with preaching, writing or travelling!'"[12]

As we all know, the church has never been the same. Wesley's disciples— Francis Asbury, for one—were mighty powers in evangelizing frontier America. Read about Wesley and his circuit riders, and you will find chronicled the most amazing love for Christ and a tenacious love for lost souls. Their lives are among the great glories of the Church Universal.

There is no such thing as a "lite" church, for a "church" that waters down its call for commitment is an imitation. Likewise, there is no such thing as a "lite" faith. A real faith is committed. It wholeheartedly follows the Master. It reflexively reaches out to those it perceives to be in need. It places its hands on the infections of the ill. It works to meet the spiritual and material needs of all.

As the wings of faith and works beat together, one's life will soar with James and Paul and John Wesley—right up to the heart of God.

Do you want to be shown, you foolish person, that faith apart from works is useless? Was not Abraham our father justified by works when he offered up his son Isaac on the altar? You see that faith was active along with his works, and faith was completed by his works; and the Scripture was fulfilled that says, "Abraham believed God, and it was counted to him as righteousness"—and he was called a friend of God. You see that a person is justified by works and not by faith alone. And in the same way was not also Rahab the prostitute justified by works when she received the messengers and sent them out by another way? For as the body apart from the spirit is dead, so also faith apart from works is dead.

2:20–26

12

Real Faith, Part 2

JAMES 2:20–26

THE ACTUALIZATION and maintenance of authentic faith has been a problem for the church from apostolic times onward. In the last century this problem was a main concern of the philosopher Kierkegaard, who addressed it with his considerable arsenal of literary weapons, variously employing logic, paradox, scorn, humor, and parable. In one memorable instance he told a parable about Duckland: It was Sunday morning, and all the ducks dutifully came to church, waddling through the doors and down the aisle into their pews where they comfortably squatted. When all were well-settled, and the hymns were sung, the duck minister waddled to his pulpit, opened the Duck Bible, and read, "Ducks! You have wings, and with wings you can fly like eagles. You can soar into the sky! Use your wings!" It was a marvelous, elevating duck scripture, and thus all the ducks quacked their assent with a hearty "Amen!"—and then they plopped down from their pews and *waddled* home.[1]

In the lives of many churchgoers today, there is a yawning chasm between profession and action, between professed faith and works—and that chasm gives the lie to people's loud claims to real faith.

As we saw in our previous study of verses 14–19, James has a passionate desire to close that deadly gap, using his own considerable literary devices to capture his readers' attention. As we take up the second half of his appeal in verses 20–26, he poses an aggressively phrased question: "Do you want to be shown, you foolish person, that faith apart from works is useless?" (v. 20). James was obviously not a student of Dale Carnegie, for "foolish" means literally "empty," suggesting in today's language shallowness. *O empty, shallow man!* He is short on tact, to be sure, but he has our attention and goes

on to answer his own question with two diverse case studies—Abraham and
Rahab, a patriarch and a prostitute. Both extremes, James will argue, dem-
onstrate the importance of active faith.

Abraham's Authentic Faith (vv. 21–24)

The first case study is detailed in verses 21–23: "Was not Abraham our father
justified by works when he offered up his son Isaac on the altar? You see that
faith was active along with his works, and faith was completed by his works;
and the Scripture was fulfilled that says, 'Abraham believed God, and it was
counted to him as righteousness'" (quoting Genesis 15:6).

In order to fully understand what James is saying, we must look at Genesis 15:6 in its context, which reveals that Abraham had just come off a great
military victory where he and 318 of his men had rescued Lot, defeating four
kings in battle (Genesis 14). Like Elijah after his great victory over the prophets of Baal, Abraham was suffering letdown. He was old, the battle had taken
a lot out of him, and he was tired. Perhaps as he drifted off to sleep he was
reflecting with weary negativism on his having been in the land for ten years,
but still having no heir to carry on. Just then God spoke in a vision: "Fear not,
Abram, I am your shield; your reward shall be very great" (Genesis 15:1).
Rousing words! Nevertheless, Abraham, still discouraged, expressed his fear
that because he was childless his estate would go to his servant Eliezer.

With Abraham at this low point, the word of the Lord came to him:
"'This man shall not be your heir; your very own son shall be your heir.' And
he brought him outside and said, 'Look toward heaven, and number the stars,
if you are able to number them.' Then he said to him, 'So shall your offspring
be'" (Genesis 15:4, 5). We do not know whether Abraham's response was im-
mediate or came after some thought, or whether it was verbal or mental, but
we do have this immortal record: "And he believed the LORD, and he counted
it to him as righteousness" (Genesis 15:6). The Old Testament scholar H. C.
Leupold calls the word "believed" here "the biggest word in the chapter, one
of the greatest in the Old Testament!"—noting that it is the first instance of
the word *believe* in Scripture! Its emphasis, says Leupold, is the permanence
of Abraham's trust.[2] The patriarch rested everything on God's word and kept
on resting in faith. As a result he was declared righteous apart from works,
fourteen years before circumcision (Genesis 17) and hundreds of years before
the Law!

This was one of the greatest events in the history of salvation, and the
Lord commemorated it with a further sign when he ordered Abraham to make
sacrifices and divide them into two piles. Then, when the sun had set, God

appeared in the night as "a smoking fire pot and a flaming torch [and] passed between these pieces" (Genesis 15:17) in the traditional figure-eight pattern of *covenant*, signifying that his promise was unconditional and that he (God) would be torn asunder like the pieces if he failed to keep his promise.

Genesis 15:6 is the locus classicus of the Old Testament on salvation through faith alone. It is not surprising then that Paul quotes it twice in arguing that all who are justified must be justified by faith alone.

> What then shall we say was gained by Abraham, our forefather according to the flesh? For if Abraham was justified by works, he has something to boast about, but not before God. For what does the Scripture say? "Abraham believed God, and it was counted to him as righteousness." . . . And to the one who does not work but believes in him who justifies the ungodly, his faith is counted as righteousness. (Romans 4:1–5)

> . . . just as Abraham "believed God, and it was counted to him as righteousness" . . . Know then that it is those of faith who are the sons of Abraham. (Galatians 3:6, 7)

With this understanding of Genesis 15:6 in mind, and realizing that James uses this verse to end his case study of Abraham, we are prepared to look at his argument: "Was not Abraham our father justified by works when he offered up his son Isaac on the altar? You see that faith was active along with his works, and faith was completed by his works" (vv. 21, 22).

What exactly did Abraham do in offering Isaac? Genesis 22 gives the full account, and we must note as we look at this experience that the offering of Isaac took place a full *thirty years after* Genesis 15:6 when "[Abraham] believed the LORD, and he counted it to him as righteousness." Now, in Genesis 22, Abraham was well over one hundred years old when God said to him, "Take your son, your only son Isaac, whom you love, and go to the land of Moriah, and offer him there as a burnt offering on one of the mountains of which I shall tell you" (Genesis 22:2). This is easily the most shocking command ever given to any human being by God! We can imagine the sickening horror that must have spread over Abraham's soul. It was contrary to his common sense, his natural affections, his lifelong dreams. This makes his ready obedience almost as equally shocking as with the first glow of dawn, without a word to aged Sarah, Abraham saddled his donkey, quietly called for two servants and his son Isaac, split wood for the sacrificial pyre, and began the terrible journey (Genesis 22:3).

How could he do it? we wonder. Our text gives us the answer: "On the third day Abraham lifted up his eyes and saw the place from afar. Then Abraham said to his young men, 'Stay here with the donkey; I and the boy will go over there and worship and come again to you'" (Genesis 22:4, 5). *Abraham was confident they would return together!* This was because, as the writer of Hebrews reveals, "He considered that God was able even to raise him from the dead, from which, figuratively speaking, he did receive him back" (Hebrews 11:19; cf. Hebrews 11:17, 18). Abraham believed God would bless him through Isaac, giving him offspring as numerous as the stars. God would certainly therefore resurrect his son!

The poignant exchange between father and son as they ascended Mt. Moriah and Isaac's dawning realization that he was the sacrifice—the construction of the altar—Isaac's voluntary submission to his aged father as he was bound—the emotion between the lines of the story: the sobbing, the kisses, the tears, the terrible blade in the father's trembling hand, the nausea, the darkness—the imminent convulsions of his only son—all this shows only the tip of Abraham's emotions.

Then the angel from Heaven called, "Abraham, Abraham!" and we know the rest of the story in all its tender redemptive glory. But do we remember the final pronouncement of the angel of the Lord?

> By myself I have sworn, declares the LORD, because you have done this and have not withheld your son, your only son, I will surely bless you, and I will surely multiply your offspring as the stars of heaven and as the sand that is on the seashore. And your offspring shall possess the gate of his enemies, and in your offspring shall all the nations of the earth be blessed, because you have obeyed my voice. (Genesis 22:16–18)

Genesis 22 thus reveals the deeds of Abraham and his well-deserved heavenly approval. Because of this, James argues, Abraham was "justified by works when he offered up his son Isaac on the altar" (v. 21), for his righteousness was demonstrated for all to see. His works in offering Isaac gave immortal testimony to the reality of the faith and righteousness that had infused his life for over thirty years.

Verse 22 explains further "that faith was active along with his works, and faith was completed by his works." The imperfect tense of "was active" tells us that his faith was not an isolated event in the offering of Isaac, but that faith and works were continual characteristics of Abraham's life before and after that event. The faith chapter, Hebrews 11, tells us that he started out in faith (Hebrews 11:8), sojourned in faith (Hebrews 11:9), and sacrificed in faith (Hebrews 11:17). Once he had come to trust in God, his subsequent works produced a beautiful ongoing synergism of faith and works. Thus, "faith was completed by his works"—not because his faith had been defective or imperfect, but because it was completed by the successive "tests" that it underwent. In time Abraham's faith reached its intended maturity.

This all served to fulfill Genesis 15:6, as James says in verse 23: "And the Scripture was fulfilled that says, 'Abraham believed God, and it was counted to him as righteousness'—and he was called a friend of God." James' point is that where there is real faith, there will be an ineluctable outworking of it in life. *Genuine faith results in works.* The authenticity of Abraham's Genesis 15:6 experience of faith meant an inevitable outworking in life that all would see—for example, in the offering of his only son.

Ultimately the progress of Abraham's faith won him the divine sobriquet "friend of God"—an astounding title. It is one thing for us to say the President is our friend; it is another for the President to say we are his friends. Even more, it is one thing for us to say that God is our friend; it is quite another for God to call us his friends! The infinite Creator of the universe calls us, his finite creatures, his *friends*. This is sublime reality for those who are justified by faith and who grow in good works. Jesus said, "You are my friends if you do what I command you. No longer do I call you servants, for the servant does not know what his master is doing; but I have called you friends, for all that I have heard from my Father I have made known to you" (John 15:14, 15).

James wraps up his case study of Abraham by saying, "You see that a person is justified by works and not by faith alone" (v. 24). James would have been shocked if anyone suggested that he was arguing for salvation by works. He simply saw faith and works as inseparable. It is said that Napoleon, while looking at some papers, let slip the bridle of his horse, which reared so that the Emperor was in danger. A corporal of the grenadiers leaped forward and caught the bridle, bringing the horse under control. Napoleon saluted the corporal and said, "Thank you, *Captain*." "Of what company, Sire?" asked the corporal. "Of my guards," replied Napoleon. The young corporal picked up his musket, hurled it aside, and walked across the field toward the Emperor's staff, tearing off his corporal's stripes as he went. When he took his place among the officers, they asked him what he was doing. He replied that he was a captain of the guards. "By whose order?" queried one of them. "The Emperor's order," he replied. A man of less faith might have picked up his musket, stepped back into the ranks, and boasted for the rest of his life that Napoleon had called him captain. This describes the difference between mental assent and true faith, which takes God at His word and acts upon it.[3]

James would say we are justified by faith alone (*sola fide*), but not by faith that is alone! He would say that if your faith is alone, you are in the grip of an eternal illusion and would urge you to experience real faith—a faith that works!

Rahab's Authentic Faith (vv. 25, 26)

It was conceivable that some of James' readers might take exception to his argument, saying that Abraham is an unfair example because he is such a towering figure in the history of religion, a man whose position and accomplishments set him far above the level of normal humankind. Perhaps for contrast, James now introduces the case of Rahab: "And in the same way was not also Rahab the prostitute justified by works when she received the messengers and sent them out by another way?" (v. 25). Abraham was a patriarch, Rahab a prostitute. He was moral, she was immoral. He was the original Jew, she a Gentile woman. He was upwardly mobile, she lived in the gutter.

Nevertheless, Rahab developed a towering faith. How did her faith flower? Abraham Kuyper, a great theologian who also served as prime minister of the Netherlands, surmised:

> The people who in Rahab's time most frequently used such houses of prostitution were the traveling merchants. From them she had repeatedly heard of the marvelous nation which was approaching from Egypt, and of the God of Israel who had perfected such striking miracles.[4]

Rahab had heard there was only one God, Jehovah. She heard bits and snatches about Israel's destiny. She heard, perhaps derisively, of the nation's high ethical and moral code. Perhaps she had become disillusioned with the culture around her, in which she was treated as chattel. All of this made her open to truth and faith. No doubt fear, a natural consequence of sensing we have offended God's holiness, also contributed to the formation of her faith. Rahab certainly knew she was a sinner. She was ready for faith.

Then there was the testimony of the spies, which opened her further to faith. Rahab must immediately have sensed the difference between the Israelite visitors and those who normally frequented her house. They were not sensualists, but men of high morals. She had never seen this before. They were sure of their God. Their ethos confirmed the reality of what she had been hearing from the merchants. This, along with her disillusionment and fear, coalesced to produce faith. Rahab's words displayed belief in the one God:

I know that the LORD has given you the land, and that the fear of you has fallen upon us, and that all the inhabitants of the land melt away before you. For we have heard how the LORD dried up the water of the Red Sea before you when you came out of Egypt, and what you did to the two kings of the Amorites who were beyond the Jordan, to Sihon and Og, whom you devoted to destruction. And as soon as we heard it, our hearts melted, and there was no spirit left in any man because of you, for the LORD your God, he is God in the heavens above and on the earth beneath. (Joshua 2:9–11)

Jericho had stood for hundreds of years. Today it is still the earliest known fortified town. Its inhabitants thought it invincible. But Rahab heard God's word and, though surrounded by her ancient culture, believed! That is why her faith has been immortalized. Hebrews 11:31 says, "By faith Rahab the prostitute did not perish with those who were disobedient, because she had given a friendly welcome to the spies." Rahab's faith produced legendary works as she not only hid the spies, assisted in their escape, and brilliantly advised their path on the hill country, but put her life in great danger. Her faith produced astounding action!

The examples of Abraham and Rahab are sufficient for his argument, so James rests his point with a concluding axiom: "For as the body apart from the spirit is dead, so also faith apart from works is dead" (v. 26). Faith without action, even if embalmed in a beautifully profound creedal statement, is a decaying corpse. It is pleasantly ironic that Martin Luther, who said such disparaging things about James, has given us, in his preface to Romans, as clear an expression of the idea of James as anyone:

Oh, it is a living, busy, active, mighty thing, this faith; and so it is impossible for it not to do good works incessantly. It does not ask whether there are good works to do, but before the question rises; it has already done them, and is always at the doing of them. He who does not these works is a faithless man. He gropes and looks about after faith and good works, and knows neither what faith is nor what good works are, though he talks and talks, with many words, about faith and good works.[5]

Two things are clear from Holy Scripture. First, *salvation is by faith alone*. When "Abraham believed God, and it was counted to him as righteousness" (v. 23, quoting Genesis 15:6), the faith alone principle was established for all time. Paul says that "just as Abraham 'believed God, and it was counted to him as righteousness' . . . Know then that it is those of faith who are the sons of Abraham" (Galatians 3:6, 7)—faith alone. Again Paul says, "And to the one who does not work but believes in him who justifies the ungodly, his faith is counted as righteousness" (Romans 4:5)—faith alone. And again, "For by grace you have been saved through faith. And this is not your own doing; it is the gift of God, not a result of works, so that no one may boast" (Ephesians 2:8, 9)—faith alone.

Belief/faith honors God more than anything else. "*Believe* in the Lord Jesus, and you will be saved" (Acts 16:31). "But to all who did receive him, who *believed* in his name, he gave the right to become children of God" (John 1:12). "And by him everyone who *believes* is freed from everything from which you could not be freed by the law of Moses" (Acts 13:39). "For God so loved the world, that he gave his only Son, that whoever *believes* in him should not perish but have eternal life" (John 3:16).

Scripture teaches that the human race is dead in its trespasses. Attempting a works salvation is no more effectual than putting makeup on a corpse or rearranging the chairs on the decks of the *Titanic*. Sinners must come to Christ with faith plus nothing.

The second thing the Scriptures are clear about is that *salvation is by a faith that is not alone.* James, the New Testament's moral theologian, says it every way he can: "What good is it, my brothers, if someone says he has faith but does not have works? Can that faith save him?" (2:14). "Show me your faith apart from your works, and I will show you my faith by my works" (2:18b). "Do you want to be shown, you foolish person, that faith apart from works is useless?" (v. 20). "You see that a person is justified by works and not by faith alone" (v. 24). "For as the body apart from the spirit is dead, so also faith apart from works is dead" (v. 26).

James understands that real faith, the kind Abraham came to in Genesis 15:6, is *potent*. It always and continually produces good works. That is the whole point of the *Hall of Faith* in Hebrews 11, which also is a *Hall of Works*. "By faith Abel offered to God a more acceptable sacrifice . . ." (Hebrews 11:4). "By faith Noah . . . constructed an ark for the saving of his household" (Hebrews 11:7). "By faith Isaac invoked future blessings on Jacob" (Hebrews 11:20). "By faith Joseph . . . made mention . . ." (Hebrews 11:22). "By faith Moses . . . [chose] rather to be mistreated with the people of God" (Hebrews 11:24, 25). "By faith the people crossed the Red Sea as on dry land" (Hebrews 11:29). If you have real faith, you are infused with a mighty potency that has shown itself in good works and must continue to do so.

Those poor ducks waddled in and out of church and never flew as they were created to do, because their "faith" was nothing more than mental assent. Few things are as inglorious as a waddle, and few things are more glorious than a duck on the wing! All God's people have wings! The first wing is faith, faith alone. The second is works, a faith that works.

The first wing is the source and inspiration of the second, for as authentic faith begins to beat, it occasions the sprouting of a second wing and its corresponding rhythm. And beating together they lift us from our inglorious waddles to the glory of lives on the wing—soaring in God's service.

Not many of you should become teachers, my brothers, for you know that we who teach will be judged with greater strictness. For we all stumble in many ways. And if anyone does not stumble in what he says, he is a perfect man, able also to bridle his whole body.

3:1, 2

13

The Peril of Teaching

JAMES 3:1, 2

HENRIETTA MEARS is undoubtedly the greatest Christian education genius of our time. As Christian education director of Hollywood Presbyterian Church during the 1940s and 1950s she built the Sunday school to the then unheard of proportions of four thousand. At the end of her life Teacher, as she was affectionately called, could count no less than one hundred young people who went into Christian service under her direct influence. Thumbing through her biography I noted photographs of seminarians who came through her college department, including such later notables as Richard Halverson, chaplain of the United States Senate, and several prominent pastors and theologians. She took young Billy Graham under her wing, and also Bill Bright, who would go on to found Campus Crusade for Christ.[1] She was a woman of immense personal influence.

Henrietta Mears's vast influence extended far beyond the walls of her church. She was a prime mover in the founding of the National Sunday School Association. Gospel Light Publications, today a major publishing house, was formed by her to provide quality Sunday school materials. She was also the visionary and tireless force behind the founding of Forest Home, the great conference center where thousands upon thousands of people have come to Christ. When Teacher died in the early sixties, officials at Forest Lawn Memorial Park said it was the largest graveside crowd in twenty years—an astounding fact, considering that many of Hollywood's most famous celebrities are buried there. Henrietta Mears's life is an eloquent testimony to the positive influence of a gifted teacher who was totally committed to Christ.[2]

Thumbing through her biography, I mentally contrasted it with the chilling experience I had in 1978 when my issue of *Time* magazine fell open to a series of pictures recording the life and death of another teacher, Jim Jones. The photographer similarly chronicled Jones's life, his coterie of disciples, his triumphs, and his end—the rotting bodies of hundreds of people in the infamous Jonestown massacre—an unforgettable testimony of the influence of a teacher for evil.

Teachers wield incredible power! Young or untaught minds in the hands of a skilled teacher are like clay in a potter's hands. Such a teacher is closely watched by his or her students, and often the teacher's attitudes and personal morals have as much influence as the information conveyed—perhaps more. Casual advice from a teacher can direct the course of one's whole life. Phrases such as "Have you considered the theater?" or "I think you would make an excellent doctor" often propel young lives into one career or another. We must realize what power teachers have at crucial times in tender lives—to crush the bloom or make it eternally flower!

The Warning (v. 1a)

In view of what we have just said, James' opening words of chapter 3 are most arresting: "Not many of you should become teachers, my brothers" (v. 1a). Power issues had produced a glut of would-be teachers in the Jewish church.

The church, and especially the Jewish church, to which James was writing, was naturally heir to the worship tradition of the synagogue, which highly honored teachers and encouraged congregational participation. The title *rabbi* meant "My great one," and those holding that office were accorded the greatest respect. One's duty to help a rabbi exceeded even the duty to help one's parents. In fact, should a rabbi and one's father and mother be captured by an enemy, duty demanded that the rabbi be ransomed first! It was considered meritorious to take a rabbi in and provide for all his needs.[3]

The problem that developed in the Jewish church was that some of this overweening respect was transferred to Christian teachers, making their position seem most enviable. This, coupled with the fact that the synagogues and the early church services were places for open discussion, invited a plague of unqualified would-be teachers—ecclesiastical climbers who promoted themselves with loud, uninformed discussions that often led to disruption and dispute.

The problem, in a word, was *ambition*, which has been and continues to be the bane of the church. Often instead of being Christ-driven people, believers are need-driven in public ministry. The need for public attention, to be thought intelligent, to show oneself wiser than others, to have influence and authority, can fuel the most ostensibly pious sermons. Such persons not only scramble to places of verbal prominence, but scheme to climb the ladder, to be president of this work or chairman of that committee. Such ambition reaches its nadir when it envies others, becoming jealous when a "rival" is elevated or praised and rejoicing when something goes wrong for the "competitor."

James was well aware that evil ambitions were driving some to become teachers, and he also knew that if such people got into teaching positions they would suffer further corruption because teaching offices are fraught with moral dangers of their own. It's a heady thing to dress in your Sunday best and stand in front of a congregation and be *the* authority for one hour—the voice of God to his people. But it can ruin your soul! This had happened to some of the rabbis. As Jesus said, "They do all their deeds to be seen by others. For they make their phylacteries broad and their fringes long, and they love the place of honor at feasts and the best seats in the synagogues and greetings in the marketplaces and being called rabbi by others" ("My great one!") (Matthew 23:5–7). The same thing has happened in the Christian church. We have had our share of arrogant buffoons.

The position of *teacher* can be deluding in any context, secular or Christian. Allan Bloom, University of Chicago professor and author of *The Closing of the American Mind*, writes of the dangers that attend the classroom when an adult teacher spends his life in the company of undergraduate youths. "Such an adult," he says, "is subject to many temptations—particularly vanity and the desire to propagandize. . . ."[4] I would add that in any situation there is the temptation to give in to a subtle egoism that gives you goose bumps at hearing yourself talk. The more you hear yourself, the less you can be taught by anyone but yourself.

With this syndrome in process, you can easily begin to harden, so that you become an autocratic little pope who can brook no other opinion or discussion but your own. Those who disagree with you are branded "intellectual" or "unspiritual," depending on the context. The result is a morally bankrupt ministry that competes for its constituency. As Paul describes it, "The former proclaim Christ out of selfish ambition, not sincerely but thinking to afflict me" (Philippians 1:17).

For these reasons, James demands (yes, it is a *command*), "Not many of you should become teachers, my brothers." Now, James is not trying to diminish the pool of teachers for the church. The church has never had too many qualified, Spirit-filled teachers or leaders at any time in its history. He is rather discouraging people from taking up the task for the wrong reasons. He also is not promoting ecclesiastical elitism that limits the teaching office to the ordained or super-educated. The church in the United States is dying from a lack of good teachers in its pulpit and Sunday schools, but we need teachers with right motives.

Reasons (vv. 1b, 2)

James follows his opening warning with some explicit reasoning as to why one should be careful in assuming the position of a spiritual teacher.

The first involves *divine judgment*. "Not many of you should become teachers, my brothers," he says, "for you know that we who teach will be *judged with greater strictness*." In saying "you know," James was indicating that the would-be teachers were aware from common understanding that becoming a teacher of the church was a serious responsibility[5] involving "greater judgment" (literal translation).

How and why do teachers incur greater judgment? The answer is, if we claim to have a full knowledge of God's Word for his people, and further claim that we are charged to deliver it, we are more responsible to deliver it clearly and obey it. I, by virtue of my professed calling and study of God's Word, and in fact possession of more knowledge of God's Word than many Christians, will undergo a stricter judgment. Increased responsibility means increased accountability. Jesus, following the Parable of the Foolish Manager, said, "Everyone to whom much was given, of him much will be required, and from him to whom they entrusted much, they will demand the more" (Luke 12:48).

Every one of us—no exceptions—will stand before the *Bema*, the Judgment Seat of Jesus Christ. The Bible is clear that while believers will *not* stand in judgment for their sin (Romans 8:1), and salvation is a free gift (Ephesians 2:8, 9), *the works of believers will nevertheless be judged*: "For we must all appear before the judgment seat of Christ" (2 Corinthians 5:10). "So then each of us will give an account of himself to God" (Romans 14:12). The picture the Bible gives of this judgment is one of individual believers presenting their lives' works to Christ in the form of buildings. The eternal foundation of each building is Christ, but the structures vary. Some are made totally of wood, hay, and straw. Others are of gold, silver, and precious stones. Still others are composite structures of all the elements. Each life will be publicly subjected to the revealing torch of Christ's judgment, and with the flames will come the moment of truth:

> Now if anyone builds on the foundation with gold, silver, precious stones, wood, hay, straw—each one's work will become manifest, for the Day will disclose it, because it will be revealed by fire, and the fire will test what sort

of work each one has done. If the work that anyone has built on the foundation survives, he will receive a reward. If anyone's work is burned up, he will suffer loss, though he himself will be saved, but only as through fire. (1 Corinthians 3:12–15)

While all Christians will be at the *Bema*, professed teachers of the church will undergo a greater judgment. Their teaching will be examined with far greater scrutiny. The preacher who prayerlessly prepares his sermons on Saturday night as he watches TV and on Sunday delivers short, anecdote-loaded topical homilies that have nothing to do with the text, and indeed are often unsound, will have his work torched!

Even more sobering, we teachers' lives will be measured against what we teach. Do we preach about the tongue and then have roast congregation for Sunday dinner? Do we castigate our people for their materialism and then lust for more? This is strong stuff for pastors, adult teachers, youth workers, and Sunday school teachers. But it is also a great encouragement because if the architecture of our souls is built with gold, silver, and costly stones, we will receive eternal reward and honor.

The second reason James gives in urging caution about becoming teachers is that *we are sinners*: "we all stumble in many ways" (v. 2a). "Stumble" means "sin" (as in 2:10), and the present tense suggests repeated stumbling— "we all sin many times in many ways." There is a persistent myth in contemporary culture that Count Leo Tolstoy was a great Christian, and even a saint. This is palpably false. In fact, he was a self-righteous egoist who felt himself to be "God's older brother." Tolstoy once arrogantly penned these words in his diary: "I have not yet met a single man who was morally as good as I. . . . I do not remember an instance in my life when I was not attracted to what is good and was not ready to sacrifice anything to it,"[6] a statement to which his inveterate womanizing and neglect of his family repeatedly gave the lie.

Paul gave a true picture of mankind: ". . . both Jews and Greeks, are under sin, as it is written: 'None is righteous, no, not one . . . All have turned aside . . . no one does good, not even one.' 'Their throat is an open grave; they use their tongues to deceive.' 'The venom of asps is under their lips.' 'Their mouth is full of curses and bitterness'" (Romans 3:9–14). "For all have sinned and fall short of the glory of God" (Romans 3:23). James is obviously saying: be careful about arrogantly assuming the position of teacher, because everyone regularly sins in many ways.

This said, the third point, so logical to the discussion of teaching, naturally follows: *the act of teaching imperils the tongue*: "And if anyone does not stumble in what he says, he is a perfect man, able also to bridle his whole body" (v. 2b). Some of the greatest saints have had trouble with the tongue. Job was a very great man whom God himself called "blameless and upright" (Job 1:8). But Job had trouble controlling his tongue, as revealed in the final chapter of his book: "Behold, I am of small account; what shall I answer you? I lay my hand on my mouth" (Job 40:4). Isaiah was as noble a man as ever served God. But hear his confession: "'For I am lost; for I am a man of unclean lips.' . . . Then one of the seraphim flew to me, having in his hand a burning coal that he had taken with tongs from the altar. And he touched my mouth and said: 'Behold, this has touched your lips; your guilt is taken away, and your sin atoned for'" (Isaiah 6:5–7). Moses was one of God's truly great men, the humblest man on the face of the earth (cf. Numbers 12:3). Yet it is written of him, "he spoke rashly with his lips" (Psalm 106:33).

Peter perpetually opened his mouth to change feet. "Though they all fall away because of you, I will never fall away," he said (Matthew 26:33). But that very night those same lips tragically denied Christ (Matthew 26:69–75). Paul, the greatest of the apostles and author of so much of the New Testament, understood his own condition: "For I know that nothing good dwells in me, that is, in my flesh. For I have the desire to do what is right, but not the ability to carry it out" (Romans 7:18). Even Paul could not always control his tongue, as when he lost it with Ananias: "God is going to strike you, you whitewashed wall!" (Acts 23:3). Luther wrote the "Ninety-five Theses" that changed the course of church history, but at times sinned in conversation, as we see in his *Table Talks*.

From these examples we get James' idea that one who never is at fault in his words is "perfect"—that is, he has come to "completeness and maturity—not sinlessness."[7] The control of the tongue is evidence of extraordinary spiritual maturity. In fact, the "perfect man" is "able also to bridle his whole body," says James. It is so natural to gossip and criticize and slander that the person who can control his tongue can easily rule the rest of his body.

If we are candid, all of us must admit it is immensely difficult not to sin with the tongue. Most of us tend to talk too much. During conversation, though we outwardly restrain ourselves, inside we are saying, "but . . . but . . . but!" We often see this in the distanced look in others' eyes as they "listen" to us as well. The fact is, nine-tenths of what is said or heard about another's character usually is better unsaid. We sin with the tongue so easily. If we could control the tongue, we could control everything else in our lives. Jesus said, "The good person out of his good treasure brings forth good, and the evil person out of his evil treasure brings forth evil" (Matthew 12:35).

James here sees anyone who is involved in a public teaching ministry but who is misusing the tongue as in particular peril. Though we may be unusually gifted in spiritual insight and verbal eloquence, if we cannot control the tongue we had better hang it up.

As we have seen, James' motivation for his command "not many of you should become teachers" is not that he wants to evacuate the church of gifted teachers, but rather that he wants people to assume such duties in the right spirit, under God's tutelage. He wants those who teach to have control over their tongues because a chaste tongue means a pure heart and a life submitted to God. How do we preachers measure up? What about those of us who are elders, leaders, Sunday school workers, club leaders?

A Christian teacher can be a Henrietta Mears or a Jim Jones. Only those with proper motivations and holiness of life should teach. Those who thus measure up *should* presume to be teachers because their character and motivations are appropriate to the calling. Not all those who are called will achieve the stature and fame of Miss Mears, but they will be used of God.

Howard Hendricks, who taught Christian education at Dallas Theological Seminary for over forty years, has told about an experience he had at a Sunday school convention:

> A number of us who were speaking there went across the street at noon to get a bite to eat at a hamburger stand. The place was crowded and people were standing in line. An elderly lady was in front of me. I guessed she was about 65—she was 83, I learned later. She wore a convention badge, so I knew she was a conferee. There was a table for four open, so two friends and I invited her to join us. I asked her the obvious question: "Do you teach a Sunday School class?" "Oh, I certainly do," she said. I visualized a class of senior citizens, but asked her: "What age group do you teach?" "I teach a class of junior high boys." "Junior high boys! How many boys do you have?" "Thirteen," she said sweetly. "Tremendous! I suppose you come from a rather large church." "No, sir, it's very small," she said. "We have about fifty-five in Sunday School." Hardly daring to go on, I said, "What brings you to this Sunday School convention?" "I'm on a pension—my husband died a number of years ago," she replied, "and, frankly, this is the first time a convention has come close enough to my home so I could afford to attend. I bought a Greyhound ticket and rode all last night to get here this morning and attend two workshops. I want to learn something that will make me a better teacher."

Hendricks went on to add, "I heard a sequel to this story some time later. A doctor told me there are eighty-four young men in or moving toward the Christian ministry as a result of this woman's influence."[8] As Howard Hendricks would say, "May her tribe increase!"

Many such of God's people should become teachers!

If we put bits into the mouths of horses so that they obey us, we guide their whole bodies as well. Look at the ships also: though they are so large and are driven by strong winds, they are guided by a very small rudder wherever the will of the pilot directs. So also the tongue is a small member, yet it boasts of great things. How great a forest is set ablaze by such a small fire! And the tongue is a fire, a world of unrighteousness. The tongue is set among our members, staining the whole body, setting on fire the entire course of life, and set on fire by hell. For every kind of beast and bird, of reptile and sea creature, can be tamed and has been tamed by mankind, but no human being can tame the tongue. It is a restless evil, full of deadly poison. With it we bless our Lord and Father, and with it we curse people who are made in the likeness of God. From the same mouth come blessing and cursing. My brothers, these things ought not to be so. Does a spring pour forth from the same opening both fresh and salt water? Can a fig tree, my brothers, bear olives, or a grapevine produce figs? Neither can a salt pond yield fresh water.

3:3–12

14

The Mighty Tongue

JAMES 3:3–12

THE BOOK OF PROVERBS speaks variously of the power of the tongue:

"With his mouth the godless man would destroy his neighbor" (11:9).
"The words of the wicked lie in wait for blood" (12:6).
"The words of a whisperer are like delicious morsels; they go down into the inner parts of the body" (18:8).
"Death and life are in the power of the tongue" (18:21).
". . . a soft tongue will break a bone" (25:15).

The power of the tongue! Lives have been both elevated and cast down by the tongue. Nations have risen, and nations have fallen to the tongue. Goodness has flowed like a sweet river from the tongue, but so has a cesspool. The tiny tongue is a mighty force in human life.

Never doubt the power of the tongue—and never underestimate it.

The Intrinsic Power of the Tongue (vv. 3–5a)

James, the Lord's brother, understood this as well as any man in history and gave it powerful expression in the analogies of the horse's bit and the ship's rudder: "If we put bits into the mouths of horses so that they obey us, we guide their whole bodies as well. Look at the ships also: though they are so large and are driven by strong winds, they are guided by a very small rudder wherever the will of the pilot directs. So also the tongue is a small member, yet it boasts of great things" (vv. 3–5a).

The horse is an awesomely powerful animal. Take 550 pounds (as much as a puffing Olympic heavyweight lifter can hoist overhead), set it on a horse's back, and it will barely snort as it stands breathing easily under the burden. The same horse, unburdened, can sprint a quarter-mile in about twenty-five seconds. A horse is half a ton of raw power! Yet place a bridle and bit in its mouth, and a one-hundred-pound woman on its back who knows what she is doing, and the animal can literally be made to dance.

James observed the same phenomenon in ancient ships, as ships small and large (as big as the 276-passenger ship that carried Paul to Rome — cf. Acts 27:37–44) were steered by an amazingly small rudder. Today it is still the same, whether it be an acrobatic ski boat or the *USS Enterprise*. He who controls the rudder controls the ship.

So it is with the mighty tongue, that "movable muscular structure attached to the floor of the mouth" (*Webster's Unabridged*). Says James, "the tongue is a small member, yet it boasts of great things" (v. 5a). Or as Phillips has helpfully paraphrased it, "the human tongue is physically small, but what tremendous effects it can boast of." This mere "two ounce slab of mucous membrane," as Charles Swindoll has called it, can legitimately boast of its disproportionate power to determine human destiny. The tongues of Adolf Hitler and Winston Churchill bear eloquent testimony to the dark and bright sides of the tongue's power. Der Führer on one side of the channel harangued a vast multitude with his hypnotic cadences. On the other side, the prime minister's brilliant, measured utterances pulled a faltering nation together for its "finest hour." But we need not look to the drama of nations to see the truth of James' words. Our own lives are evidence enough. Never doubt the power of the tiny tongue, and never underestimate it.

The Destructive Power of the Tongue (vv. 5b, 6)

James' concern about the destructive power of the tongue is a most provocative statement: "How great a forest is set ablaze by such a small fire! And the tongue is a fire, a world of unrighteousness. The tongue is set among our members, staining the whole body, setting on fire the entire course of life, and set on fire by hell" (vv. 5b, 6).

The tongue has awesome potential for harm, as the forest fire analogy suggests. One Sunday evening in October 1871, the great Chicago Fire blackened three and one half miles of the city, destroying over seventeen thousand buildings before it was checked by gunpowder explosions on the south line of the fire. The fire lasted two days and cost over 250 lives.

But, ironically, that was not the greatest inferno in the Midwest that year. Historians tell us that on the *same* day that dry autumn a spark ignited a raging fire in the north woods of Wisconsin that burned for an entire month, taking more lives than the Chicago Fire. A veritable firestorm destroyed billions of yards of precious timber—all from one spark!

The tongue has that scope of inflammatory capability. James is saying that those who misuse the tongue are guilty of spiritual arson. A mere spark of an ill-spoken word can produce a firestorm that annihilates everything it touches.[1] "And the tongue is a fire,[2] a world of unrighteousness . . . set among our members" (v. 6). *Kosmos* is translated here as "world" and means "sinful world-system."[3] The tongue contains and conveys all the world system's wickedness. It is party to every evil there is, and it actively obtrudes its evil into our lives.[4]

The effect of the tongue's cosmic wickedness is, as James further states, that it "[stains] the whole body, setting on fire the entire course of life" (v. 6b). "Course of life" is literally "the wheel of our genesis," "genesis" referring to our life or existence. New Testament scholar Douglas Moo says,

> . . . the phrase, and others parallel to it, were used in the Orphic religion to describe the unending cycle of reincarnations from which deliverance was sought. But there is sufficient evidence to show that what had originally been a technical religious or philosophical expression had become "popularized" and was used in James' day as a way of describing the course of human life, perhaps with an emphasis on the "ups and downs" of life.[5]

What an apt description of human experience! About nine-tenths of the flames we experience in our lives come from the tongue.

Having grabbed his readers' imaginations with his graphic language, James adds the final touch: "and [it is] set on fire by hell" (v. 6c). Here the present participle means *continually* set on fire by Hell. James used the same word for Hell that his brother Jesus used—Gehenna—derived from the perpetually burning garbage dump outside Jerusalem,[6] a place of fire and filth where, as Jesus said, "their worm does not die and the fire is not quenched" (Mark 9:48). Can anyone miss the point? The uncontrolled tongue has a direct pipeline to Hell! This pipeline is reciprocal. Fueled by Hell, it burns our lives with its filthy fires. But it is also, as Calvin says, an ". . . instrument for catching, encouraging, and increasing the fires of hell."[7]

Taking James' words seriously, we recognize that the tongue has more destructive power than a hydrogen bomb, for the bomb's power is physical and temporal, whereas the tongue's is spiritual and eternal. In fact, the tongue controls the bomb! As to how this all works out in life, James is not specific, leaving the varied applications of the tongue's destructiveness to the spiritual mind.

Gossip. The tongue's destructive power in gossip leads the list, of course. A physician in a Midwestern city was a victim of a disgruntled patient who tried to ruin him professionally through rumor, and almost did. Several years later the gossiper had a change of heart and wrote the doctor asking his forgiveness, and he forgave her. But there was no way she could erase the story, nor could he. Vigorous denial would only bring more suspicion—"He protests too much!" The damage was done. Hereafter the innocent doctor would always look into certain eyes and wonder if they had heard the story—and if they believed it.[8]

Gossip often veils itself in acceptable conventions such as "Have you heard. . . ?" or "Did you know. . . ?" or "They tell me . . ." or "Keep this to yourself, but . . ." or "I don't believe it's true, but I heard that . . ." or "I wouldn't tell you, except that I know it will go no farther." Of course, the most infamous such rationalization in Christian circles is, "I am telling you this so you can pray." This seems so pious, but the heart that feeds on bearing evil reports is a tool of Hell, and it leaves flaming fires in its wake. Oh, the heartache that comes from the tongue.

Innuendo. A cousin of gossip is innuendo. Consider the ship's first mate who after a drunken binge was written up by the captain on the ship's log: "mate drunk today." The mate's revenge? Some months later he surreptitiously wrote on his own entry, "captain sober today." So it goes with the word unsaid, the awkward silence, the raised eyebrows, the quizzical look—all freighted with the misery of Hell.

Flattery. Gossip is saying behind a person's back what you would never say to his or her face; flattery is saying to a person's face what you would never say behind his or her back.[9] The Scriptures warn us repeatedly against flatterers, for they are destructive people who carry a legion of unwholesome motives.

Criticism. Criticism can take many forms, but it is always motivated by self-doubt and jealousy. Byron had it right:

> He who ascends to mountain-tops, shall find
> The loftiest peaks most wrapt in clouds and snow;
> He who surpasses or subdues mankind,
> Must look down on the hate of those below.
>
> Byron, *Childe Harold's Pilgrimage*

There are many other ways the tongue can destroy—meanness, sarcastic humor, boasting—but at the very bottom is *blasphemy*. When one attributes the work of the Holy Spirit to Satan, he does it not with his hands or feet but with his tongue (cf. Matthew 12:31, 32). "To call evil good, and good evil—to see the Divinest good, and call it Satanic evil—below this lowest deep there is not a lower still."[10] This ultimate destruction of one's own soul is accomplished by the tongue.

God's word through James to us about the tongue is, "How great a forest is set ablaze by such a small fire! And the tongue is a fire, a world of unrighteousness. The tongue is set among our members, staining the whole body, setting on fire the entire course of life, and set on fire by hell" (vv. 5b, 6). Believe it! And never forget it!

The Uncontrollable Power of the Tongue (vv. 7, 8)

I have seen whales playing jump rope and so have you, at Sea World or some other great aquarium, as their trainers hoisted the rope high and the whales sailed over it. I have seen African lions cowed and submissive to the wizardry of Gunther Gebal Williams. I have seen eagles kill their prey and humbly lay it at their master's feet. I have seen a woman obediently kissed on the lips by a deadly cobra. But I have never seen a man or woman who in their own power could tame the tongue.

I say this, of course, on good Biblical authority: "For every kind of beast and bird, of reptile and sea creature, can be tamed and has been tamed by mankind, but no human being can tame the tongue. It is a restless evil, full of deadly poison" (vv. 7, 8). This is true of all of us every day. People who have been delivered from alcohol or gambling or hard drugs find their most difficult opponent to be the tongue.

Moreover, the uncontrolled tongue is deadly—"It is a restless evil, full of deadly poison" (v. 8b)—verbal cyanide. Like the deadliest poisons, those that are most effective are tasteless and odorless: subtle criticism and slander, verbal venom which has done its work before the victim can react. By exposing the untamable tongue James is driving us to grace, as we shall see.

The Revealing Power of the Tongue (vv. 9–12)

Evidently James had observed a contradictory phenomenon in his church. Jewish Christians were perpetuating the beautiful old Hebrew custom of saying, "Blessed be he" after each utterance of God's name, so that their worship times were continually punctuated by choruses of praise. Yet these same people, with the blessings still on their lips, would sometimes, after leaving worship, actually curse someone who had angered them! This was a shameful sin, and James would not tolerate it! The Law, as James well knew from the teaching of Jesus, is fulfilled by loving God with all one's heart and loving one's neighbor as oneself (cf. Mark 12:28–31). But to affirm devotion for God and then hate a fellow man made in God's image scandalizes one's profession of loving God (see 1 John 4:20, 21).

James concludes his teaching here by passionately denouncing this terrible inconsistency: "With [the tongue] we bless our Lord and Father, and with it we curse people who are made in the likeness of God. From the same mouth come blessing and cursing. My brothers, these things ought not to be so. Does a spring pour forth from the same opening both fresh and salt water? Can a fig tree, my brothers, bear olives, or a grapevine produce figs? Neither can a salt pond yield fresh water" (vv. 9–12). His overpowering point is, whatever comes out of the mouth unfailingly reveals what is on the inside.

He is saying, "Be honest. Are you skilled in your religious vocabulary so that at church you appear holy and good, but at home you are sarcastic with your family and critical of others?" What about us? Do we enjoy the gossipy tidbits that come our way at the office, and even pass on a few ourselves? What do we laugh at or about? How do we respond to others? Would the answers to these questions give the lie to our profession of love for God?

Do we feel deflated by James' teaching? Good! For as Augustine said, ". . . he does not say that no one can tame the tongue, but no one of men; so that when it is tamed we confess that this is brought about by the pity, the help, the grace of God."[11]

In view of all this, what are we to do?

First, *we must ask God to cauterize our lips*, confessing as Isaiah did, "Woe is me! For I am lost; for I am a man of unclean lips, and I dwell in the midst of a people of unclean lips; for my eyes have seen the King, the LORD of hosts!" (Isaiah 6:5). Then we need to submit to the cleansing touch: "Then one of the seraphim flew to me, having in his hand a burning coal that he had taken with tongs from the altar. And he touched my mouth and said: 'Behold, this has touched your lips; your guilt is taken away, and your sin atoned for'" (Isaiah 6:6, 7). Next we can prepare to serve: "And I heard the voice of the Lord saying, 'Whom shall I send, and who will go for us?' Then I said, 'Here I am! Send me'" (Isaiah 6:8). Isaiah's outline as a spiritual exercise, performed with all one's heart, will work wonders in our lives! Let us all do this today!

Second, hand-in-hand with the first step there must be *an ongoing prayerfulness* regarding our tongues—regular, detailed prayer. This, coupled with the first step, will work a spiritual miracle.

Third, we must resolve to *discipline ourselves* regarding the use of the tongue—not to criticize, not to give or receive gossip, not to belittle or demean or falsely flatter, not to lie, not to boast.

The tongue, so tiny, is immensely powerful. The tongue is mightier than generals and their armies. It can fuel our lives so they become fiery furnaces, or it can cool our lives with the soothing wind of the Spirit. It can be forged by Hell, or it can be the tool of Heaven.

Offered on the altar, the tongue has awesome power for good. It can proclaim the life-changing message of *salvation*: "And how are they to hear without someone preaching? And how are they to preach unless they are sent? As it is written, 'How beautiful are the feet of those who preach the good news!'" (Romans 10:14b, 15). It has power for *sanctification* as we share God's Word: "Sanctify them in the truth; your word is truth" (John 17:17). It has power for *healing*:

> For even when we came into Macedonia, our bodies had no rest, but we were afflicted at every turn—fighting without and fear within. But God, who comforts the downcast, comforted us by the coming of Titus, and not only by his coming but also by the comfort with which he was comforted by you, as he told us of your longing, your mourning, your zeal for me, so that I rejoiced still more. (2 Corinthians 7:5–7)

It has power for *worship*: "Through him then let us continually offer up a sacrifice of praise to God, that is, the fruit of lips that acknowledge his name" (Hebrews 13:15).

Few sections of Scripture are so graphically relentless in making a point. In addition, this is the most penetrating (and convicting) exposition of the tongue anywhere in literature, sacred or secular. One must also conclude that it was not just James' local concern for his churches that occasioned the writing, but also the Holy Spirit's desire that the church at large learn to control the tongue.

> May the mind of Christ my Savior
> Live in me from day to day,
> By His love and pow'r controlling
> All I do and say.

Who is wise and understanding among you? By his good conduct let him show his works in the meekness of wisdom. But if you have bitter jealousy and selfish ambition in your hearts, do not boast and be false to the truth. This is not the wisdom that comes down from above, but is earthly, unspiritual, demonic. For where jealousy and selfish ambition exist, there will be disorder and every vile practice.

3:13–16

15

Wisdom from Below

JAMES 3:13–16

J. I. PACKER, a gifted and personable theologian, has shown how many go wrong in their thinking about wisdom via the illustration of a British railway station, the kind with which all visitors to England quickly become very familiar. He says that if you stand at the end of a platform you will readily observe the constant movement of trains in and out, but you will only be able to form a general idea of the overall plan of what is going on, catching only glimmers of the subtle minute-by-minute alterations that are part and parcel of a smooth-running station.

However, if you are privileged to be taken into the signal box room, you will see on a long wall a detailed diagram of all the tracks for five miles around the station, with little "glowworm lights" indicating the positions of every engine on the track—some moving slowly or swiftly, some stationary. In a glance you will be able to survey the entire situation through the eyes of those in control. You will see why one engine is signaled to a halt, and why another has been diverted, and why another sits unmoving on a siding. The reasoning for all the movements will become perfectly plain once you see the great diagram and its glowing dots. Says Dr. Packer:

> Now the mistake that is commonly made is to suppose that this is an illustration of what God does when He bestows wisdom: to suppose, in other words, that the gift of wisdom consists in a deepened insight into the meaning and purpose of events going on around us, an ability to see why God has done what He has done in a particular case, and what He is going to do next.[1]

People who think this is what wisdom is imagine that if they walk close enough to God, they will be in God's signal box and will understand everything that happens. Such people are always analyzing the events of life: why this or that happened, whether specific happenings are signs to stop, park on a siding, or go ahead. When they are confused, they suppose themselves to have a spiritual problem. It is true that God sometimes uses unusual signs to confirm the way we should go by, but this is very different from getting a message from every unusual thing that comes our way.

On the contrary, explains Dr. Packer, the experience of God's wisdom is like learning to drive a car. When driving it is important to make appropriate responses to the constantly changing scene, to exercise soundness of judgment regarding speed, distance, and braking. If you are going to drive well, you must not fret over the highway engineer's reasoning for an S curve; the philosophy that produced red, green, and yellow traffic lights; or why the lady in front of you is accelerating while her foot is on the brake. Rather, "You simply try to see and do the right thing in the actual situation that presents itself. The effect of divine wisdom is to enable you and me to do just that in the actual situations of life."[2] In order to drive well, you need to keep your eyes wide open to what is before you and use your head. To live wisely, you must be clear-eyed about people and life, seeing life as it is, and then responding with a mind dependent on the wisdom of God.

Being wise does not mean we understand everything that is going on because of our superior knowledge, but that we do the right thing as life comes along. Some drivers may have immense knowledge about everything, but they cannot drive well at all. Others who are less knowledgeable consistently do the right thing as they wisely drive through life.

How does wisdom from God come to us? The Scriptures identify four specific avenues:

Reverence. The first is reverence or a respectful fear of God. Again and again God's Word says, "The fear of the LORD is the beginning of wisdom" (Psalm 111:10; Proverbs 9:10; cf. Job 28:28; Proverbs 1:7; 15:33). When we see God for who he is—holy, awesome, loving, and sovereign—and embrace a proper fear of him, we are at the doorway of wisdom. And we step through that door when we acknowledge our own finiteness and inability to direct our lives. There can be no wisdom apart from a quaking, fearful vision of God and our own contrasting littleness. This vision is the missing element today in evangelical Christianity. Christians, in their desire to be relevant and relational in their worship, have minimized the awesomeness of God and have falsely maximized their own virtues and importance. But when we truly see God and truly see ourselves, we become humble and meek, and therefore teachable and receptive to God's wisdom. As Proverbs 11:2

says, "with the humble is wisdom." Whole libraries can exist in a man or woman's head without even a whiff of wisdom, but in humble relationship with God—WISDOM!

Conversion. When we became Christians we became what the Scriptures describe as "in Christ," a term that Paul uses over and over again (some 161 times!) to indicate our dynamic relationship with God through Christ. In respect to wisdom, believers are "in Christ Jesus, who became to us wisdom from God" (1 Corinthians 1:30). Since all God's wisdom resides in Christ, when we came to be "in him," we become rooted in wisdom. Thus we personally experience the infinite wisdom of God. Our relationship with Christ assures a transfer of this wisdom to us and opens us to further wisdom. "Christ Jesus . . . became to us wisdom from God." Hallelujah!

Scripture. The 119th Psalm repeatedly affirms that wisdom comes from God's Word, but no more eloquently than in verses 97–100:

> Oh how I love your law!
>   It is my meditation all the day.
> Your commandment makes me wiser than my enemies,
>   for it is ever with me.
> I have more understanding than all my teachers,
>   for your testimonies are my meditation.
> I understand more than the aged,
>   for I keep your precepts.

In accord with this Paul commands us in the New Testament to "Let the word of Christ richly dwell within you, with all wisdom teaching and admonishing one another . . ." (Colossians 3:16, NASB). None of us will ascend to the heights of wisdom God wishes for us without spending long hours reading and meditating on God's Word. Do we spend as much time with the Bible as with our daily newspaper? What fools we will be—and so remain all of our lives—if we do not take the time to avail ourselves of God's wisdom![3]

Prayer. The last avenue to wisdom is prayer. As James so memorably stated in 1:5, "If any of you lacks wisdom, let him ask God, who gives generously to all without reproach, and it will be given him." Anyone who asks believing will get wisdom—no exceptions! God will always keep his word. There is wisdom for the many decisions that have to be made in your life—simply *ask for it.*

The formula for wisdom is simple enough: 1) *reverence/fear*, for "the fear of the LORD is the beginning of wisdom" (Psalm 111:10); 2) *conversion*, receiving Christ who is "wisdom from God" (1 Corinthians 1:30); 3) *the*

Scriptures, which convey the wisdom of God; and 4) *prayer*, which brings wisdom for the asking. As we follow this formula we will know how to conduct our lives with ultimate wisdom.

Also, we will begin to manifest the sublime characteristic of a truly wise person: *humility/meekness*. This is because the true root of wisdom is, as we have seen, a profound understanding of the greatness of God and our own finiteness and sin, which in turn facilitates the God-glorifying character trait of meekness. Wisdom and meekness are interrelated. No one can be considered wise who is not at the same time meek. Meekness is the *moral characteristic* of wisdom.

This insight makes the opening question and command of our brief text come alive: "Who is wise and understanding among you?" (v. 13). After voicing this question James states rhetorically, "By his good conduct let him show his works in the meekness of wisdom" (v. 13). The ambitious would-be teachers who had been devastating the church with their incendiary tongues were claiming to be superior in their wisdom and understanding. They imagined those who disagreed to be mentally inferior. In their thinking wisdom had to do with the mind, intellectual prowess.

But James, the practical theologian, knew better and brought them down to earth by informing them that real wisdom is demonstrated by two qualities: first by "good conduct" (that is, a noble and beautiful life), and, second, by "his works in the meekness of wisdom" — a quality they were definitely lacking. This was a penetrating rebuke because in their frame of mind meekness was an obvious sign of weakness.

Meekness, of course, is not weakness at all. Israel's powerful ruler Moses was himself called "very meek, more than all people who were on the face of the earth" (Numbers 12:3). In addition, Jesus said of himself, "I am gentle [meek] and lowly in heart" (Matthew 11:29). Meekness does not denote cowardice or any of its parallel characteristics such as spinelessness, timidity, or a "peace at any cost" attitude. Neither does meekness suggest indecisiveness, wishy-washiness, a lack of confidence, shyness, or a withdrawn personality. Nor can it be reduced to wimpy niceness.

Seeing what meekness is not, we must note that the popular rendering of "meek" and "gentle" are fairly adequate. In classical Greek the word was used to describe tame animals, soothing medicines, a mild word, and a gentle breeze.[4] "It is a word with a caress in it."[5] The New Testament bears the same sense. John Wycliffe translated it "mild."[6]

James gives a penetrating moral test for any who think themselves to be wise — the test being not pride, but *gentleness, meekness, mildness* in dealing with others. The wise know that God is in control, and they know who they are as redeemed sinners. Thus they can confidently meet their problems and their detractors with the gentle assurance that God will vindicate them. The meek/wise know how to do the right thing as they pass through the traffic of life.

Having established the moral shape of true wisdom, James goes on to describe the outworking, character, and results of pseudo-wisdom.

The Outworking of False Wisdom (v. 14)

James assails the bogus wisdom of the pseudo-wise in verse 14 by saying, "But if you have bitter jealousy and selfish ambition in your hearts, do not boast and be false to the truth." The hearts of the would-be wise were wrought with "bitter jealousy," or literally a *harsh zeal*.[7] They could not stand to see others in possession of the position and influences they so desired. They experienced an inner frenzy at what they saw and set themselves to subvert it.

The story is told of two men who lived in a certain city. One was envious and the other covetous. The ruler of the city sent for them and said he wanted to grant them one wish each—with this proviso, that the one who chose first would get exactly what he asked for, while the other man would get exactly twice what the first had asked for himself. The envious man was ordered to choose first, but immediately found himself in a quandary. He wanted to choose something great for himself, but realized that if he did so the other would get twice as much. He thought for a while and then asked that one of his eyes be put out.[8] In the church this type of person could honestly pray, "Lord, I would sooner your work was not done at all than done by someone better than I can do it."[9]

The wretched twin of this bitter jealousy in our text is *erithia*, "selfish ambition"—political ambition in the church.[10] The same word is used by Paul in Philippians 1:17 where he describes rival brethren who "proclaim Christ out of selfish ambition [*erithia*], not sincerely but thinking to afflict me in my imprisonment." This brought party splits to the church—vile little support groups[11] that mutually envenomed one another in sustained attacks. And to top things off, they were boasting about it.

James says, "do not boast and be false to the truth" (v. 14b). In other words, stop claiming that your bitter envy and party spirit are a result of God's wisdom. James' insightful reproach is still a sharp challenge to us today who presume to be wise in doing God's work, but inwardly are driven by pride, so that our conversation is full of subtle gibes and witty ripostes aimed at those we envy.

The Character of False Wisdom (v. 15)

In verse 15 James gives the diabolical bloodline of pseudo-wisdom: "This is not the wisdom that comes down from above, but is earthly, unspiritual, demonic." There is an ascending order of negative strength here: "earthly"—"unspiritual"—"demonic." This pseudo-wisdom is "earthly"—the world is its source and boundary. Further, this wisdom from below is "unspiritual" (*pseuchike*), natural as opposed to spiritual. Paul's use of the same word in 1 Corinthians 2:14 clarifies this idea: "But a natural [*pseuchikos*] man does not accept the things of the Spirit of God, for they are foolishness to him; and he cannot understand them, because they are spiritually appraised" (NASB). Thus we see that "unspiritual" or "natural" describes a wisdom that comes from the mind of depraved fallen humanity and is hopelessly flawed. Last, and lowest, this wisdom is "demonic." This wisdom that produces "bitter jealousy," "selfish ambition," and proud boasting is radically evil, for it is authored by the devil.[12]

The truth is clear—proud, ambitious, fighting "wisdom" comes from the world, the flesh, and the devil. We must never let anyone convince us that such conduct is "common sense," or that if we don't learn "to give as good as we get" we will never succeed in life, or that meekness is "unmanly" (or "unwomanly"), or that the wise must always have the last word. Such wisdom is from below and can only take us down, down, down, down!

The Result of False Wisdom (v. 16)

James concludes his discussion of false wisdom by summing up its unhappy results: "For where jealousy and selfish ambition exist, there will be disorder and every vile practice" (v. 16). One of the words that came out of World War II was *snafu*, which is an acronym for "situation normal, all fouled up." According to the *Chicago Tribune*, the Pentagon has now scrapped that word for a new one, *fubb*—"fouled up beyond belief." Sadly, both words describe any church where the false wisdom of the world prevails. Over the years, speaking at pastors' conferences, I have repeatedly been told horror stories that would tax the credulity of those unfamiliar with the ravages of worldly "wisdom" in the church—situations truly fouled up beyond belief.

James' message is simple: there is no place in the church for pride, jealousy, or selfish ambition. Anyone who says pseudo-wisdom is okay is an unwitting messenger of the devil. We must allow no place for harshness, criticism, or clever comments masquerading as "wisdom."

We have seen that one becomes wise through fear of the Lord, through conversion, through the Word, and through prayer. True wisdom is within reach.

But what about meekness/gentleness, apart from which there is no wisdom? This, too, is within reach. In fact, it is one of the fruits of the Spirit listed in Galatians 5:22, 23. We also know it is possible because Jesus blessed it: "Blessed are the meek, for they shall inherit the earth" (Matthew 5:5). And most of all we know it is possible because as Christians we are "in Jesus," who urged us to "Take my yoke upon you, and learn from me, for I am gentle [meek, mild] and lowly in heart, and you will find rest for your souls. For my yoke is easy, and my burden is light" (Matthew 11:29, 30). He promises that if we consciously yoke ourselves to him, we will learn meekness and humility and will find rest for our souls.

In Biblical times a young ox was yoked to an older, experienced ox, so that the older might train him to perform properly. By bearing the same yoke, the untrained ox learned the proper pace and how to heed the direction of the master. Jesus calls us to yoke ourselves to him. What a privilege and joy!

But the wisdom from above is first pure, then peaceable, gentle, open to reason, full of mercy and good fruits, impartial and sincere. And a harvest of righteousness is sown in peace by those who make peace.

3:17, 18

16

Wisdom from Above

JAMES 3:17, 18

IN 1845 Royal Navy Rear Admiral Sir John Franklin and 138 specially chosen officers and men left England to find the Northwest Passage. They sailed in two three-masted ships with the daunting names the *Erebus* (the dark place, according to Greek mythology, through which souls pass on their way to Hades) and the *Terror*. Each ship was equipped with an auxiliary steam engine and a twelve-day supply of coal, should steam power be needed sometime during the anticipated two- to three-year voyage. But instead of loading additional coal, each ship made room for a 1,200-volume library, an organ, and full, elegant place settings for all—china, cut-glass goblets, and sterling flatware. The officers' sterling was of especially grand Victorian design, with the individual officers' family crests and initials engraved on the heavy handles. "The technology of the Franklin expedition," says Annie Dillard, ". . . was adapted only to the conditions in the Royal Navy officers' clubs in England. The Franklin expedition stood on its dignity."[1] The only clothing that these proud Englishmen took on the expedition were the uniforms and greatcoats of Her Majesty's Navy.

The ships sailed off amidst imperial pomp and glory. Two months later a British whaler met the two ships in the Lancaster Sound, and reports were carried back to England of the expedition's high spirits. He was the last European to see them alive.

Search parties funded by Lady Jane Franklin began to piece together a tragic history from information gathered from Eskimos. Some had seen men pushing a wooden boat across the ice. Others had found a boat, perhaps the same boat, and the remains of thirty-five men at a place now named Starvation Cove. Another thirty bodies were found in a tent at Terror Bay. Simpson

Strait had yielded an eerie sight—three wooden masts of a ship protruding through the ice.

For the next twenty years search parties recovered skeletons from the frozen waste. Twelve years later it was learned that Admiral Franklin had died aboard ship. The remaining officers and crew had decided to walk for help. Accompanying one clump of bodies were place settings of sterling silver flatware bearing the officers' initials and family crests. The officers' remains were still dressed in their fine, buttoned blue uniforms, some with silk scarves in place.

The Franklin Expedition was a monumental failure by all estimations. It was foolishly conceived, planned, equipped, and carried out. The expedition itself accomplished absolutely nothing. Yet it is universally agreed that it was the turning point in Arctic exploration. The mystery of the expedition's disappearance and its fate attracted so much attention in Europe and the United States that no less than thirty ships made extended journeys in search of the answer. In doing so, they mapped the Arctic for the first time, discovered the Northwest Passage, and developed a technology suitable to Arctic rigor. It was upon the shipwreck of Rear Admiral Franklin's "wisdom" that Amundsen would one day stand victorious at the South Pole and Peary and Henson at the North.[2] Similarly, the shipwreck of worldly wisdom ought to motivate us to seek wisdom from above, so we can wisely navigate through life.

This is what James had in mind when he contrasted two kinds of wisdom in 3:13–18. In verses 13–16 he demonstrated the follies of the "wisdom" from below by parading its skeletons before us. He says in verses 15, 16, "This is not the wisdom that comes down from above, but is earthly, unspiritual, demonic. For where jealousy and selfish ambition exist, there will be disorder and every vile practice." A close look at those rotting bones, hopes James, will cause us to swear off the vanity of earthly pride and wisdom.

By contrast there is the lure of the meek/gentle wisdom (v. 13) from above, and James skillfully describes its seven beautiful characteristics in verses 17, 18.

Wisdom from Above: Its Profile (v. 17)

Pure. James begins, "But the wisdom from above is first pure . . ." It is pure in the sense of being undefiled[3]—morally pure. This purity comes when one has been cleansed by Christ's blood, who is himself pure (the very same word is used of Christ in 1 John 3:3), has received Christ's purity, and as a result is leading a morally pure life. Those who are pure have put aside sensuality, pride, and covetousness, which lie at the root of earthly wisdom.

But even more, this person's heart is pure in its unmixed devotion to God. James will repeat this idea later in 4:8: "purify your hearts, you double-minded." That is, get rid of your mixed motives, your double-mindedness; be committed and pure in your devotion. This carries the idea of being pure in one's focus on God, concentrating on serving him. So we see that the purity that characterizes a life full of heavenly wisdom is utterly dynamic. It involves *moral* purity before God and *devotional* purity in one's focus on him.

It is most significant that purity is positioned as the very first characteristic of wisdom from above. The scholar James Adamson says it is the key to all the qualities of wisdom to follow.[4] Others agree, calling it the "overarching attribute."[5] The authenticity and intensity of one's purity determines the outworking of the other qualities of wisdom.

James' opening declaration that "the wisdom from above is first pure" teaches that all who possess it are to make perfect purity in one's moral and devotional life a primary goal. The Christian who wants to live in wisdom can ask no better question regarding his thoughts, words, actions, and devotion than, "Am I pure?"

James had apparently given much thought to the arrangement of the remaining six characteristics of wisdom because he has artfully ordered them so that in the Greek the first four began with the *e* sound and the last two with a pleasant *a* sound. Also, the last two have an almost metrical rhyming.[6] He wanted his hearers to remember this wisdom.

Peace-loving. The next of wisdom's characteristics, which our translation renders as "peaceable," is literally "peaceful." This does not suggest, as some may hear it, an attitude of peace by abdication—like the couple who had just celebrated their fiftieth wedding anniversary. Someone asked the gentleman the secret of their marital bliss. "Well," the old man drawled, "the wife and I had this agreement when we first got married. It went like this: When she was bothered about somethin' she'd jus' tell me and git it off her chest. And if I was mad at her about somethin', I was able to take a long walk. I s'ppose you could attribute our happy marriage to the fact that I have largely led an outdoor life."

There are indeed proper times to "take a walk," but James is not recommending a peace that depends on walking away from conflict. Rather, he is commending a peaceful spirit. The hearts of those with such peace have met Christ, who is himself their peace (Ephesians 2:14). They have the peace he gives, which is totally unlike the peace the world gives (John 14:27). Their spiritual war is over, they are at peace with God, and they have a deep sense of well-being—*shalom.* The person walking in heavenly wisdom longs for peace. At times he or she may make some "waves" because a Biblical principle is at stake, but ordinarily they refrain from turbulence and rejoice in making peace. They are "eager to maintain the unity of the Spirit in the bond of peace" (Ephesians 4:3) and they "pursue what makes for peace and for mutual upbuilding" (Romans 14:19). They live out Paul's injunction, "If possible, so far as it depends on you, live peaceably with all" (Romans 12:18). St. Francis understood this, as his prayer beautifully recalls:

Lord, make me an instrument of Thy peace;
Where there is hatred, let me sow love.
Where there is doubt, faith;
Where there is despair, hope;
Where there is darkness, light;
Where there is sadness, joy.

You and I have met many people more capable than us, with far greater knowledge and gifts, some far more accomplished and esteemed. But if they are pugnacious and trouble-making, they are, despite their great abilities, unwise. The wise are peace-loving, says God's Word.

Gentle. The wisdom from above also makes one "gentle." The great linguist Archbishop Trench said there is no word in English or Latin to adequately translate this word.[7] Nevertheless, the idea is fairly clear. It describes the kind of person who though wronged and possessing the "right" not to bend nevertheless forgoes his rights.[8] I saw this quality in the pastor under whom I served for nine years. On one particular occasion, when slandered and with a right to just recourse, he refused any such action. Instead he gently began to defend his slanderer, listing the pressures his attacker was under and the necessity of tolerance. The man or woman with this quality makes allowances for the weaknesses and ignorance of others and takes the kindest perspective whenever possible.

Heavenly wisdom is "gentle," or as the *Jerusalem Bible* has it, "kindly." The honest personal application of this is humbling, to say the least. But if we are to be wise we must take this to heart.

Open to Reason. The ESV's rendering of the fourth characteristic as "open to reason" implicitly indicates a willingness to submit to persuasion[9] or to be open to reason.[10] A moving example of such submissive wisdom is seen in the case of David and Abigail. David's generous and friendly overtures to Abigail's foolish husband Nabal had been outrageously rejected. So David and his men armed themselves and set out for redress. Fortunately they were met by Abigail, who eloquently argued against violence. David responded by saying, "'Blessed be the LORD, the God of Israel, who sent you this day to meet me! Blessed be your discretion, and blessed be you, who have kept me this day from bloodguilt and from working salvation with my own hand!'" (1 Samuel 25:32, 33). Those who are filled with Heaven's wisdom will submit to reason.

On one occasion Abraham Lincoln, to please a certain politician, issued a command to transfer certain regiments. When Secretary of War Edwin Stanton received the order, he refused to carry it out, saying the President was a fool. When Lincoln was told of this, he replied, "If Stanton said I'm a fool, then I must be, for he is nearly always right. I'll see for myself." As the two men talked, the President quickly realized that his decision was a serious mistake, and without hesitation he withdrew it. A teachable, open spirit is often a major key in defusing conflict.

A man or a woman is in a bad way when he or she is no longer persuadable. "Foolish" is the Biblical designation for such a state. Are some of us playing this part in our marriages—or at work—in our theology? The wise are open to reason—they are submissive.

Mercy. Next, the wise are characterized as "full of mercy and good fruits." Recently a friend of mine, Olena Mae Welsh, received this note:

> I was very excited one day when I was listening to the "Geraldo" program on TV in California. They were having a discussion about abused children, and this one man—in his 20's I would say—told of how a neighbor lady named Olena Welsh had been such a help to him. He would be beaten and sitting forlornly outside his home, as a child, probably wishing he were dead, when Olena Welsh came and put her arms around him and told him how much God loved him and that God had a purpose for his life. He said that was the redeeming factor in his life. I knew it had to be you.

This happened because Olena Mae overflows with Biblical mercy. Mercy, in Biblical theology, is not just compassion that results in pity and sympathy. It is *compassion in action.*[11]

James, the unrelenting moral theologian, ties wisdom (seemingly so cerebral and esoteric) to action. Thus we may teach the Bible and be viewed by everyone as fountains of wisdom, refreshing those around with pithy sayings and sage advice. But if we are not full of mercy and good works we are not wise! How radical and countercultural this is. It condemns many modern-day dispensers of so-called "wisdom"—consider, for example, Ernest Hemingway and Jean-Paul Sartre—as fools!

Impartial. The sixth characteristic of true wisdom is that it is "impartial" or steady. It does not vacillate, taking one position in one circumstance and another in a different situation.[12] It operates on consistent principle. I remember once viewing a conversation between Groucho Marx and William Buckley in which Groucho excused a contradiction by quoting Thoreau: "consistency is the hobgoblin of little minds." At which Buckley rolled his eyes and faced the camera with a winning grin as he corrected Groucho with the exact quotation: "A *foolish* consistency is the hobgoblin of little minds." Consistency—being "impartial"—is a hallmark of wisdom from Heaven.

Sincere. Finally, wisdom from above is "sincere," or literally *without hypocrisy*. Sir Arthur Conan Doyle, the author of the Sherlock Holmes mysteries, used to tell how he sent a telegram to each of twelve friends, all men of great virtue and considerable position in society. The message was worded: "Fly at once, all is discovered." Within twenty-four hours, the story goes, all twelve had left the country! No doubt there was some playful exaggeration here, but the point is generally true that so many people, including Christians, are not what they seem to be.

But those full of wisdom from above never play-act. What you see is what you get. No masks—no feigned sincerity—no pretense. How refreshing this is in a world full of off-stage actors who believe a little hypocrisy is part of the essential wisdom of life. Christian wisdom demands and demonstrates the sincerity of Christ. "For our boast is this," says Paul, "the testimony of our conscience, that we behaved in the world with simplicity and godly sincerity, not by earthly wisdom but by the grace of God, and supremely so toward you" (2 Corinthians 1:12).

Wisdom from Above: Its Fruit (v. 18)

Having given the seven characteristics of heavenly wisdom, James now reaches for a fitting summary and appropriates what most believe to be a popular proverb of the day: "And a harvest of righteousness is sown in peace by those who make peace." The sense is: "peacemakers produce, in the atmosphere of peace they create, the harvest (fruit) of righteousness."[13] Righteousness cannot be produced in the climate of bitterness and selfish ambition fostered by wisdom from below. Righteousness can only grow in a climate of peace.

This is a call to reject the decaying skeletons of earthly wisdom: "This is not the wisdom that comes down from above, but is earthly, unspiritual, demonic. For where jealousy and selfish ambition exist, there will be disorder and every vile practice" (vv. 15, 16). The bones and grinning skulls of such false "wisdom" are clumped everywhere along the shores of modern culture, and among them are the remains of many believers and their churches.

We need to be like the ships that followed Franklin's Expedition, learning from the folly of the past and embracing new wisdom for the journey. We must consciously take hold of the wisdom from Heaven.

This is a good point at which to consider again the promise given earlier in James' letter: "If any of you lacks wisdom, let him ask God, who gives generously to all without reproach, and it will be given him" (1:5). Let us pray frequently for Heaven's wisdom with full assurance.

Our only wise God, we pray that you will make us "pure" in our moral lives and in the purity of our devotion to you. With all our hearts we desire this first-named characteristic of wisdom—the foundational element of wisdom from above.

We pray that you will further fill us with Heaven's wisdom, making us "peaceable." Give us your shalom, and help us promote peace with our brothers and sisters.

God, we entreat you to make us "gentle" so we will make allowances for the weaknesses of others and will be reasonable and kind in all our dealings with difficult people.

Make us "open to reason" so we will submit to reason, abandon unthinking stubbornness, and be open to the changing of our minds when we are wrong.

Lord, Heaven's wisdom is "full of mercy and good fruits," compassion that brings merciful action. Help us to go beyond pity and sentiment so that we do merciful acts, becoming the hands of Christ.

Grant us the wisdom to be "impartial," unwavering in respect to Biblical principle, so our lives will exude fairness.

Finally, make us "sincere," clear-eyed, honest, forthright, without masks—so others will perceive the wisdom of Christ in us.

Lord, give us wisdom from Heaven.

We pray this in Jesus' name.

Amen.

What causes quarrels and what causes fights among you? Is it not this, that your passions are at war within you? You desire and do not have, so you murder. You covet and cannot obtain, so you fight and quarrel. You do not have, because you do not ask. You ask and do not receive, because you ask wrongly, to spend it on your passions.

4:1–3

17

Troubles' Source

THE MODERN CATHOLIC AND EPISCOPALIAN LITURGIES contain a pleasing segment in their worship called "passing the peace." It requires that one shake hands with those around him and sincerely say, "Peace be with you." The other then responds, "Peace be with *you*." This new "tradition" is a nice touch, but it can have problems. The people of one small New York congregation found it beyond their limits. They could not bear shaking hands with people with whom they bore lifelong grudges. So they fired the priest and found a new one sympathetic to their needs![1] The story is humorous, but its tragic note is firmly rooted in all communions.

James Robert Johnstone, the nineteenth-century Scottish theologian and preacher, remarked:

> Men and women who on the Sabbath have sat side by side at the Lord's table and drunk of the common cup of love, will scowl at and calumniate and thwart each other all the week. And the feeling between congregations or denominations, which are but different companies or brigades in the army of the Captain of salvation, is not unfrequently such as to remind one of the host of Midian in the night of Gideon's victory, when "every man's sword was turned against his fellow, throughout all the host."[2]

Our individualistic American tradition has been particularly receptive to church strife. Recently I read of a congregational business meeting that turned into a brawl that was finally stopped by the local police! Stories like this are such a part of our American folklore that the caricature of a feuding church is found everywhere, as a young father learned from his children. Hearing a commotion in his backyard, he looked outside and saw his daughter and several playmates in a heated quarrel. When he intervened, his daughter called back, "Dad, we're just playing church!"[3]

The Origin of Trouble (v. 1)

James now poses a challenging question to his troubled churches: "What causes quarrels and what causes fights among you?" (v. 1a). The hounded Jewish congregations of the Dispersion were shot through with strife. They were experiencing class conflicts between the gold-fingered rich and their many poor (cf. 2:1–11). Rival would-be teachers grasped at the imagined good life of being Christian rabbis (literally "great ones") (cf. 1:19–26; 3:1). They boiled with "bitter jealousy" and "selfish ambition" and fell to "disorder and every vile practice" (3:14, 16). They praised God in church at every mention of his name, saying "Blessed be he! Blessed be he!" and then verbally cursed their fellow parishioners on the street (3:9, 10). Some of the new believers in these congregations were former Zealots, violent political activists. Because of this, many prominent scholars believe some may have actually become violent in the churches.[4]

The literal root meaning of the phrase "quarrels and . . . fights" is "wars and fights," which I think better conveys the raw realities of the situation in James' churches. Moreover, James' use of compressed language—deleting the verbs, so that his question is "From where wars and where fights among you?"—suggests his immense passion in asking this question.[5]

Some say today that the modern church needs to return to the purity and simplicity of the early church. I'm not so sure, especially in light of what Paul later reveals about the early church (cf. Acts 6:1ff.; 1 Corinthians 1:11; 2 Corinthians 12:20; Philippians 4:2).

James has posed a passionate rhetorical question, "From where wars and where fights among you?" And he answers it with a second rhetorical question that takes us to the heart of the subject: "Is it not this, that your passions are at war within you?" (v. 1b). The obvious answer is, "Yes!" In fact, this is the answer to all questions about conflict in the church. One word here bares the heart of this verse—the word "passions." In the Greek this is *hedone*, from which we derive the English word *hedonism*, the belief that pleasure is the chief good in life. Its primary sense here is *pleasures*.[6] James is saying in essence, "Don't your fights come from your *desire for pleasures* that battle within you?"[7] The strife and trouble in the church for the last two thousand years has been rooted in the overreaching personal desires of her people for personal pleasure and enjoyment.

Pleasure is not sinful per se, but what *is* wrong is a driving desire for pleasures. The only other uses of this word in the New Testament suggests this idea: Luke 8:14, where Jesus describes those who fall among thorns as "choked by the. . . pleasures of life," and Titus 3:3, which refers to people as "slaves to various passions and *pleasures*." James' emphasis is on a feverish search for one's own pleasures and gratifications.

In the phrase "passions [for pleasure] . . . at war within you" (v. 1c), James is explicit about how this searching for pleasure works misery in one's life. As a person is victimized by conflicting desires, his or her inner life becomes a battleground.[8] The old nature, with its self-seeking focus on personal pleasure, battles against the new nature (cf. Romans 7:21–23; Galatians 5:17), and selfish pleasure-seeking dominates. This in turn fosters a self-focus that naturally diminishes the importance of others and enthrones one's pleasures as the goal of life. This brings relational war with those around us, especially others in the church. Such narcissistic embrace of one's own pleasure as the chief end of life, whether it be sensual, materialistic, professional, or positional, is the bane of the church.

James' insights come down hard on us Christians who live in a profoundly pleasure-seeking culture. Years ago two famous men produced two opposite but equally chilling visions for the twentieth century. George Orwell wrote *1984* in which he warned that our culture would be overcome by externally imposed opposition. In *The Animal Farm* he explicitly identified it as communism. On the other hand, Aldous Huxley's *Brave New World* portrayed the danger not as some collectivistic oppressors, but as pleasure-giving technologies. Orwell feared those who would ban books. Huxley feared there would be no reason to ban books because no one would read them. Orwell feared we would become a captive culture. Huxley feared we would become a trivialized culture, preoccupied with pleasures. In *1984* Orwell envisioned a people controlled by inflicting pain. In *Brave New World* Huxley saw us as controlled by inflicting pleasure.[9]

Huxley was right! Marxism is crumbling, and pleasure is the ruler, especially in our land. We spend billions on this counterfeit "chief end of man." And, ironic tragedy of tragedies, even the church has become a purveyor of pleasure-centered theology. Christianity is often presented as the unfailing source of the affluent, successful life. For many, Christianity has become the spiritual equivalent of designer clothes and Chivas Regal—something to make life more enjoyable. The significance of this, in terms of our text, is that pleasure-seeking Christians are walking civil wars whose lust for pleasure brings fighting to the church and even to the world.

Are our lives filled with interpersonal conflicts, especially with believers? If so, it is probably because we have been profoundly infected by our

Brave New World and, however subtly and piously, are putting our personal
pleasure above everything else.

The Pathology of Trouble (v. 2a)

Having established that the root of fighting is the pursuit of pleasure, James
proceeds to introduce its miserable pathology in verse 2a: "You desire and
do not have, so you murder. You covet and cannot obtain, so you fight and
quarrel." This is a jarring indictment, to say the least, because James says
of *the church* "you murder." This is shocking! Some have dismissed this as
an error or, more commonly, have seen it as a metaphorical statement. But
there is no compelling evidence for either view.[10] Moreover, the case of King
David's murder of Uriah the Hittite is almost a letter-for-letter acting out
of what we have here, as the *New American Standard Bible* better puts it:
"You lust and do not have; so you commit murder" (see also NEB and GNB).[11]

Very likely something like this had happened in one of the churches,
scandalizing everyone and bringing disgrace on the name of Christ. Whatever
the exact case, Christians were brought to terrible lows in their frustrated
pursuits of pleasure and became homicidal in heart (cf. Matthew 5:21, 22).
Murder went to church and grinned fraternally at its brothers and sisters.
How degenerating are the effects of "pleasure first" upon the Body of Christ.

This section oozes with the frustration and disappointment of unrequited
pleasure-seeking. "You desire [literally: lust for] and do not have, so you
murder [frustration]. You covet [literally: hotly desire] and cannot obtain
[frustration], so you fight and quarrel."

The frantic pleasure-first life invariably goes after that which cannot
satisfy.

An intriguing experiment shows that a male butterfly will ignore a living
female butterfly of his own species in favor of a painted cardboard one, if the
cardboard one is big. If the cardboard one is bigger than he is, bigger than any
female butterfly ever could be, the male butterfly courts the piece of cardboard.
Nearby, the real, living female butterfly opens and closes her wings in vain.[12]

Similarly, the cardboard pleasures of this age have a whole world
fluttering after them in perpetual dissatisfaction.

When the pleasure-seeking person gets what he wants, it does not satisfy.
Dr. Samuel Johnson wisely said:

> Of all that have tried the selfish experiment, let one come forth, and say
> that he has succeeded. He that has made gold his idol, has it satisfied him?
> He that has toiled in the fields of ambition, has he been repaid? He that

has ransacked every theatre of sensual enjoyment, is he content? Can any answer in the affirmative? Not one![13]

John MacMurray put it even more succinctly: "The best cure for hedonism is an attempt to practice it."[14]

The Prayerlessness of Trouble (vv. 2b, 3)

The Bible is repeatedly clear that a driving desire for pleasure is ruinous to the prayer life: "You do not have, because you do not ask. You ask and do not receive, because you ask wrongly, to spend it on your passions" (vv. 2b, 3). The way this works is that, first, the pleasure-mad Christian, who has some spiritual sensitivity, realizes his prayers are inappropriate. Somehow he senses that his desire for a Maserati may not be a spiritual essential. So he asks for nothing. In fact, he doesn't pray much at all because few of the things he wants are high on the divine priority list.

Secondly, some pleasure-seeking believers do express their wrongly motivated desires in prayer, but do not receive. When John Ward, a member of the British Parliament, died, a prayer was found among his papers:

> O Lord, thou knowest that I have mine estates in the City of London, and likewise that I have lately purchased an estate in the county of Essex. I beseech thee to preserve the two counties of Middlesex and Essex from fire and earthquake; and as I have a mortgage in Hertfdordshire, I beg of thee likewise to have an eye of compassion on that county. As for the rest of the counties, thou mayest deal with them as thou are pleased.[15]

This is hardly the way to win friends or influence God. A pleasure-driven prayer life finds Heaven made of brass. The petty circumference of its requests simply do not interest the Father.

Is James saying Christians are never to passionately desire pleasure? The answer is a resounding "No!" It is OK to enjoy a day in the sun, the pleasures of sightseeing, a run in the country, a fine meal at your Chez Dreams, a barbecue, brats and a ball game, the joys of marital intimacies, the pleasures of tennis or golf or a roller-coaster ride, a good book or concert. The Christian life is not a life of negation, but of affirmation and enjoyment. In fact, in a way Christians ought to be the biggest pleasure-seekers in the universe. How is this?

First, we must understand that God is the author of all pleasure. There is a revealing passage in C. S. Lewis's *Screwtape Letters*, when he has the Senior Devil say to his understudy, Wormwood:

Never forget that when we are dealing with any pleasure in its healthy and normal and satisfying form, we are, in a sense, on the Enemy's ground. I know we have won many a soul through pleasure. All the same, it is His invention, not ours. He made the pleasures: all our research so far has not enabled us to produce one. All we can do is to encourage the humans to take the pleasures which our Enemy has produced, at times, or in ways, or in degrees, which He has forbidden. Hence we always try to work away from the natural condition of any pleasure to that in which it is least natural. An ever increasing craving for an ever diminishing pleasure is the formula.[16]

Lewis inventively states an unchanging theological reality: *all true pleasures are authored by God*. The Scriptures, especially the Psalms, are filled with the language of enjoyment—joy—pleasure. "Delight yourself in the LORD, and he will give you the desires of your heart" (Psalm 37:4). "Oh, taste and see that the LORD is good" (Psalm 34:8). "In your presence there is fullness of joy; at your right hand are pleasures forevermore" (Psalm 16:11).

This is why the Psalmist pursued God. "As a deer pants for flowing streams, so pants my soul for you, O God. My soul thirsts for God, for the living God" (Psalm 42:1, 2). "My soul thirsts for you; my flesh faints for you, as in a dry and weary land where there is no water" (Psalm 63:1).

Second, man is naturally made to seek pleasure. Blaise Pascal wrote in his *Pensees*:

All men seek happiness. This is without exception. Whatever different means they employ, they all tend to this end. The cause of some going to war, and of others avoiding it, is the same desire in both, attended with different views. The will never takes the least step but to this object. This is the motive of every action of every man, even of those who hang themselves.[17]

Pascal's point is that it is part of our humanness to seek pleasure. The problem is that men and women in delusive sinfulness, even as Christians, so often seek it from the wrong source and in the wrong way. Consider, for example, the words of God through the prophet Jeremiah: "For my people have committed two evils: they have forsaken me, the fountain of living waters, and hewed out cisterns for themselves, broken cisterns that can hold no water" (Jeremiah 2:13).

Third, God wants us to immerse ourselves in his pleasure by immersing ourselves in him. John Piper put it this way, making a slight alteration of the Westminster Confession's opening line:

The chief end of man is to glorify God
BY
enjoying Him forever.[18]

His desire to be *glorified* and your desire to be *satisfied* are not irreconcilable!
Pursue him with all you have, for every genuine pleasure is from his hand.

> We taste Thee, O Thou living Bread,
> And long to feast upon Thee still;
> We drink of Thee, the Fountainhead,
> And thirst our souls from Thee to fill.

Bernard of Clairvaux

You adulterous people! Do you not know that friendship with the world is enmity with God? Therefore whoever wishes to be a friend of the world makes himself an enemy of God. Or do you suppose it is to no purpose that the Scripture says, "He yearns jealously over the spirit that he has made to dwell in us"? But he gives more grace. Therefore it says, "God opposes the proud, but gives grace to the humble."

4:4–6

18

He Gives Us More Grace

JAMES 4:4–6

IN TODAY'S WORLD truly free people are exceptions. Most are like marionettes suspended and animated by a thousand strings of purported "pleasure." Some bounce puppet-like on the terrible strings of alcohol and drugs. Others' animus comes from pleasure-giving technology—cars, hot tubs, water beds, or stereos. Still others lay lifeless until they are "brought to life" by sports and entertainment. Millions of people rise and shower, drive their cars, walk the streets, ride elevators, return home, and go out in apparent freedom while actually never making a move not due to the tug of a self-centered pleasure. Even Christians are not immune to such bondage.

How does God regard his children who live for their self-centered pleasures, and what does he do to help them? These are the questions that our current text answers.

The Hostility of God (v. 4)

First, God regards pleasure-dominated believers adversarily, as verse 4 makes so clear: "You adulterous people! Do you not know that friendship with the world is enmity with God? Therefore whoever wishes to be a friend of the world makes himself an enemy of God." Thus we understand that a Christian, someone who has trusted in Christ alone for salvation, can become "an enemy of God"—God's adversary. This is horrifying!

This requires some reverent and careful thought. James is not saying friendship with *people* in the world is hatred toward God or makes anyone his adversary. Rather, friendship with the *world*—the *kosmos*, the evil world system that lies under the power of Satan—this friendship makes one God's enemy (cf. John 14:30; 2 Corinthians 4:4; Galatians 1:4; 1 John 5:19).

Believers who choose to pursue the pleasures of the world are ineluctably drawn to friendship with the forces of the world-system, which are at the very least indifferent to God and at the worst openly hostile to him. These friendships will ultimately spawn in the believer's heart the same indifferences and hostilities, thereby turning a true Christian into a practical enemy of the God he claims and desires to love.

These are painful thoughts—that a Christian for whom Christ died when he was still an enemy (Romans 5:10) should in effect lower himself to live as a redeemed enemy of God! Yet this is the very focus of our text because *James is writing to Christians*. And it rings true to our Christian experience. Many Christians, believers who have not disclaimed God or announced their allegiance to the world, derive their pleasures and entertainments in things that are patently hostile to God. Their "friends" are degraded videos and movies and CDs that demean the God they profess to love. There are also many who participate in evanescent pleasures God specifically forbids. Such become practical enemies *by choice*. "Whoever," says James, "wishes to be a friend of the world makes himself an enemy of God" (v. 4b).

It must be said that those who persist in living as friends of the world are very likely without grace, not Christians, despite their claims to faith. Paul says of such, "For many, of whom I have often told you and now tell you even with tears, walk as enemies of the cross of Christ. Their end is destruction, their god is their belly, and they glory in their shame, with minds set on earthly things" (Philippians 3:18, 19). They are friends of the world!

James is certainly direct and hard-hitting with his moral theology. Recently I was discussing this with one of my colleagues, who humorously suggested that James' letter ought to be entitled *In Your Face!*—an aggressive term borrowed from the sports world. *James, The In Your Face Epistle*. James gets in our faces that he might get into our hearts.

James' teaching suggests several penetrating questions. Are we today better friends with the world than we were a year ago? With God? From which do we derive our primary pleasure? Are we God's adversaries or his friends? How would God answer these questions?

The Jealousy of God (v. 5)

Having vividly instructed us that God becomes the *adversary* of those who pursue the accepted pleasures of the world, James proceeds to tell us that this also provokes God to *jealousy*: "Or do you suppose it is to no purpose that the Scripture says, 'He yearns jealously over the spirit that he has made to dwell in us' . . ." (v. 5). This is the most difficult passage in James, for two reasons. First, its statement that the "Scripture says" leads us to look for an Old Testament source, but none can be found in canonical (or even non-canonical) writings. So we conclude that James probably is referring to the general theme of God's jealousy as it is expressed in various places in the Old Testament (cf. Exodus 20:5; 34:14; Zechariah 8:2).[1]

Second, there is a dispute over how this verse ought to be translated. Without going into all the complexities of the problem, the translations are divided over whether the word "spirit" refers to the human spirit or the Holy Spirit. If it is the human spirit, as the *New International Version* has it, the verse refers to the universal tendency we all have toward envy and jealousy of one another. Or it could mean that God yearns over the plight of our human spirits which were given to us in creation, as the *English Standard Version* has it. If, however, this is referring to the Holy Spirit, it means that the indwelling Holy Spirit is jealous that we not fall to the error of friendship with the world. The *New International Version* footnotes' second alternative reads this way: "the Spirit he caused to live in us longs jealously." Other translations render it similarly: the *New King James Version*—"the Spirit who dwells in us yearns jealously"; *Jerusalem Bible*—"the spirit which he sent to live in us wants us for himself alone"; and *The Living Bible*—"the Holy Spirit, whom God has placed within us, watches over us with tender jealousy."

I am convinced that the text refers to the Holy Spirit's jealousy over us because it best fits the argument of the context[2] and because it touches on that grand truth so indispensable to the New Testament theology—the indwelling of the Holy Spirit.

Understanding that the Holy Spirit's jealousy for us is what is meant here opens a heart-changing truth to us: even when we sin by seeking our pleasures in friendship with the world, we are greatly loved, for jealousy is an essential element of true love. We are brides of Christ, and the Holy Spirit does not want us to go somewhere else to "have our needs met." The Holy Spirit's true love for us evokes a proper intolerance of straying affection. The personalness of this ought to steel us against wandering.

This jealous Spirit is *inside* us. When we sin, he is pained! Furthermore, his jealousy is passionate, for the idea in the Greek is that he longs or yearns for us with an intense jealousy.[3]

To realize that the awesomely holy God who transcends the universe and is wholly other and self-contained is at the same time personally and passionately and lovingly jealous for our affection—this realization ought to stop any of our "affairs" with the world and cause us to prostrate our souls adoringly before him. How we are loved! And how we ought to love! For as John informs us, "We love because he first loved us" (1 John 4:19).

Though God is the author of all true pleasures and desires us to enjoy life, the illicit tugging strings of self-centered hedonism constantly pull at us. And many of us have become friends of the fallen world order and are thus God's enemies. What are we to do?

The Grace of God (v. 6)

The answer is to remove the question mark from the middle of verse 6 and put it at the end of verse 5 where it belongs, and then read the opening words of verse 6 not as a question, but as a declaration: "But he gives more grace." That is the answer—more grace! This is not saving grace, for every believer has that. Rather, it is literally "greater grace"—God's gracious supply to live as we ought in a fallen world. As Augustine put it, "God gives what he demands."[4] There is always, for the believer, greater grace. This is without doubt one of the most comforting texts in all of Scripture.

This verse means there will always be enough grace regardless of our situation or need—always. The writer of Hebrews confidently tells us, "Let us then with confidence draw near to the throne of grace, that we may receive mercy and find grace to help in time of need" (Hebrews 4:16). We have no need that outstrips his grace, and we never will! Even if we fall into abject sin there is a stream of grace, as Paul said: "But where sin increased, grace abounded all the more" (Romans 5:20b). "For daily need there is daily grace; for sudden need, sudden grace; for overwhelming need, overwhelming grace," says John Blanchard.[5] John Newton, author of "Amazing Grace," knew this well:

> Through many dangers, toils and snares,
> I have already come:
> 'Tis grace has brought me safe thus far,
> And grace will lead me home.

There is always more grace.

An artist once submitted a painting of Niagara Falls for an exhibition, but neglected to give it a title. The gallery, faced with the need to supply one, came up with these words: "more to follow."[6] Old Niagara Falls, spilling over billions of gallons per year for thousands of years, has more than met the needs of those below and is a fit emblem of the flood of God's grace. There is always more to follow! The Apostle John referred to this reality, saying, "For from his fulness we have all received, grace upon grace" (John 1:16).

This is literally "grace instead of grace" or as others have rendered it, "grace following grace" or "grace heaped upon grace."

> He giveth more grace when the burdens grow greater;
> He sendeth more grace when the labours increase;
> To added afflictions He addeth His mercy,
> To multiplied trials His multiplied peace.
>
> When we have exhausted our store of endurance,
> When our strength has failed ere the day is half done:
> When we reach the end of our hoarded resources,
> Our Father's full giving is only begun.
>
> His love has no limits, His grace has no measure,
> His power has no boundary known unto men;
> For out of His infinite riches in Jesus,
> He giveth, and giveth, and giveth again.
>
> Annie Johnson Flint

Whatever our condition or situation, he always gives us more grace. He gives grace to overcome *personal weaknesses*. If to your alarm you find that you are repeatedly succumbing to a burning pursuit of hedonism, God will give you more grace if you ask. If you are a victim of an imploding self-centeredness that repeatedly sucks you into its nothingness, and you want deliverance, there is grace for the asking.

Perhaps you are so stubborn that you have never lost an argument. Perhaps you are such a knothead that you never listen to anyone. Now you find that your most intimate relationships are impaired, so that your spouse and friends find your presence a burden, but you want to change. God will give you more grace. If you have fed on cherished hatreds, but now see that the feast has really been the devil's feast and the main course your soul, and you want deliverance, he will give you more grace.

Perhaps your life has *insurmountable obstacles*. Perhaps a terminal disease. There is more grace. Or a loved one's death. There is more grace. Or a shattering divorce. There is more grace. Or the bitter ashes of failure. There is more grace.

There is also grace to do the *impossible*. If God is calling you to sell all and go to the ends of the earth to share the gospel or to take up a social crusade—whatever he asks—there will always be more grace.

> For out of His infinite riches in Jesus,
> He giveth, and giveth, and giveth again.

Is there any condition to receiving this river of grace? Yes—a very slight one for some people, a Donner Pass for others. James quotes Proverbs 3:34—"Therefore it says, 'God opposes the proud, but gives grace to the humble'" (v. 6b).

"Oh Sir," said a lady to the victorian preacher Charles Spurgeon one day. "I pray for you every day that you may be kept humble!" She was a wonderfully fine looking woman, and splendidly dressed—and Spurgeon replied, "Thank you much; but you remind me of a failure in my duty. I have never prayed for you that you might be kept humble." "Dear Sir," she cried, "there is no need for such prayers, for I am not tempted to be proud." Observed Spurgeon wryly, "How proud she was to have obtained such a delusion."[7]

A proud life is hard to grace. That is why Jesus said, "But woe to you who are rich. . . . Woe to you who are full now. . . . Woe to you who laugh now. . . . Woe to you, when all people speak well of you" (Luke 6:24–26). He knew that the rich, well-fed, laughing, those who are spoken well of, are naturally weighted with the relentless gravity of pride and thus find it difficult to open up to God's love and mercy.

It is true that "he gives more grace," that there is always greater grace, grace upon grace, grace heaped on grace. But it is also true that "God opposes the proud, but gives grace to the humble" (v. 6). Have we provoked our Maker's jealousy? If so, he will give us more grace.

Lord, we come humbly to you asking for more grace!

Submit yourselves therefore to God. Resist the devil, and he will flee from you. Draw near to God, and he will draw near to you. Cleanse your hands, you sinners, and purify your hearts, you double-minded. Be wretched and mourn and weep. Let your laughter be turned to mourning and your joy to gloom. Humble yourselves before the Lord, and he will exalt you.

4:7–10

19

The Gravity of Grace

JAMES 4:7–10

THE GRAVITY OF GRACE works like the earth's water system, which always flows from the highest to the lowest. Just as the waters of Niagara roll over the falls and plunge down to make a river below, and just as that river flows ever down to the even lower ranges of its course, then glides to still more low-lying areas where it brings life and growth, so it is with God's grace. Grace's gravity carries it to the lowly in heart, where it brings life and blessing. Grace goes to the humble.

This is the spiritual law behind Proverbs 3:34, which James has quoted in verse 6: "God opposes the proud, but gives grace to the humble." The unbowed soul standing proudly before God receives no benefit from God's falling grace. It may descend upon him, but it does not penetrate and drips away like rain from a statue. But the soul lying humbly before God is immersed—and even swims—in a sea of grace. So while there is always "more grace," it is reserved for the lowly—the humble.

The problem, of course, is that authentic humility has never been in vogue and most certainly is not today. Our rebellious world has embraced "the illusion that the human species is the sole crown of the cosmos, generator of the good, touchstone of truth, fashioner and designer of destiny,"[1] to use Carl Henry's words. Our modern-day human icons are not religious figures, but those who have been strong enough to climb to the top of the pile—and it does not matter to us how they got there.

Even the church has not been immune to this disease. Despite recent disgraces, it appears that much of the church is under the sway of the proud—those who, to use Woodrow Wilson's phrase, can "strut sitting down"[2]—hardly the posture in which to receive God's grace! With examples like this, the predictable result is that there are multitudes in the pew who haven't the foggiest idea of what God wants from them, and thus they live frustrated, graceless lives.

What is to be done? Fortunately God's Word still speaks, just as it did in James' day, for in verses 7–10 we find the antidote. This is a tidy unit consisting of a series of terse commands, beginning with the dominant call to submit to God and then giving three couplets of matching commands, and finally issuing a summary command.[3] In the Greek the language is even more clipped, so that the commands come in a jackhammer burst. James wants to so fire the souls of his people that they will swim triumphantly in the river of grace. May it be so for us as well!

James' opening command grates like fingernails across the chalkboard of contemporary culture: "Submit yourselves therefore to God" (v. 7a). Today people flood to classes on assertiveness and pay big money to learn the techniques of dominance. But can you imagine anyone attending a class on submissiveness? "Assert yourselves!"—that sounds better to the ear. "Assert yourselves before the Lord, and he will lift you up!"—that is a gospel people would like. The truth is, the language of grace may be grating, but submission is the only way to go. None of us came to Christ unbowed. Many of us had the fear we couldn't get low enough. That was my experience. I was ignorantly afraid he wouldn't take me, but he did.

James is calling us back to this initial submissiveness. It is to be our everyday experience. This is no small task because, though children of grace, we naturally rebel against many of the things God providentially allows in our lives. We want to be accomplished and highly regarded, but we Salieris just do not have the gifts some of our Mozart friends have, and we resent the ways of God, the bestower of gifts (1:17). Or perhaps our friends' children all excel in school, but ours have trouble, and we seethe toward God. Or we have a love that is not returned, and we are angry at Heaven. Or our health fails us, so we rebel. Many Christians have a sort of private feud with God, sit down with Jonah under the withered vine, and mutter, "I do well to be angry, angry enough to die" (Jonah 4:9).

If this is where we are, we must understand that this dead-end road is as futile as Jonah's display. Is there hidden rebellion in our lives? Is it so hidden that perhaps only those closest to us see it when they hear our morose humor and momentary bitternesses? If so, there is only one answer: submit to God, let go and say, "Though I do not understand my situation, I bow before you and submit my whole life to you." The last words of Richard Baxter provide a perfect prayer: "Lord, what thou wilt, where thou wilt, and when thou wilt."

Some of us need to pray this right now, and if we do, grace will flood our souls. Will you do it?

Resist . . . Come Near (vv. 7b, 8a)

James launches into the first of his coupled commands by stating the negative and positive sides of a mutual call. The *negative* expression is, "Resist the devil, and he will flee from you" (v. 7b). The *positive* side is, "Draw near to God, and he will draw near to you" (v. 8a).

"Resist" is a military metaphor that means to *stand against*, as in combat. This martial language suggests the parallel language of Ephesians 6 where we are told how to prepare to resist the devil. The primary element is an understanding of the enemy, which Paul memorably gives us in Ephesians 6:12: "For we do not wrestle against flesh and blood, but against the rulers, against the authorities, against the cosmic powers over this present darkness, against the spiritual forces of evil in the heavenly places." From this we learn that the struggle is *supernatural*, supra-flesh and blood. We also learn that it is *personal*, for the word for "wrestle" suggests hand to hand combat—swaying back and forth in sweaty battle. Finally, it is *futile* if fought with conventional weapons because we are fighting against serried ranks of evil angels led by fallen angelic princes.

Once we understand the nature of the enemy, we must put on the proper armament. For this let us picture the old warrior Paul in his own spiritual armor. He has worn his warbelt so long that it is sweat through and salt-stained and comfortable like an old horse's bridle, and it holds everything perfectly in place. "*The belt of truth,*" God's truth, has girt him tight for years, so that it permeates his life and truth reigns within. He is armed with the clear eyes of a clear conscience. He can face anything.

His torso is sheathed with a battle-tarnished breastplate. It is criss-crossed with great lateral grooves from slicing sword blows and dented from enemy artillery. "*The breastplate of righteousness*" has preserved his vitals intact. His holy life has rendered his heart impervious to the spiritual assaults of Satan.

His gnarled legs are comfortable in his ancient war boots. He has stood his ground on several continents. The boots are "*the gospel of peace,*" the peace *with* God that comes through faith in him, and the resultant peace *of* God—the sense of well-being in wholeness—*shalom.* He stands in peace, and being rooted in peace he cannot be moved.

Paul's great shield terrifies the eyes, for the broken shafts and the many charred holes reveal him to be the victor of many fierce battles. He has held *"the shield of faith"* as he repeatedly believed God's Word and so extinguished every fiery dart of doubt and sensuality and materialism. None have touched him.

On his old gray head he wears a helmet that has seen better days. Great dents mar its symmetry, reminders of furtive blows dealt him by the enemy. *"The helmet of salvation,"* the confidence of knowing that he is saved and will be saved, has allowed him to stand tall against the most vicious assaults. His imperial confidence gives him a regal bearing.

Then there is his sword. He was equal to a hundred when his sword flashed. *"The sword of the Spirit, which is the word of God,"* the ultimate offensive weapon, cut through everything—armor, flesh, glistening bone, and running marrow—even the soul (cf. Hebrews 4:12).

These are the weapons: *truth, righteousness, peace, faith, salvation, the Word of God*—and any believer who resists with these will put the devil and his armies to flight! This is not arrogance. This is the truth! You and I can withstand the devil if we wear the armor God provides. "Resist the devil, and he will flee from you" (v. 7).

Such resources are available to us! But there is another half to this: "Draw near to God, and he will draw near to you" (v. 8a). There are two views that the Christian ought to cultivate with all that he has: the devil's back and the face of God.

The soul-tingling truth here is, if you go after God, he will go after you! This was the prodigal son's experience when he neared his home: "But while he was still a long way off, his father saw him and felt compassion, and ran and embraced him and kissed him" (Luke 15:20). The father smothered him with kisses. Inch toward God, and he will step toward you. Step toward God, and he will sprint toward you. Sprint toward God, and he will fly to you!

What is James' overall point here in this positive call to draw near? In a word, *prayer*. The essence of prayer is the heart drawing near to God. Prayer is the soul's desire to come to him, to receive his love, to feel his power as we conform to his will. This is exactly what Paul's soldier in spiritual armor does. Every piece is in place. The spiritual forces of wickedness approach, and there will be lethal battle. But first the soldier falls to his knees and prays in the Spirit with all kinds of prayers (cf. Ephesians 6:18).

There is only one view more welcome than the backside of the devil—and that is the face of God.[4] Paul tells us, "But now in Christ Jesus you who once were far off have been brought near by the blood of Christ" (Ephesians 2:13). As his children and *in his Son*, we are near. But there is a *nearer nearness* available to all: "Draw near to God, and he will draw near to you." If you will take that step, a new nearness to God will be yours, and with it buoying tides of his grace.

Wash . . . Purify (v. 8b)

The next couplet of commands is in the last half of verse 8, which gives the external and internal aspects of the same action. The external is, "Cleanse your hands, you sinners," and the internal is, "purify your hearts, you double-minded" (v. 8b). This is a call to clean up one's acts and inner life.

James is bitingly aggressive, because up to now he has been courteously referring to his correspondents as "brothers," but now insultingly calls them "sinners" and "double-minded." The latter literally means *two-souled* and describes them as having a double allegiance to God and the world. This is a spiritual impossibility.

When I was growing up, the newspapers and magazines were full of a famous gangster named Mickey Cohen. It seems that Cohen once attended an evening evangelistic meeting and appeared interested. As a result many Christian leaders began to visit him, imagining what an impact his conversion would make. After one long evening service he was urged to open his heart and let Christ in, based on Revelation 3:20—"Behold, I stand at the door and knock. If anyone hears my voice and opens the door, I will come in to him and eat with him, and he with me." Cohen did this, but as the months passed it was evident he had not left his life of crime. When he was confronted about this, his response was that no one had told him he would have to give up his work or his friends. After all, there were Christian football players, Christian cowboys, and Christian politicians—why not a Christian gangster?[5]

Ridiculous! we think. But it is just as much (or even more) absurd for a true child of God to serve two masters. The Lord calls us to a single-minded allegiance to himself. He wants us to have eyes only for him! Jesus said, "Blessed are the pure in heart [the single-minded], for they shall see God" (Matthew 5:8). Jesus meant they would see him in this life, because this purity of focus invites deeper spiritual understanding. Seeing God in life is the highest good—the summum bonum—because all those who see him become like him. "And we all, with unveiled face, beholding the glory of the Lord, are being transformed into the same image from one degree of glory to another. For this comes from the Lord who is the Spirit" (2 Corinthians 3:18).

Are we two-souled Christians—having wandering eyes, one raised to Heaven, one focused on earth—absurd Mickey Cohens? If so, there is only one thing to do: *repent!* "Cleanse your hands . . . purify your hearts"—and get ready for more grace!

Grieve . . . Change (v. 9)

The final challenging couplet is in verse 9: "Be wretched and mourn and weep. Let your laughter be turned to mourning and your joy to gloom." Before applying this, it must be said that Christianity is preeminently a religion of joy and that the Bible is a joyous book. Solomon said, "A joyful heart is good medicine" (Proverbs 17:22), and this is eternally true. J. Oswald Sanders underlines the need for laughter in the church with these questions:

> Should we not see that lines of laughter about the eyes are just as much marks of faith as are the lines of care and seriousness? Is laughter pagan? We have already allowed too much that is good to be lost to the church and cast many pearls before swine. A church is in a bad way when it banishes laughter from the sanctuary and leaves it to the cabaret, the nightclub, and the toastmasters.[6]

Despite this, some Christians have misinterpreted this verse as calling for a life of gloom. I once knew a man who dourly maintained that the Scriptures never record that Jesus laughed or smiled (obviously our Lord repeatedly did many things not described in Scripture)—and therefore he wrongly maintained that truly Christlike believers do not laugh or smile either. When around this pious brother, I felt guilty for smiling or feeling good. Robert Louis Stevenson met some preachers like this and wrote facetiously in his diary, "I've been to church today and am not depressed." Spurgeon wrote, "Some men appear to have a white cravat twisted round their souls, their manhood is throttled with that starched rag."[7]

Nevertheless, while gloom is not a Christian characteristic, mourning over our sin is. "Be wretched" describes the grief one ought to experience when he falls to sin. "Be devastated" is the perfect expression of what "wretched" means.[8] "Mourn" expresses inner grief, and "weep" refers to a funeral lament. "Let your laughter be turned to mourning and your joy to gloom" is a scathing denunciation of Christians who are so insensitive and superficial that they are laughing when they ought to be weeping! Some laughter indicates a sickness of soul that only tears can cure. Have we wept over our sins?

An old preacher was informed that in one of his services a certain woman had gotten "joy in the Lord" (i.e., conversion). His penetrating question was: "Did she ever get any sorrow?" He knew that a proper grief precedes real joy. Have you gotten any sorrow? "Blessed are those who mourn, for they shall be comforted" (Matthew 5:4), for grace will wash over their lowly souls.

Years ago, at a great convention, Dr. Donald Grey Barnhouse stood before a vast throng and began his address dramatically by saying, "Up is down!" and then after a lengthy pause, "Down is up!" In doing so, he was intoning an unbreakable spiritual law: God exalts the humble and debases the proud.

Jesus himself lived this out, for Paul tells us in Philippians 2 that after Jesus' humiliation in his incarnation and death, "Therefore God has highly exalted him and bestowed on him the name that is above every name, so that at the name of Jesus every knee should bow, in heaven and on earth and under the earth, and every tongue confess that Jesus Christ is Lord, to the glory of God the Father" (Philippians 2:9–11). Jesus was subject to and verified his own spiritual law through his own life. During his time on earth Jesus repeated this on three separate occasions: "For everyone who exalts himself will be humbled, but the one who humbles himself will be exalted" (Luke 18:14; cf. Matthew 23:12; Luke 14:11).

God evidently wants his people to get the point. I hope we do, because this law will never be broken, ever! When the stars turn to ashes, it will still be intact. Everyone who has ever lived, including every angel and spirit, will be subject to this irrefragable law.

The gravity of grace will always channel the rivers of divine favor to the lowly—to those 1) who submit to God, 2) whose soul's momentum is away from the devil and toward God, 3) who purify their inner and outer lives, 4) who mourn over their sins, and 5) who obey the final summary command, "Humble yourselves before the Lord, and he will exalt you" (v. 10).

We are not to wait passively for this to somehow happen. We are not to wait for someone else to humble us, nor should we wait for the vicissitudes of life to do it. Rather, self-humbling is *our* Christian duty. We must take inventory of our sinfulness and weakness, then bow in total submission to God, yielding our total being, our dreams, our future, our *everything* to him. It is then that he will pour on the grace—grace upon grace—grace heaped upon grace—"and he will exalt you."

Do not speak evil against one another, brothers. The one who speaks against a brother or judges his brother, speaks evil against the law and judges the law. But if you judge the law, you are not a doer of the law but a judge. There is only one lawgiver and judge, he who is able to save and to destroy. But who are you to judge your neighbor?

4:11, 12

20

Watch What You Say

JAMES 4:11, 12

WALTER WANGERIN, in his collection of short stories *Ragman and Other Cries of Faith*, begins one of his stories with what seems to be a lesson in entomology, the study of insects (specifically spiders). But he surprisingly turns it into an unforgettable metaphor of spiritual truth. He explains that a female spider is often a widow for embarrassing reasons—she regularly eats those who come her way. Lonely suitors and visitors alike quickly become corpses so that her dining room is a morgue. A visiting fly, having become captive, will be granted the illusion of wholeness, but she will have drunk his insides so that he has become his own hollow casket. Not a pleasant thought, especially if you have a touch of arachnaphobia, as I do!

The reason for this macabre procedure is that she has no stomach and so is incapable of digesting anything within her. Through tiny punctures she injects her digestive juices into a fly so that his insides are broken down and turned into a warm soup. "This soup she swills," says Wangerin as he makes the point, "even as most of us swill souls of one another after having cooked them in various enzymes: guilt, humiliations, subjectives, cruel love—there are a number of fine, acidic mixes. And some among us are so skilled with the hypodermic word that our dear ones continue to sit up and to smile, quite as though they were still alive."[1]

This is a gruesome but effective metaphor to describe the destructive power of evilly intended words. Words do not dissolve mere organs and nerves but *souls*! This world is populated by walking caskets because countless lives have been dissolved and sucked empty by another's words.

This is the evil that the Holy Spirit addresses through James in verses 11, 12, where we find a command against evil speech and the reasoning behind it.

The command is unadorned and to the point: "Do not speak evil against one another, brothers" (v. 11a). It is important that we understand the precise wording of this command as the Greek has it, because it actually forbids more than slander. Literally the command is, "Do not speak down on one another, brothers,"[2] or "Do not speak against one another, brethren" (NASB). Slander is malicious speech that is untrue. But the command here forbids *any speech* (whether it is true or false) that runs down another person.[3]

Certainly no Christian should ever be a party to slander—making false charges against another's reputation. Yet some do. But even more penetrating is the challenge to refrain from any speech that intends to run down someone else, even if it is totally true. Personally I can think of few commands that go against commonly accepted conventions more than this. Most people think it is okay to convey negative information if it is *true*. We understand that lying is immoral. But is passing along damaging truth immoral? It seems almost a moral responsibility! By such reasoning, criticism behind another's back is thought to be all right as long as it is true. Likewise, denigrating gossip (of course it is never called gossip!) is okay if the information is true. Thus many believers use truth as a license to righteously diminish others' reputations.

Related to this, some reject running down another behind his or her back, but believe it is OK if done face-to-face. These persons are driven by a "moral" compulsion to make others aware of their own faults. Fault-finding is, to them, a spiritual gift. I once knew a young man who, after reading the list of the seven gifts mentioned in Romans 12, decided he had the gift of prophecy. The prophets, he observed, were confrontational, acerbic, and sharp-tongued, just as he was, so he must have the gift! Thus he had a spiritual rationale for an abrasive, critical personality. He was called to conduct spiritual search-and-destroy missions—or so he thought.

What people like this do not know is that most people are painfully aware of their own faults—and would so like to overcome them—and are busy trying. Then someone mercilessly assaults them believing they are doing their spiritual duty—and, oh, the hurt!

This destructive speaking down against others can also manifest itself in the subtle art of minimizing another's virtues and accomplishments. After being with such people, your mental abilities, athletic accomplishments, musical skills, and domestic virtues seem not to be quite as good as they were a few minutes earlier. Some of this feeling came, perhaps, from their words about your Steinway—"what a nice little piano"—and surprised exclamations about what you didn't know. It was also the tone of the voice, the cast of the eye, and the surgical silences.

There are many sinful reasons why brothers and sisters in Christ talk down one another. Revenge over some slight, real or imagined, may be the motivation for Christian slander. Gossip and criticism may be rooted in an overweening sense of self-righteousness. Our spirituality and sensitivity, we think, equips us to pull others from their pedestals and unmask their hypocrisies. Gideon once righteously cried, "A sword for the LORD and for Gideon!" (Judges 7:20)—and we may do the same, but in our case it is too often a sword of self-righteousness.

Talking down others may also come from the need to elevate oneself—like the Pharisee who thanked God he wasn't like other sinners "or even like this tax collector" (Luke 18:11). We thus enjoy the dubious elevation of walking on the bruised heads of others.

Sometimes this talking down of others simply comes from too much empty talk. People don't have much to talk about, so they fuel the fires of conversation with the flesh of others. The manifestations and motivations of the Body of Christ to run itself down could fill a library.

James' command to desist from harmful speech tells us that those in the early church (so historically near to Christ that Jesus' brother was one of its pastors!) were often engaged in mutually speaking against each other. They were puncturing one another repeatedly with fine gastric mixes of slander, gossip, and criticism, both behind the back and face-to-face. It was a devil's feast.

Is James' command only for another age? I think not. We're all skillful in rationalizing our corrosive speech. We've all done it and do it. We bite and are bitten. So God's Word comes to us with equal force and application: "Do not speak evil against one another, brothers [fellow believers]."

James realizes that some of his readers may take exception to his command, perhaps rationalizing that it is too stringent, that the miserable things being said about them by other Christians demands a return in kind, that "the best way to fight fire is with fire." James answers this with two parallel arguments.

Self-Elevation above the Law (v. 11b)

James' first argument is that when you speak against other believers, you exalt yourself above the Law. "The one who speaks against a brother or judges his brother, speaks evil against the law and judges the law. But if you judge the law, you are not a doer of the law but a judge" (v. 11b).

In order to clarify what James means here, it is helpful to understand that he is not saying Christians are never to make judgments about others or tell them what is what. Some reason that the greatest saints never judge anyone and that the ideal preacher is indifferent to people's moral choices, treating everyone the same. Their favorite verse is Matthew 7:1—"Judge not, that you be not judged." They interpret Christ's word as meaning that if you dare make a judgment about someone's actions you will be in big trouble with God. They neglect to read the saying's context (it is directed to people who are overlooking the logs in their own eyes while they judge others). Jesus does not forbid judgment. Rather, he forbids flagrant sinners from exercising it while refusing to deal with the sin in their own lives.

In point of fact, it is the Christian's *duty* to exercise judgment. For example, we are to beware of false prophets (Matthew 7:15). How can we determine a false prophet except by judging him against the standard of the Word of God? Likewise we are told, "You will recognize them by their fruits" (Matthew 7:16). Recognition hinges on careful judgment. We are to judge adultery, murder, lying, and theft as sins, and if anyone does these things, we must judge them as being sinful! Jesus said, "Do not judge by appearances, but judge with right judgment" (John 7:24). What the Scriptures forbid is *judgmentalism*, a critical and censorious spirit that judges everyone and everything, seeking to run others down.

It is this unkind, judgmental spirit that James attacks in verse 11. His point is, when anyone speaks uncharitably against a fellow believer and judges him, he breaks the law of love, the royal law (2:8)—"love your neighbor as yourself" (Leviticus 19:18)—which then makes him guilty of breaking the whole Law of God (James 2:10). His failure to keep the Law amounts to judging it, in that he has judged it to be invalid and unnecessary.[4] "Such a person," says Douglas Moo, "becomes a judge of the law and sits himself 'outside' and 'above' the law. Thus the law is not kept but is 'disdained.'"[5] If we think thus, we evidently view our opinions as better than God's. We imagine that given the chance we could improve the Law. Thus we become like Tolstoy, who said he was God's older brother.

The argument here is meant to deliver us from mind games that tell us it's okay to be judgmental because we are so spiritually sensitive and insightful, or because we have the kingdom's good as the motivation behind our judgments. God says this is stupid arrogance of cosmic dimensions. Perhaps we should have been on Sinai with Moses!

Self-Elevation above God (v. 12)

The second parallel argument takes the absurdity of a critical spirit a step higher, suggesting that a judgmental person sets himself not only above the

Law, but above God. Says James, "There is only one lawgiver and judge, he who is able to save and to destroy. But who are you to judge your neighbor?" (v. 12). God's sovereign capacity "to save and to destroy" is repeated many times in the Bible, as in Deuteronomy 32:39—"See now that I, even I, am he, and there is no god beside me; I kill and I make alive." In 1 Samuel 2:6 Hannah acknowledges this in her prayer: "The LORD kills and brings to life." In Job 40:7–14 we read how the Lord gloriously held up those realities to Job when he answered him from the whirlwind:

> Dress for action like a man;
>   I will question you, and you make it known to me.
> Will you even put me in the wrong?
>   Will you condemn me that you may be in the right?
> Have you an arm like God,
>   and can you thunder with a voice like his?
>
> Adorn yourself with majesty and dignity;
>   clothe yourself with glory and splendor.
> Pour out the overflowings of your anger,
>   and look on everyone who is proud and abase him.
> Look on everyone who is proud and bring him low
>   and tread down the wicked where they stand.
> Hide them all in the dust together;
>   bind their faces in the world below.
> Then will I also acknowledge to you
>   that your own right hand can save you.

In Matthew 10:28 Jesus warned his followers not to fear men who could kill the body but not the soul, but to fear God "who can destroy both soul and body in hell."

These Scriptures illustrate James' logic here: since God is the only one who can save and destroy, only God has the right to judge! Therefore, for us to judge one of his creatures is to usurp a right that only God has. Thus judgmentalism is not only arrogant but blasphemous![6] This alone ought to seal our judgmental, demeaning lips for eternity.

James' concluding rhetorical question is powerful: "But who are you to judge your neighbor?" (v. 12b). Would we take God's place? *Ignorance* mars our best judgments. We can judge external sins to be sins, but only imperfectly. We certainly do not know what is in the heart of another. God, however, knows every subtlety. "Therefore do not pronounce judgment before the time, before the Lord comes, who will bring to light the things now hidden in darkness and will disclose the purposes of the heart" (1 Corinthians 4:5).

Sin also inhibits our judgments. We are all such sinners that our subjective judgments are clouded by our fallenness. As the Puritan William Beveridge so perfectly said:

> I cannot pray,
> except I sin;
> I cannot preach,
> but I sin;
> I cannot administer, nor
> receive the holy sacrament,
> but I sin.
> My very repentance needs
> to be repented of;
> And the tears I shed
> need washing in the
> blood of Christ.

Let us thank God with all our hearts that we will not be judged by our sinful human counterparts.

Normally we would probably agree that speaking against our brothers and sisters and judging them is a serious sin. But James has set the record straight—it is one of the *worst* of sins because 1) it is self-exaltation above the Law, and 2) even worse, it is self-exaltation above God. We must agree that judgmentalism/evil-speaking is a terrible sin, for there is one thing even worse than this—namely, denying that it is so. We must agree with God or experience terrible consequences.

If we acknowledge our sin, what then? Here again the lowly spider has a lesson for us. Sometimes a tiny famine descends upon the mother spider and her offspring. There are no flies to eat, and the spiders will die. Says Wangerin:

> But then, privately, she performs the deed unique among the living. Into her own body this spinster releases the juices that digest. Freely they run through her abdomen while she holds so still, digesting not some other meat, but her own, breaking down parts of her that kept her once alive, until her eyes are flat. She dies. She becomes the stomach for her children, and she herself the food.[7]

There is, of course, no morality in this. The spider, whether swilling the life of another or becoming soup for her children, is simply acting according to instinct. Nevertheless, it is a picture of what Christ did for us on the cross when God "made him to be sin who knew no sin, so that in him we might become the righteousness of God" (2 Corinthians 5:21). It was our sin that Christ took upon himself. What horror rolled over him as wave after wave of *all* the sins ever committed rolled over him and through him as he became a curse. "Christ redeemed us from the curse of the law by becoming a curse for us—for it is written, 'Cursed is everyone who is hanged on a tree'" (Galatians 3:13). He cooked on the cross in the juices of our sins!

The resurrected Christ is food for our souls. Jesus said, "Truly, truly, I say to you, unless you eat the flesh of the Son of Man and drink his blood, you have no life in you. Whoever feeds on my flesh and drinks my blood has eternal life" (John 6:53, 54). We are called to spiritually dine upon his flesh and blood: "This is my body which is for you. Do this in remembrance of me. . . . This cup is the new covenant in my blood. Do this, as often as you drink it, in remembrance of me" (1 Corinthians 11:24, 25).

We have the life of Christ in us. And when we draw deeply on him, the same submissive love that caused him to become sin for us courses through us. Then, like him, when insulted we do not retaliate or make threats but entrust ourselves "to him who judges justly" (1 Peter 2:23). Like him, we do not run down others but rather are channels of divine love. It is possible to lead lives that heal instead of bite, that sustain instead of take.

Lord Jesus Christ, give us the grace, we ask. Amen.

Come now, you who say, "Today or tomorrow we will go into such and such a town and spend a year there and trade and make a profit"—yet you do not know what tomorrow will bring. What is your life? For you are a mist that appears for a little time and then vanishes. Instead you ought to say, "If the Lord wills, we will live and do this or that." As it is, you boast in your arrogance. All such boasting is evil. So whoever knows the right thing to do and fails to do it, for him it is sin.

4:13–17

21

Deo Volente

JAMES 4:13–17

The United Nations complex sits on sixteen acres of New York City's choicest real estate, bordering the East River and Manhattan. The lean, immense Secretariat building rises into the sky, the sun reflecting off its window walls. Bright flags of the nations of the world fly in the breezes off the river. The most prominent is the blue and white UN flag, its two white reeds of olive branches surrounding the world.

A visitor is immediately struck by the grandeur of the building, stirred by the sight of dignitaries stepping out of black limousines to cross the massive plaza. He realizes that if this place represents the powers of the world, one might well want to see the place of worship, where the nations bow before the One under whose rule they govern.

The information personnel are bemused. "The chapel? We don't have a chapel. If there is one, I believe it's across the street."

The visitor darts across the thoroughfare, dodging New York's taxis, and successfully arrives at the opposite building's security-clearance desk.

"Well, there's a chapel here," responds the officer, "but it's not associated with the UN." He thumbs through a directory. "Oh, I see, all right, here it is. It's across the street. Tell them you're looking for the meditation room."

Again the visitor dashes across the pavement. An attendant tells him the room is not open to the public; it's a "nonessential area," and there has been a personnel cutback. But a security guard will escort the visitor through long, crowded hallways and swinging glass doors. Again there is the pervasive sense of weighty matters being discussed in the noble pursuit of world peace.

The guide pauses at an unmarked door. He unlocks it and gingerly pushes it open. The small room is devoid of people or decoration. The walls are stark white. There are no windows. A few wicker stools surround a large square rock at the center of the room. It is very quiet. But there is no altar, rug, vase, candle, or symbol of any types of religious worship.

Lights in the ceiling create bright spots of illumination on the front wall. One focuses on a piece of modern art: steel squares and ovals. Beyond the abstract shapes, there is nothing in those bright circles of light. They are focused on a void. And it is in that void that the visitor suddenly sees the soul of the brave new world.[1]

So writes Charles Colson as he brilliantly underscores the view of God that lies at the heart of the secular world. The nations have come together for a noble pursuit—the peace and prosperity of all mankind, but without any reference to God. Indeed, there is a calculated indifference to God, even a skepticism about his existence. Our brave new pleasure-dominated, pleasure-seeking world is increasingly filled with people who live their lives with no reference to God.

This, of course, is not new. The early nineteenth-century politician Lord Melbourne said, "Things have come to a pretty pass when religion is allowed to invade public life." But whereas Melbourne's comment raised at least a few eyebrows in his day, today it would be hardly noticed, for his thesis is a cultural given. As the late Walker Percy's protagonist said in *The Moviegoer*, "one hundred percent of people are humanists and ninety-eight percent believe in God."[2] God simply is not a part of daily life.

So pervasive is our culture's arrogant independence of God that even many (most?) Christians attend church, marry, choose their vocations, have children, buy and sell homes, expand their portfolios, and numbly ride the currents of culture without substantial reference to the will of God. More Christians never seriously pray about God's will regarding their vocation, family direction, or entertainments than actually seek God's will. They change Augustine's "Love God and do as you please" to "Do as you please and say that you love God."

The Holy Spirit challenges this casual arrogance through the hard-hitting words of James in verses 13–17. The challenge falls into two sections: what we *must not say* as we plan our lives and what we *must say*.

What We Must Never Say (vv. 13, 14)

James immediately goes on the attack saying, "Come now, you who say, 'Today or tomorrow we will go into such and such a town and spend a year there and trade and make a profit'" (v. 13). His attack is specifically aimed at the materialistically focused Christian merchants in his congregations who arrogantly mapped out their destinations and sojourns on the basis of profitability, with no reference to the will of God. It had not been easy for them when they first became Christians. In fact, their conversions had cost them socially and economically. But in the initial flush of spiritual forgiveness they had borne the difficulties with grace, for they hung on to Christ with everything they had.

But as life settled down, the cares of making a living began to dominate again. They came to assume that profit and God's will were one and the same. Soon they reverted to being self-made, self-assured men who, though now Christians, live as if this world is all there is. If they prayed in reference to their lives, it was not to ask God where and what they should do, but to ask his blessing on their plans.

They were so like us. We are such children of our times that we cannot conceive it would ever be God's will that we not become rich and prosperous. Sadly, we have often advised our children the same way: "Be sure you get into a profession where you will make a good living, son, so you won't have to struggle like I did." Some have even objected to their children going into Christian work because it is not lucrative. Despite Christian trappings and evangelical nods, we often live without serious reference to God's will. This is practical atheism. God is about as relevant to our real life as the void in the heart of the United Nations.

James flays such a mind-set with powerful spiritual logic: "Yet you do not know what tomorrow will bring. What is your life? For you are a mist that appears for a little time and then vanishes" (v. 14).

One Memorial Day our family traveled in several cars to Lake Geneva, Wisconsin for the day. My wife, Barbara, and I traveled in the glorious role of grandparents with three of our grandchildren strapped into the backseat (Brian, then three and a half, Catherine, two, and Caroline, five months). As we drove along a major highway, a white car coming the opposite direction accelerated as he attempted to pass the car in front of him. There was no room, but instead of braking he accelerated even more—so that he was coming right at us at about 70 mph. We were skidding, and I thought, *This is it!* Then he accelerated even more, whipped onto the shoulder to the right of my car, on *our* side of the road, missing me and the two cars behind me, and then careened back across the center line to his side of the road—apparently never taking his foot off the accelerator!

I was numb, my wife was in tears, and the children were terrified—but alive. A second more and I think all five of us would have been dead. That could very easily have been the end of our lives! But the truth is, death could come to any of us any day, for we "do not know what tomorrow will bring" (v. 14).

None of us knows what tomorrow holds—a financial reversal or McDonald's millions, an accident or a memorable serendipity, a tornado or the return of Christ. *Maranatha*—"Our Lord, come!" (1 Corinthians 16:22).

It is fleshly presumption to say we are going to do this or that, travel here or there, without humble reference to the will of God. This is not only because of life's uncertainty, but also because of its *brevity*. "For you are a mist that appears for a little time and then vanishes" (v. 14). This is an eloquent simile. When I take an early-morning crisp jog, I see my warm breath rhythmically appear with each exhale and disappear before it clears my face. As I jog by a park I observe a mist hanging above the warm grass, but when I return that way it is gone. Smoke wafts from a campfire, almost palpable, and a moment later is gone! Steam rises from a kettle but disappears against the ceiling. Such is the span of our lives! This is serious stuff.

Evidently the Spirit of God wants us to grasp and internalize the brevity of our lives because the Old Testament contains so many parallel similes. Job says, "My days are swifter than a weaver's shuttle" (Job 7:6). They fly by—zip zip! In another place he says, "As the cloud fades and vanishes, so he who goes down to Sheol does not come up" (Job 7:9). A cloud floats aloft, separates before one's eyes, and is borne silently away, never to be seen again. And again Job says, "My days are swifter than a runner" (Job 9:25). Here he comes—there he goes. That is my life! Again says Job of his days, "They go by like skiffs of reed" (Job 9:26). As a sail is seen on the horizon, then is gone, so is my life.

King David sang, "My days are like an evening shadow" (Psalm 102:11). The shadow is there, but in a minute its shade fades, and it is swallowed before one's eyes by the night and is gone forever. In the same Psalm we read, "For my days pass away like smoke" (Psalm 102:3). Poof! In another place David says, "You have made my days a few handbreadths" (Psalm 39:5). Here one imagines David holding his hand up before his people as he sings and pointing to the short journey across his palm. And then, of course, there is his famous, "As for man, his days are like grass" (Psalm 103:15). It sprouts, greens, withers, *and is gone.*

Words are piled on words, simile upon simile, rich metaphors interwoven, to get the idea across to us. Mike Mason says, "Lives are curlicues of fire cut briefly in the dark with a glowing stick."[3] Have you ever made orange curlicues in the dark with a hot stick or a spent sparkler and watched them fade away? One after another for thousands of years men and women have been living short lives, and the total of them is not a second compared to the endless duration of eternity.

Oh, how I wish the Spirit's message would sink into the hard brain patterns of our lives. I especially wish this for those in high school and college. It is said that long ago when an eastern emperor was crowned at Constantinople, the royal mason would set before his majesty a certain number of marble slabs. One he was to choose then and there for his tombstone. The ancients thought it wise for him to remember his funeral at the time of his elevation, for his life would not last forever. Perhaps this would be a profitable ceremony, say, at graduation. If those who are young or in the best of health could sense how short it all is, and how unpredictable, it would perhaps be so much easier to give it all to Christ. May we all do this.

Holy Spirit of God, teach us to number our days that we may have a heart of wisdom! (Cf. Psalm 90:12.)

What We Must Say (vv. 15, 16)

Having shown the folly of announcing what we are going to do tomorrow or next year without reference to God's will, James gives us a godly alternative: "Instead you ought to say, 'If the Lord wills, we will live and do this or that'" (v. 15). Interestingly, the expression "If the Lord wills" appears nowhere in the Old Testament, though it is used several times in the New Testament. Paul promised the Ephesians, "I will return to you if God wills" (Acts 18:21). To the Corinthians he said, "But I will come to you soon, if the Lord wills" (1 Corinthians 4:19; cf. Romans 1:10; 1 Corinthians 16:7; Philippians 2:19, 24; Hebrews 6:3). However, in similar instances he talks confidently about his future plans without using the phrase (cf. Acts 19:21; Romans 15:28; 1 Corinthians 16:5). The right mind-set—dependence on God—is more important than saying the right words.

Despite this, the phrase has been immensely popular at different times in church history. The Puritans loved it and filled their speech and correspondence with the Latin equivalent *Deo Volente*, "God willing." And the Methodists followed the same practice. In fact, godly Methodists regularly signed their letters with the initials D.V., and placards and circulars about coming events also had D.V.

I think this was a beautiful custom, but of course I realize the danger inherent in its becoming a cliché. (We all know we do not need more Christian clichés!) Words are so much more easily counterfeited than the reality they represent. Nevertheless, I wonder if the reason we don't use D.V. today is not so much the fear of cliché, but rather the influence of our modern world that rejects a transcendent God. It is not without significance that the Puritan epoch, as well as the Wesleyan revivals, were golden ages of evangelical Christianity. "God willing" is the posture of a burning heart.

However that may be, one thing is for sure—*Deo Volente* is to be the constant refrain of our hearts as we conduct the affairs of our lives. "If God wills" must be written over students' plans—the choice of a life partner, future education, all everyday activities. Older people need to say from the heart, "If God wills, I will spend my time . . . If God wills, my children will become . . . If God wills, I will take up this ministry . . . If God wills, I will wake up tomorrow." All of us should have this heart attitude.

D.V. before and after everything in life presupposes a life of dependent prayer in which all is taken before God. It means, further, a profound submission, for "God willing" truly said from the heart cannot produce anything else.

When my family and I moved from Southern California to Illinois, we underwent an understandably difficult adjustment. This was especially hard for my wife. We left a church that we had founded. Not only were our families left behind, but friends from fifteen years of ministry. We had expected to spend our lives at that church, to have our daughters married there, to be surrounded by old friends at life's big events, some of whom had known us from childhood. We never thought we would move, ever! But we did. And the passage that gave my wife greatest joy and wisdom was, "Come now, you who say, 'Today or tomorrow we will go into such and such a town and spend a year there and trade and make a profit'—yet you do not know what tomorrow will bring. What is your life? For you are a mist that appears for a little time and then vanishes. Instead you ought to say, 'If the Lord wills, we will live and do this or that'" (vv. 13–15). Our years have turned out to be wonderful, and we will never, ever move again *D.V.*!

Have we been planning our own way, with little thought of God's will? Are we being pulled along by life's events in a direction we have not chosen, though we sense God is behind it? If either is the case, we ought to say, "Lord, I will do it if it is your will."

James interjects a jarring note after his lofty call to do God's will: "As it is, you boast in your arrogance. All such boasting is evil" (v. 16). Here the Greek would be better rendered, "As it is, you boast about your pretensions. All such boasting is evil"[4] (as in the Moffatt and Williams translations). Apparently some of James' parishioners were actually bragging around about their independent accomplishments apart from God. The same word is used in 1 John 2:16 of "the boastful pride of life" (NASB). "Look what I have done

on my own. Sure, God gave me life, but it is *my* brains, *my* plans, *my* energy."
This was amazing arrogance. James says, "All such boasting is evil."

Most of us would not be so crass as to outwardly boast. We're far too
urbane and culturally "cool" to do that. But inwardly? God knows, and God
has his ways of dealing with us.

The greatest of the Babylonian kings, Nebuchadnezzar, learned this the
hard way. As head of Babylon at its zenith, he strode one bright day on his
palace roof. Below stretched Babylon's busy canals and the glistening tiled
walls of the city. Before him rose the famous Hanging Gardens, one of the
ancient world's Seven Wonders. He could not contain himself as he cried,
"Is not this great Babylon, which I have built by my mighty power as a royal
residence and for the glory of my majesty?" (Daniel 4:30). Swift came divine
judgment as Nebuchadnezzar fell to all fours, thinking himself an ox and
began to dine on the grass until he came to his senses years later (cf. Daniel
4:34, 35). If God did this with pagan King Nebuchadnezzar, how much less
will he suffer his children to go on in arrogance.

James closes with a challenge to do the truth here enjoined and not succumb to the sin of *omission*"[5] "So whoever knows the right thing to do and
fails to do it, for him it is sin" (v. 17).

In 1744 Louis XV of France was smitten with a malady that threatened
to cut his days short. The historian Thomas Carlyle tells us that France was in
terror, and Paris seemed like a city taken by storm. The churches resounded
with supplications and groans, and the prayers of priests and people were
continually interrupted by their sobs. This widespread manifestation of tender interest and deep affection for Louis XV brought him the surname of
"Louis the Well-beloved." The love of the people for their young king was
not inspired by what he had done, but by what they hoped he would do. For
years the nation had been crushed under the heel of a cruel tyrant, and they
regarded the accession of Louis XV as the dawn of a brighter and happier
day. They loved him because in him rested all their hopes. That was in 1744.

Thirty years later, Louis XV again lay sick. But the churches did not re-
sound with excessive groanings. Sobs did not now interrupt any prayers, for
no prayers were being offered. In fact, "Louis the Well-beloved" had become
the most hated man in France. In 1744 he might have asked, "What have I
done to be so loved?" and in 1774, "What have I done to be so hated?" The
truth is, he had done *nothing*.[6]

"So whoever knows the right thing to do and fails to do it, for him it is
sin" (v. 17). What is "the right thing" here in our text? It is this: we are to
reject the modern delusion that sees God as, even if he exists, irrelevant to

life—and this being done, we are to embrace the truth that our life is short and we have no control over its brief span, finally saying with all our heart, *Deo Volente.*

Is God calling you or me to do his specific will? Perhaps to give up something? If so, may we say, "Lord, I am willing."

Is God calling us to go somewhere and we are resisting? If so, may we say, "Lord, I am willing."

Perhaps he is calling us to accept a difficult responsibility. If so, may we say, "Lord, I am willing."

The spiritual logic here is inescapable. "What is your life? For you are a mist that appears for a little time and then vanishes" (v. 14), but our destiny is eternity with God.

May our heart-cry in all of life be, *Deo Volente.*

Come now, you rich, weep and howl for the miseries that are coming upon you. Your riches have rotted and your garments are moth-eaten. Your gold and silver have corroded, and their corrosion will be evidence against you and will eat your flesh like fire. You have laid up treasure in the last days. Behold, the wages of the laborers who mowed your fields, which you kept back by fraud, are crying out against you, and the cries of the harvesters have reached the ears of the Lord of hosts. You have lived on the earth in luxury and in self-indulgence. You have fattened your hearts in a day of slaughter. You have condemned and murdered the righteous person. He does not resist you.

5:1–6

22

Riches That Corrode

JAMES 5:1–6

JAMES' ATTACK in the opening paragraph of chapter 5 can only be described as seething. It is so fierce that Upton Sinclair, the novelist and social reformer, once read a paraphrase of this section to a group of ministers after attributing it to Emma Goldman, an anarchist agitator. The ministers were so enraged they declared she ought to be deported![1] So we must take heed as we preach and teach this passage lest we be likewise disposed of! But we must also take heed, for this is God's Word, and we will all answer to him who will judge our souls for eternity.

Actually James' invective is aimed at his wealthy, nonbelieving countrymen[2] who were exploiting the poor, many of whom were in the church. Specifically, James' targets were wealthy farmers who owned large tracts of land and were squeezing everyone and everything for profit. But though these persons were the calloused unbelieving rich, the message is also meant to benefit the church. James understood that the natural human tendency to envy the rich, if sustained, would lead many Christians astray. Thus, this scathing warning to the ungodly rich is also meant to steel his people against such folly. In addition, James' terrifying description of the judgment awaiting these rich countrymen is meant to ensure the exploited poor that justice is coming and they ought to bear their indignities with patience.

This is a timely message for us as we all live under the lure of "The Lifestyles of the Rich and Famous"—the seductive delusion that "you are what you buy." May the Holy Spirit help us step inside James' smoldering human spirit, hear the hammer blows as he pounds the arrogant rich, and allow those blows to shape *our* lives as well.

James begins, "Come now, you rich, weep and howl for the miseries that are coming upon you" (v. 1). Some feel that this command suggests that the rich are intrinsically happy. Consider recently deceased Malcolm Stevenson Forbes Sr., who owned *Forbes Magazine* that annually lists the four hundred wealthiest Americans—devoting over four hundred pages to their motivations, spending habits, divorces, and hobbies. Forbes's wealth was estimated from $400 million (*London Daily Mail*) to one billion (*New York Daily News*). He possessed a 400-square mile ranch in Colorado, a South Sea island, a palace in Tangiers, a chateau in France, a mansion in London, twelve hot air balloons, a huge yacht that helped keep his income tax down.[3] Was he happy? Probably not.

I do know that Paul Wachtel in his book *The Poverty of Affluence* cites a survey that reveals that a higher percentage of those with grammar school educations and poverty-level incomes report themselves "very satisfied with life" than do college graduates with high incomes.[4]

So we must understand that James, in commanding the rich to mourn, is not necessarily calling them from a state of happiness to mourning. He is calling the unrighteous rich (be they happy or not) to mourn because of what awaits them in the final judgment. Their materialistic focus places them in terrifying peril.

Next we should note that James is not making an indiscriminate attack on the rich. Some notable saints have been rich: Abraham, Job, David, Josiah, Philemon, Joseph of Arimathea, and Lydia, for example. Moreover, there is not a word here against riches *per se*. The Bible does not say money is the root of all evil, but that "*the love of money* is a root of all kinds of evils" (1 Timothy 6:10). The focus, again, is on those who gain their wealth in an ungodly manner, make it the center of their lives, and fail to use it to benefit others—those who smugly think:

> The rich man in his castle
> The poor man at his gate
> God made them high and lowly
> And orders their estate.[5]

To such comes James' drastic command to "weep and howl"—"howl" being the onomatopoeic word *olouzo*, which one of the classic commentators renders "lament with howls of misery."[6] The picture is of sobbing lament punctuated with repeated howlings as they face the final judgment. We ought to let the subjective horror of this seep into our hearts. This is God's Word!

These words suggest a solemn, forgotten truth—that wealth is not an advantage, but rather a *spiritual handicap*. Toward the end of the Sermon on the Mount Jesus says, "No one can serve two masters, for either he will hate the one and love the other, or he will be devoted to the one and despise the other. You cannot serve God and money" (Matthew 6:24). In answer to a question that precipitated the Parable of the Rich Fool, Jesus began, "Take care, and be on your guard against all covetousness, for one's life does not consist in the abundance of his possessions" (Luke 12:15). After the parable he stated, "For where your treasure is, there will your heart be also" (Luke 12:34). When a rich young ruler came to Jesus and was told that he must sell all to inherit eternal life, "He went away sorrowful, for he had great possessions" (Mark 10:22).

> And Jesus looked around and said to his disciples, "How difficult it will be for those who have wealth to enter the kingdom of God!" And the disciples were amazed at his words. But Jesus said to them again, "Children, how difficult it is to enter the kingdom of God! It is easier for a camel to go through the eye of a needle than for a rich person to enter the kingdom of God." And they were exceedingly astonished, and said to him, "Then who can be saved?" Jesus looked at them and said, "With man it is impossible, but not with God. For all things are possible with God." (Mark 10:23–27)

Jesus' unrelenting point is, it is *impossible* for one who trusts in riches to get into Heaven.

Material possessions tend to focus one's thoughts and interests on the world only. Wealth gradually enslaves those who are attached to it and perverts their values. The more we have, the easier it is to be possessed by our possessions, comforts, and recreations. Jesus says, "the cares of the world and the deceitfulness of riches and the desires for other things enter in and choke the word" (Mark 4:19). Most tragic of all, as with the rich young ruler, wealth can steel one against the objective requirement for entering the kingdom. That is, when your hands are full, it is difficult to say:

> Nothing in my hand
> I bring
> Simply to thy cross
> I cling.

With this withering reality in mind, we turn to James' indicting blows, the force of which we should apply to our needy souls. There are four distinct blows: (1) hoarding, (2) fraud, (3) self-indulgence, and (4) murder.

Indicted for Hoarding (vv. 2, 3)

Bertha Adams was seventy-one years old. She died alone in West Palm Beach, Florida on Easter Sunday, 1976. The coroner's report read: "Cause of death . . . malnutrition." After wasting away to fifty pounds she could no longer stay alive. When the state authorities made their preliminary investigation of her place, they found a veritable "pigpen . . . the biggest mess you can imagine." One seasoned inspector declared he'd never seen a dwelling in greater disarray. The pitiable woman had begged food from neighbors and gotten what clothes she had from the Salvation Army. From all appearances she was a penniless recluse—a pitiful and forgotten widow. But such was not the case.

Amid the jumble of her unclean, disheveled belongings, two keys were found that led officials to safe-deposit boxes at two different local banks. The discovery was absolutely unbelievable. The first box contained over seven hundred AT&T stock certificates, plus hundreds of other valuable certificates, bonds, and solid financial securities, not to mention a stack of cash amounting to nearly $200,000. The second box had no certificates, only more currency—$600,000 to be exact. Adding the net worth of both boxes, the woman had well over a million dollars. Bertha Adams's hoarding was tragic, and her death was an unusually grim testimony to the shriveled focus of her life. Her great wealth did her no good whatsoever. Its proper use could have meant good health for her and many others.

Such hoarding is obscene, as James makes so clear in verses 2, 3: "Your riches have rotted and your garments are moth-eaten. Your gold and silver have corroded, and their corrosion will be evidence against you and will eat your flesh like fire. You have laid up treasure in the last days."

The agrarian ancient world had three standard sources of wealth: harvested grain, clothing, and precious metals and jewels, and James points out that hoarding is ruinous to all three. Their great stocks of grain have soured through the futile attempt to preserve them. Their clothing, so important to their status and maintenance of position—the changes of robes for occasions throughout the day, etc.—are ruined in storage. Moth-eaten, they are worthless![7] And their gold and silver? James knew they could not corrode, but he appropriates the language of wisdom literature to emphasize that even these are temporal, despite careful accumulation (cf. the non-canonical Ecclesiasticus 29:10 and Epistle of Jeremiah 10). "Your gold and silver," James says, "have corroded."[8] James' conscience-convicting meaning is, "While God's needy children are all around you, your heartless act of stockpiling to preserve your wealth has turned it to spiritual rot in your souls!"

Their wealth became a self-destructive curse. "Their corrosion will be evidence against you and will eat your flesh like fire." Their hoarded wealth eats them "in the last days"—in the time just before the return of the Lord.[9]

What does this warning mean to us today? While the Bible does not discourage saving and prudential provision for one's needs, it is dead set against the vast accumulation of self-directed wealth focused solely on perpetuating one's own comforts and pleasures. Jesus was very clear about this, using words that James consciously borrowed: "Do not lay up for yourselves treasures on earth, where moth and rust destroy and where thieves break in and steal, but lay up for yourselves treasures in heaven, where neither moth nor rust destroys and where thieves do not break in and steal. For where your treasure is, there your heart will be also" (Matthew 6:19–21). A wise Christian will submit to these convicting words of God.

Indicted for Fraud (v. 4)

The Old Testament repeatedly warns against defrauding workers. Deuteronomy 24:14, 15 commands, "You shall not oppress a hired worker who is poor and needy, whether he is one of your brothers or one of the sojourners who are in your land within your towns. You shall give him his wages on the same day, before the sun sets (for he is poor and counts on it), lest he cry against you to the Lord, and you be guilty of sin." Leviticus 19:13 similarly says, "You shall not oppress your neighbor or rob him. The wages of a hired worker shall not remain with you all night until the morning." And Proverbs 3:27, 28 says, "Do not withhold good from those to whom it is due, when it is in your power to do it. Do not say to your neighbor, 'Go, and come again, tomorrow I will give it'—when you have it with you" (cf. Jeremiah 22:13; Malachi 3:5; also the non-canonical Ecclesiasticus 34:22 and Tobit 4:14).

Nevertheless, these landlords were doing this to the poor, so James erupts: "Behold, the wages of the laborers who mowed your fields, which you kept back by fraud, are crying out against you, and the cries of the harvesters have reached the ears of the Lord of hosts" (v. 4). This was a heinous crime for two reasons. First, the poverty-stricken workers were living hand-to-mouth, and a day without wages was a day without food! Second, the owners were doing this at harvesttime when their barns were full and the wine red in the press. Imagine an employer sitting in a Thanksgiving Eve service before a sumptuously decorated table aglow in the flickering amber light of candles, singing, "Now thank we all our God/With hearts and hand and voices/Who wondrous things has done/In whom his world rejoices," while his employees cannot afford a turkey. And don't think this hasn't happened! This sin is not confined to a Dickens novel. In fact, it is one of the reasons one-time evangelist Vincent Van Gogh gave up the faith.[10] This also happens today—for example, to illegal aliens who have come to *El Norte*, the promised land.

James says two cries go up here. The cry of unpaid wages rises again from the bank accounts of the rich, like the blood of Abel (Genesis 4:10). This cry is *loud* like the scream of an expelled demon[11] and demands vengeance. The other cry is a shout from the workers. This pathetic duet does not go unheard, for it reaches "the ears of the Lord of hosts." The hosts are the angelic armies of Heaven. This is the name young David invoked when he stood before Goliath and cried, "You come to me with a sword, a spear, and a javelin, but I come to you in the name of the LORD of hosts, the God of the armies of Israel, whom you have taunted. This day the LORD will deliver you up into my hands" (1 Samuel 17:45, 46, NASB). This awesome, martial God hears and will avenge!

This prophetic cry is against any person or nation who reaps riches at the expense of the poor. It is against unbelievers. But sadly it is also sometimes true of Christians. Christian employer, it is far better to pay your employees what they are worth and to provide good benefits than to increase your profit and give more to "Christian causes." All who employ others must ask themselves if there are any voices calling out to God because of them.

Indicted for Self-Indulgence (v. 5)

Self-indulgence in the accumulation of wealth is progressively addictive. Lance Morrow tells how, when a collegian, he visited Pocantico, the great Rockefeller estate:

> We passed through the Rockefellers' parks and forests. Here, off the public roads, came a sense of kingdom and privacy and magnificent exemption. We pulled up to Kykuit. . . . John D. Rockefeller, Jr. had built it at the beginning of the century. It looked like an ornate and compact and private museum of gray stone. The stone suggested a permanence almost too permanent; an air of the mausoleum clung there. Yet it was summer. The place was gay with bright striped awnings, and trees and flowers. Beside the house lay the profligate garden of art—a reckless millionaire litter of Henry Moores and Calders and Giacomettis and Noguchis, all strewn across the grass, among the boxwood. I felt the casual and overbearing power of that display, the sheer unanswerable force that commanded so much of the world's artistic imagination to come and lie down upon the grass of one man's lawn. And it was all private—family decor—not the work of institutions or governments but of an individual's whim and will. Such a display belonged to an earlier civilization, to the feudal.[12]

Such self-centered accumulation and indulgence is, and always has been, sub-Christian, even if the perpetrators are Christians.

James excoriates such living: "You have lived on the earth in luxury and in self-indulgence. You have fattened your hearts in a day of slaughter" (v. 5) James' reference to luxurious living is very descriptive in its literal rendering: "You have *lived delicately*"[13]—a soft, pampered life. His mention of "self-indulgence"—literally "taken your pleasure"—evokes the wasteful living of the prodigal, wanton self-indulgence. This is *conspicuous consumption*, a sin that assaults us every hour as we walk through a shopping mall, watch television, or go through the day's mail.

This is a powerful temptation, but the divine statement for those who reject God's grace and pursue an indulgent lifestyle is even more powerful: "You have fattened your hearts in a day of slaughter" (v. 5). What a terrible thought, especially if you have ever dressed out an animal for the table. "The wealth of the rich becomes a wasting disease."[14] Calvin quaintly says:

> Not for nothing does the Lord by His prophets throw sharp words at those who sleep on ivory couches, who pour on precious unguents, who entrance their palates with sweetness to the notes of the zither, to all intents like fat cattle in rich pastures. All this is said to make us keep a perspective in all our creature comforts; self-indulgence wins no favour with God.[15]

James' scathing words to the unregenerate must also find their mark in us. There are times for sumptuous celebration—holidays, birthdays, or anniversaries. There are times to feast and lavish our loved ones. But a life of conspicuous consumption—delicate, soft luxury—is *not* Christian. Do not be fooled by the evangelistic gigolos who tell eager ears, "You are children of the King—live like it!"

Indicted for Murder (v. 6)

In this final indictment James' accusations reach the greatest intensity: "You have condemned and murdered the righteous person. He does not resist you" (v. 6). Literally this reads, "the righteous man; he does not resist you," as the ESV reflects, but other translations are correct in taking this as a generic reference to the kind of man these landed rich had victimized.[16] James is referring to *judicial* "murder"—primarily referring to taking away the means of making a living. The landed gentry controlled the courts. The poor could not oppose them because they had no way to use the system, and thus were helpless.

So it often is today in the cold, hard, secular world. Despite attempts to protect the poor, the power still largely resides with the moneyed. This ought to never be true of Christians. We who have advantages of education and wealth and perhaps position must take great care not to harm others, especially those less fortunate, as we pursue our livings. God sees all!

James has been so painfully explicit with his pounding indictments of the money-mad, unbelieving world. Material fixation spawns a miserable quartet in one's life: 1) hoarding, 2) fraud, 3) self-indulgence, and 4) murder.

Though this is a characterization of the world without Christ, we must never imagine ourselves to be immune. We must each ask ourselves: Do I hoard? Am I guilty of overaccumulation of wealth? Have I ever or am I now defrauding someone? Is there financial deception in my life? Have I succumbed to the culture's Siren song of self-indulgence? Are there sub-Christian excesses in my life? Have I "murdered" another—that is, have I victimized someone because of a power advantage I possess?

The key to a healthy Christian life is regular submission to the searchlight of God's Word. We must honestly do so for our soul's sake and the sake of the church. Many of us, in comparison with others, are rich. Our lifestyles, due to modern invention and education, make the lifestyles of the ancients seem very shabby. Depending on our mind-set and soul-dependence, our souls may be in great peril.

How then should we live? Timothy gives us Heaven's wisdom for those who *want* to get rich: "But those who desire to be rich fall into temptation, into a snare, into many senseless and harmful desires that plunge people into ruin and destruction. For the love of money is a root of all kinds of evils. It is through this craving that some have wandered away from the faith and pierced themselves with many pangs" (1 Timothy 6:9, 10).

Heaven's wisdom for the rich is this: "As for the rich in this present age, charge them not to be haughty, nor to set their hopes on the uncertainty of riches, but on God, who richly provides us with everything to enjoy" (1 Timothy 6:17). May God's Word find a place in our hearts!

> Christ stands at the bar of the world today,
> As He stood in the days of old.
> Let each man tax his soul and say,—
> "Shall I again my Lord betray
> For my greed, or my goods, or my gold?"
>
> John Oxenham[17]

Be patient, therefore, brothers, until the coming of the Lord. See how the farmer waits for the precious fruit of the earth, being patient about it, until it receives the early and the late rains. You also, be patient. Establish your hearts, for the coming of the Lord is at hand. Do not grumble against one another, brothers, so that you may not be judged; behold, the Judge is standing at the door.

5:7–9

23

Patient Till He Comes

JAMES 5:7–9

THE BRIEF PASSAGE under consideration in this chapter was written to people who ached for the second coming of Christ. The author—James, the Lord's brother—had been with the apostolic band on the Mount of Olives at Christ's ascension. He had seen the *Shekinah* glory, the luminous cloud of God's presence, overshadow the mount, and then watched his elder brother/ Savior disappear into its shimmering folds (Acts 1:9). The glow of the receding cloud was still on James' rapt face when the angels issued their challenge: "Men of Galilee, why do you stand looking into heaven? This Jesus, who was taken up from you into heaven, will come in the same way as you saw him go into heaven" (Acts 1:11). Jesus will come back in a similar cloud of glory!

In retrospect James and the others recalled some of Jesus' words given earlier on this same mountain in his Olivet Discourse: "For as the lightning comes from the east and shines as far as the west, so will be the coming of the Son of Man" (Matthew 24:27). What glory that will be! Of course, none of them knew when, for Jesus had told them even he did not know the day (Matthew 24:36). They also remembered that on Olivet he had said his return would come without warning, just as the flood surprised the inhabitants of the earth in Noah's time (Matthew 24:37–39).

They didn't know *when* he was coming, whether it would be in their lifetime or not, but they believed it would be *soon*. They lived in the exhilarating expectancy of Christ's return. The New Testament contains over three hundred references to Christ's return—one of every thirteen verses! The Scriptures ooze with the return of Christ.

But it wasn't just Christ's promise that made those believers ache for the second coming—it was *the difficulties of life*. James' scattered Jewish church was being kicked around the Mediterranean like a soccer ball. The verses that immediately precede our text are a seething denunciation of their rich oppressors who had reduced them to miserable poverty. Life was hard, and this hardness particularly made them long for the return of Christ.

In my ministry I have noticed that when people are hurting, they frequently express their hope for Christ's return—"Oh, I wish the Lord would return today!" But I have never heard anyone say, "Things are going so well . . . I wish Christ would return right now!" Hard times make us long for Christ's return. It is no surprise that almost all the hymns that center on the return of Christ were written when life was more difficult than it is today. It is also revealing that Black hymnody especially focused on Christ's return precisely because the slaves had nothing in *this* world. So their hymns rang with longings about "crossing over Jordan" to the "land that is fairer than day."

Ellen Thompson has written, "Life is too comfortable and things too important for us to want to leave this world, making it hard to sing with integrity, 'On Jordan's stormy banks I stand/And cast a wishful eye/To Canaan's fair and happy land/Where my possessions lie.'"[1] The modern western church simply has too much *here* to sing words like these today.

As we have seen, the early Christians had no such problem. Their implicit belief in Christ's promised return, coupled with the grinding realities of life, made them constantly breathe, "Even so, come Lord Jesus!"—an enviable cry we should cultivate, as we shall see.

Three great words in the New Testament refer to the Lord's second coming. *Epiphania* means an appearing or a showing or a manifestation of Christ. Another great word is *apokalupsis*, which means an unveiling, a laying bare, a revelation, and refers to the full display of Christ's power and glory.[2] The third word, the one for the Lord's "coming" in verses 7, 8 of our text, is *parousia*, which emphasizes Christ's physical presence, literally meaning "being alongside of." It is used in this way fifteen times in the New Testament in reference to Christ's return,[3] denoting "the physical arrival of a ruler." The significance of the word as James uses it here is that *his suffering people longed for the presence of Christ their King*. They knew that when Jesus came to be *with* them, everything would be all right.

Be Patient (v. 7)

James' Spirit-directed wisdom for his afflicted brothers and sisters was given in the form of a command: "Be patient, therefore, brothers, until the coming of the Lord" (v. 7a). This is not passive resignation, but rather patient, expectant waiting on the Lord.[4]

To make sure they understand exactly what he means, James provides a rich example: "See how the farmer waits for the precious fruit of the earth, being patient about it, until it receives the early and the late rains" (v. 7b). The "early" rains come in late October and early November in Palestine. Farmers still eagerly await these because they aid planting and make seed germination possible. Heavy rains come in December through February. And finally the spring rains come in April and May. These rains represent a *process* apart from which there can be no harvest. All farmers must patiently submit to this process. To fight against it, to bite their nails, to insist they must have fruit in the middle of the process, is futile.

In submitting to God's process, they will inevitably undergo stressful times when it appears the rains will never come. But these times can be spiritually beneficial to them as they call upon their faithful God. "The soul would have no rainbow if the eye had no tears."[5] So they wait in positive confidence that the process will take place and that there will be a harvest/second coming. During this time they grow spiritually, the fullness of time grows, and Jesus will come. The key is to submit expectantly to his hidden timetable, trusting wholeheartedly in his goodness.

Be Double-Patient (v. 8)

James apparently understands that patience won't come easily to his harried church, so he repeats his command: "You also, be patient. Establish your hearts, for the coming of the Lord is at hand" (v. 8). Modern naysayers have had their day spouting that the New Testament writers were in error when they said the Lord's coming was near. But their argument is nothing new. It was heard—and effectively answered—in James' day by Peter:

> Knowing this first of all, that scoffers will come in the last days with scoffing, following their own sinful desires. They will say, "Where is the promise of his coming? For ever since the fathers fell asleep, all things are continuing as they were from the beginning of creation." For they deliberately overlook this fact, that the heavens existed long ago, and the earth was formed out of water and through water by the word of God, and that by means of these the world that then existed was deluged with water and perished. But by the same word the heavens and earth that now exist are stored up for fire, being kept until the day of judgment and destruction of the ungodly. But do not overlook this one fact, beloved, that with the Lord one day is as a thousand years, and a thousand years as one day. The Lord is not slow to fulfill his promise as some count slowness. (2 Peter 3:3–9a)

The apostles knew that "with the Lord one day is as a thousand years," and none of them predicted Christ would return in their lifetime. Even the incarnate Son of God said he didn't know the time of his return (Matthew 24:36; Mark 13:32). But the apostles were sure Christ's return was near (James 5:8). What Christians, as well as scoffers, must realize is that "at hand" is a relative term. Nature provides an illustration. The life of a mayfly (*ephemeron*) is exactly one day. Suppose a mayfly hovering over a pool for the one spring day of its life was capable of observing the tadpole offspring of a frog in the water below. In the mayfly's aged afternoon, having seen no change in the tadpole, it would be impossible for the mayfly to conceive that the tadpole's becoming a frog was very *near*![6] So it is with us in our mayfly existence in Christ's calendar. Our ephemeral day does not negate the nearness of his coming.

Similarly, to a child in October Christmas may seem an eternity away, but to the aged, white-haired grandmother who has weathered the snows of many winters and numerous trips to the best department stores, Christmas is not just near—it is here! Thus when James says Christ's coming is "at hand," he is writing as one who has been taught to see the years of his life according to the unbeginning, unending "lifetime" of the Most High.[7]

We should note that the aged Apostle John, at the end of his life, writing the very final chapter in Revelation, closing the entire written canon of Holy Scripture, records the resurrected Christ three times saying that his coming is near. Verse 7: "And behold, I am coming soon. Blessed is the one who keeps the words of the prophecy of this book." Verse 12: "Behold, I am coming soon, bringing my recompense with me, to repay each one for what he has done." Verses 20, 21: "He who testifies to these things says, 'Surely I am coming soon.' Amen. Come, Lord Jesus! The grace of the Lord Jesus be with all. Amen."

Brothers and sisters, the coming of Christ is *near*. The ultimate epiphany is just around the corner. If we think otherwise, we tragically impoverish our souls. Most Christians think little of Christ's return, or if they do think about the day they will see Christ, they associate it with the day of their death. This is a proper hope, but death is not a pleasant thing, and thus the expectation of seeing Christ is mixed with a certain fear of the dark veil. But it is not so with his second coming. It is all joy! And that singular joy is meant to be a boon to our souls.

The Scriptures say his coming is near, and we are not only to believe this, but to embrace it! If logic be worth anything, we are much nearer his return than the apostles were. We are much nearer than the Apostle John who ended Scripture with Christ saying, "I am coming soon." He could come today! And if he does, all the mysterious Scriptural teachings about the end-times will be clearer to us than our children's picture books. *Jesus is coming soon!*

James didn't have to convince his people of this. His task was rather to get them to be patient and stand firm (v. 8). This is the same positive, confident patience, but this time laced with the resolve to "put iron into their hearts" (cf. the Williams translation). They were to be tough in their resolve to wait for the return of the Lord Jesus Christ.

Be Positive (v. 9)

Finally, James commands that positive waiting for Christ be matched by positive relationships with other waiting believers: "Do not grumble against one another, brothers, so that you may not be judged; behold, the Judge is standing at the door" (v. 9).

It is one thing to get along with other believers when things are going well. It is quite another when we are all under stress. For example, my pastoral staff and I get along great. We each have our own homes, our own offices, our defined duties, as well as mutual goals and commitments. But how would we get along if we were marooned on a desert island? It would probably take some doing not to provide fresh material for a new book—*The Lord of the Pastors*! We would need abundant prayer not to fall to the wiles of Beelzebub.

James was writing to people in such a miserable state that they were easily at each other's throats. Close pressures had made them jumpy and quick to take offense. This had to stop. So James focused the imminency of Christ's return on the problem, for Christ's imminent return meant that Christ, the great Judge of all, was right at the door. Calvin said, "No bridle is more suited to holding back our headstrong temper than the thought that our imprecation does not go off into the air, but close at hand there is the judgment of God."[8] This is a dramatic image. The Son of God, to whom is committed the judgment of the world, is at the doors of the judgment hall, ready to throw them wide open as he strides to the judgment seat.

If we have been grumbling victimizers of the Body of Christ, we may be saved as if by fire, but our works will be burned to nothing (cf. 1 Corinthians 3:10–15). James says the Judge is coming sooner than we think.

The layers of application in this passage are many, but the primary one for us who live in the affluent West today is this: we must believe and embrace the truth that "the coming of the Lord is at hand" (v. 8). Dr. John Piper described his further realization of this great truth in these words:

I was flying at night from Chicago to Minneapolis, almost alone on the plane. The pilot announced that there was a thunderstorm over Lake Michigan and into Wisconsin. He would skirt to the west to avoid turbulence. As I sat there staring out into the total blackness, suddenly the whole sky was brilliant with light and a cavern of white clouds fell away four miles beneath the plane and then vanished. A second later, a mammoth white tunnel of light exploded from north to south across the horizon, and again vanished into blackness. Soon the lightning was almost constant and volcanoes of light burst up out of cloud ravines and from behind distant white mountains. I sat there shaking my head almost in unbelief. "O Lord, if these are but the sparks from the sharpening of your swords, what will be the day of your appearing!" And I remembered the word of Christ,

> As the lightning comes from the east,
> and shines as far as the west,
> so will be the coming of the Son of Man.

Even now as I recollect that sight, the word glory is full of feeling for me.[9]

> Christ is coming! let creation
> From her groans and travail cease;
> Let the glorious proclamation
> Hope restore and faith increase.
> Christ is coming! Christ is coming!
> Come Thou blessed Prince of Peace.
> Long Thine exiles have been pining,
> Far from rest, and home, and Thee:
> But in heav'nly vestures shining,
> They their loving Lord shall see:
> Christ is coming! Christ is coming!
> Haste the joyous jubilee.
>
> Joachim Neander, 1680

Whatever one's theological tradition, we are to take great comfort in this great truth, as Paul so eloquently testifies:

> But we do not want you to be uninformed, brothers, about those who are asleep, that you may not grieve as others do who have no hope. For since we believe that Jesus died and rose again, even so, through Jesus, God will bring with him those who have fallen asleep. For this we declare to you by a word from the Lord, that we who are alive, who are left until the coming of the Lord, will not precede those who have fallen asleep. For the Lord himself will descend from heaven with a cry of command, with the voice of an archangel, and with the sound of the trumpet of God. And the dead in Christ will rise first. Then we who are alive, who are left, will be caught up together with them in the clouds to meet the Lord in the air, and so we

will always be with the Lord. Therefore encourage one another with these words. (1 Thessalonians 4:13–18)

The imminence of Christ's return makes its demands upon us. We must be prepared. Peter wrote, "The end of all things is at hand; therefore be self-controlled and sober-minded for the sake of your prayers" (1 Peter 4:7). We need to discipline our spiritual lives and be in regular prayer. Are you ready? Am I? If you are not a believer, the call to preparation is even more compelling, for:

> But concerning that day and hour no one knows, not even the angels of heaven, nor the Son, but the Father only. For as were the days of Noah, so will be the coming of the Son of Man. For as in those days before the flood they were eating and drinking, marrying and giving in marriage, until the day when Noah entered the ark, and they were unaware until the flood came and swept them all away, so will be the coming of the Son of Man. Then two men will be in the field; one will be taken and one left. Two women will be grinding at the mill; one will be taken and one left. Therefore, stay awake, for you do not know on what day your Lord is coming. But know this, that if the master of the house had known in what part of the night the thief was coming, he would have stayed awake and would not have let his house be broken into. Therefore you also must be ready, for the Son of Man is coming at an hour you do not expect. (Matthew 24:36–44)

Are we ready? We must purify ourselves. Again as Peter says:

> But the day of the Lord will come like a thief, and then the heavens will pass away with a roar, and the heavenly bodies will be burned up and dissolved, and the earth and the works that are done on it will be exposed. Since all these things are thus to be dissolved, what sort of people ought you to be in lives of holiness and godliness, waiting for and hastening the coming of the day of God, because of which the heavens will be set on fire and dissolved, and the heavenly bodies will melt as they burn! (2 Peter 3:10–12)

We must live in daily expectancy.

> For the grace of God has appeared, bringing salvation for all people, training us to renounce ungodliness and worldly passions, and to live self-controlled, upright, and godly lives in the present age, waiting for our blessed hope, the appearing of the glory of our great God and Savior Jesus Christ. (Titus 2:11–13)

"Our Lord, come! [*Maranatha!*]" (1 Corinthians 16:22)

As an example of suffering and patience, brothers, take the prophets who spoke in the name of the Lord. Behold, we consider those blessed who remained steadfast. You have heard of the steadfastness of Job, and you have seen the purpose of the Lord, how the Lord is compassionate and merciful.

5:10, 11

24

The Perseverance of Job

JAMES 5:10, 11

AGNOSTIC STEPHEN CRANE, famous as the author of *The Red Badge of Courage*, nowhere expressed his bitter agnosticism more eloquently than in his poem "God Is Cold," in which he uses the image of a drowning sailor to portray God's indifference (if there be a God) toward humanity.

A man adrift on a slim spar
A horizon smaller than the rim of a bottle
Tented waves rearing lashy dark points
The near whine of froth in circles.
God is cold.
The incessant raise and swing of the sea
And growl after growl of crest
The sinkings, green, seething, endless
The upheaval half-completed.
God is cold.
A horizon smaller than a doomed assassin's cap,
Inky, surging tumults
A reeling, drunken sky and no sky
A pale hand sliding from a polished spar.
God is cold.
The puff of a coat imprisoning air;
A face kissing the water-death
A weary slow sway of a lost hand
And the sea, the moving sea, the sea.
God is cold.[1]

Crane's angry lyrics reflect the despairing heart-song of today's secular consensus: if God is there, he cares little about humankind's needs—God has an arctic heart.

"Disgraceful blasphemy!" we protest. But if the truth be known, most Christians have had similar thoughts of God, and some of us have even voiced them at times. The predictable atheism of our sinful natures naturally quarrels with God when we go through hard times. Many of us, when young and undergoing the common experience of having our romantic love rebuffed, have defamed God. The loss of a job, professional disappointment, the loss of property have brought many otherwise faithful Christians to the point of blasphemy. Not a few ministers have succumbed to similar conduct when their "ministries" have failed. The loss of dear friends or loved ones sometimes produces an ugly indictment of God by his children.

If we submit to Biblical authority, we know that such thoughts and words about God are wrong. Anytime we have not thought and spoken well of his name, we have thought and spoken amiss. And if we have not repented, we will repent one day with all our hearts if we yield to God.

Nevertheless, the proclivity persists in bad times to think bad things of God. James certainly saw this evidenced during the hard times his churches were undergoing, and the present text is an attempt to help them avoid such disgraceful conduct. James gave them real-life examples of those who shone in the midst of adversity because he knew that suffering people have little patience with theory or fiction. Real stories bring real comfort.

The Perseverance of the Prophets (vv. 10, 11a)

James begins this brief section by recalling the prophets: "As an example of suffering and patience, brothers, take the prophets who spoke in the name of the Lord. Behold, we consider those blessed who remained steadfast."

Perhaps at the top of his list was Jeremiah, who because of his unrelenting faithfulness in preaching God's Word was cast into an empty water cistern where he was left to sink in the cold mud. Had he not been rescued by Ebed-Melech the Cushite and thirty men who gently extricated the prophet, he would have died suspended in the muck (Jeremiah 38:4–13).

Courageous Micaiah withstood the lying prophets before King Ahab, delivering the true prophecy of the downfall of the kingdom. For this he was slapped around, thrown into prison, and fed only bread and water (1 Kings 22:24–27).

And so it was for Moses, with his grumbling detractors; and David, fleeing Saul; Elijah on Mount Carmel; and Daniel in the lions' den.

By New Testament times the persecution of the prophets was proverbial, being referenced in at least eleven passages (Matthew 5:12; 21:35, 36; 22:6; 23:29–37; Luke 13:33; Acts 7:51, 52; Romans 11:3; 1 Thessalonians 2:15;

Hebrews 11:32–38; Revelation 16:6; 18:24). In Stephen's sermon, which led to his own martyrdom, he shouted, "Which of the prophets did your fathers not persecute?" (Acts 7:52). Hebrews 11:35b–38 says of the faithful prophets:

> Some were tortured, refusing to accept release, so that they might rise again to a better life. Others suffered mocking and flogging, and even chains and imprisonment. They were stoned, they were sawn in two, they were killed with the sword. They went about in skins of sheep and goats, destitute, afflicted, mistreated—of whom the world was not worthy—wandering about in deserts and mountains, and in dens and caves of the earth.

James' point is that the prophets suffered not because they did anything wrong, but because they were doing *right*, for they "spoke in the name of the Lord" (v. 10). And as these righteous suffered, they did it with class, with brave endurance.[2]

We are not without examples of this suffering in our own day. One immediately thinks of Corrie ten Boom in Ravensbrueck or Dietrich Bonhoeffer in Flossenberg. But there are less famous who have died far away and relatively unknown, like Regions Beyond Missionary Union's Stan Dale and Phil Masters, who were martyred in Irian Jaya by mountain tribesmen. As Yemu, their helper, and Nalimo, one of their killers, tell it, when Stan saw what was going to happen he commanded Yemu to leave and raised his staff, grimly facing his murderers.

> "All of you, turn around and go home!" he commanded.
> A priest of *Kembu* named Bereway slipped around behind Stan and—at point blank range—shot an arrow in under his upraised right arm. Another priest, Bunu, shot a bamboo-bladed shaft into Stan's back, just below his right shoulder.
> Yemu was crying now and shouting at them to stop. As the arrows entered his flesh, Stan pulled them out, one by one, broke them and cast them away. Dozens of them were coming at him from all directions. He kept pulling them out, breaking them and dropping them at his feet until he could not keep ahead of them. Nalimo reached the scene after some thirty arrows had found their mark in Stan's body.
> *How can he stand there so long?* Nalimo gasped. *Why doesn't he fall? Any one of us would have fallen long ago!* A different kind of shaft pierced Nalimo's own flesh—fear! *Perhaps he is immortal!* Nalimo's normally impassive face melted with sudden emotion. Because of that emotion, Nalimo said later, he did not shoot an arrow into Stan's body.
> Stan faced his enemies, steady and unwavering except for the jolt of each new strike. Yemu ran to where Phil stood alone. Together they watched in anguish at Stan's agony. As some fifty or more warriors detached from

the main force and came toward them, Phil pushed Yemu behind him and gestured speechlessly—*run!* Phil seemed hardly to notice the warriors encircling him. His eyes were fixed upon Stan.

Fifty arrows—sixty! Red ribbons of blood trailed from the many wounds, but still Stan stood his ground. Nalimo saw that he was not alone in his fear. The attack had begun with hilarity, but now the warriors shot their arrows with desperation bordering on panic because Stan refused to fall. *Perhaps Kusaho was right!* Perhaps they were committing a monstrous crime against the supernatural world instead of defending it, as they intended.

"Fall!" they screamed at Stan. "Die!" It was almost a plea—*please die!*

Yemu did not hear Phil say anything to the warriors as they aimed their arrows at him. Phil made no attempt to flee or struggle. He had faced danger many times but never certain death. But Stan had shown him how to face it, if he needed an example. That example could hardly have been followed with greater courage.

Once again, it was Bereway who shot the first arrow. And it took almost as many arrows to down Phil as it had Stan.[3]

The story is a gory microcosm of the long history of the endurance of the saints through the centuries as they have suffered for the name of our Lord. All the character necessary for fifty years of endurance was pressed into those bloody minutes. For me it is a sanctifying vision of how we ought to receive the sufferings that come our way whether they be greater or lesser, longer or shorter.

From the divine and Scriptural perspective, such conduct deserves a beatitude. "Behold," says James, "we consider those blessed who remained steadfast" (v. 11a). Those who have persevered to death, or more commonly through the multiple trials that come to committed believers over the long span of life, are called "blessed." Notice that it says "blessed," not "happy" (as the RSV has it), for what is meant here is not the *subjective*, emotional state of happiness, but the *objective*, unalterable approval and reward of God.[4] The smile of God rests upon such a life.

How is this so? In answer, we must begin with the universal truth that life without struggle and difficulty is bland and tasteless. Malcolm Muggeridge wrote in his book *Jesus Rediscovered*:

Suppose you eliminated suffering, what a dreadful place the world would be. I would almost rather eliminate happiness. The world would be the most ghastly place because everything that corrects the tendency of this unspeakable little creature, man, to feel over-important and over-pleased with himself would disappear. He's bad enough now, but he would be absolutely intolerable if he never suffered.[5]

In other words, our moral development—our character—is largely dependent upon the experience of suffering. Without trials we would be morally dwarfed. In fact, the study of the lives of great people reveals there is a consistent link between the crucible and true greatness. No wise person would seek to be exempt from the healthy discipline of trouble.

For one thing, *trouble promotes trust.* We children of God seldom trust God as we do when we are in big trouble. Troubles knock secondary things away. They sharpen our focus and increase our grip on God. When all our attempts at self-deliverance fail, we are forced to trust in the only One who can truly help us.

Troubles bring us near to God. When our regular comforts do not suffice, we draw near to him. It is hard to learn to swim on dry land, but when we are in the water we *have* to swim. Our troubles are waters in which we are obliged to swim toward God.

Troubles strengthen our communion with God. Without troubles we would not learn prayer. James says in effect, "we consider those blessed who [have] remained steadfast" because they learn *trust*, because they *draw near* to God, and because their *communion* with God becomes what it ought to be. These are great blessings. Jesus said, "Blessed are those who are persecuted for righteousness' sake, for theirs is the kingdom of heaven. . . . Rejoice and be glad, for your reward is great in heaven" (Matthew 5:10, 12a). Those who endure suffering are going to receive a vast reward. Paul put it this way: "I consider that the sufferings of this present time are not worth comparing with the glory that is to be revealed to us" (Romans 8:18). Those who persevere are *blessed*.

The Perseverance of Job (v. 11b)

The examples of the prophets ought to be enough, but James adds the greater example of Job, the greatest man of the East: "You have heard of the steadfastness of Job, and you have seen the purpose of the Lord, how the Lord is compassionate and merciful" (v. 11b).

The opening scene in Job presents a man who prospered in every way. He had a healthy *soul*. The divine assessment was that he was "blameless and upright, one who feared God and turned away from evil" (Job 1:1). He was so spiritually sensitive that when his ten children feasted, he would send for them and have them purified, and then he would sacrifice a burnt offering for each of them (Job 1:4, 5). Job had his spiritual priorities in order. He also had a beautiful *family*: seven boys and three girls. And Job was *wealthy*:

seven thousand sheep, five hundred yoke of oxen, five hundred donkeys, and multiple servants. And he was *healthy.*

The next scene transpires in Heaven. All the angels came to present themselves before God, and among them was the fallen angel, Satan. "The LORD said to Satan, 'From where have you come?' Satan answered the LORD and said, 'From going to and fro on the earth, and from walking up and down on it.' And the LORD said to Satan, 'Have you considered my servant Job, that there is none like him on the earth, a blameless and upright man, who fears God and turns away from evil?'" (Job 1:7, 8). Satan knew, of course, who the great man was and responded with a sneer.

> Does Job fear God for no reason? Have you not put a hedge around him and his house and all that he has, on every side? You have blessed the work of his hands, and his possessions have increased in the land. But stretch out your hand and touch all that he has, and he will curse you to your face. (Job 1:9–11)

Here Satan puts forth his great argument that no one serves God for who he is, but for what he or she can get. So God allowed Satan to take everything, save Job himself (Job 1:12).

With that, four flattening blows fell on unsuspecting Job. A messenger arrived and breathlessly told him that the Sabeans had taken all his oxen and donkeys and killed his servants (Job 1:15). Before he finished, a second messenger informed him that fire from Heaven had consumed all Job's sheep and attendant servants (Job 1:16). Then came another messenger with news that the Chaldeans had taken all his camels and executed his servants (Job 1:17). And while he was still reeling from these blows, a fourth messenger came with a report of transcending tragedy—all Job's children were dead, having perished when the house fell on them (Job 1:18, 19). Oh, the pain! Darkness and nausea rolled across the righteous man's writhing soul.

But amazingly Job did not do what Satan said he would do. He didn't curse and renounce God but rather, as the Scriptures record, "arose and tore his robe and shaved his head and fell on the ground and worshiped. And he said, 'Naked I came from my mother's womb, and naked shall I return. The LORD gave, and the LORD has taken away; blessed be the name of the LORD'" (Job 1:20, 21). He proved he did not serve God for what God gave him.

At the second council of Heaven, when God pointed to Job's integrity, Satan snarled, "'Skin for skin! All that a man has he will give for his life. But stretch out your hand and touch his bone and his flesh, and he will curse you to your face.' And the LORD said to Satan, 'Behold, he is in your hand; only spare his life'" (Job 2:4–6).

So Satan came to Job and afflicted him with running sores from the pink soles of his feet to the crown of his head. Job went to the town garbage heap, found a broken piece of pottery, and began to scrape his festering sores. Then his grief-stricken wife came and said to him, "'Do you still hold fast your integrity? Curse God and die.' But he said to her, 'You speak as one of the foolish women would speak. Shall we receive good from God, and shall we not receive evil?' In all this Job did not sin with his lips" (Job 2:9, 10). Ancient Job was certainly a great man!

Next came Job's three friends, who began so well by keeping their mouths shut in an eloquent silence of compassion. But then they spoke, three times each in rotating order: Eliphaz, Bildad, and Zophar. At first they were gentle with him, but when it became apparent that he did not agree that his calamity came because he was a great sinner, they became brutal. Finally a long-silent observer, Elihu, seethingly rebuked Job for his self-righteousness and urged him to repent. The stage was set for God to answer Job from the whirlwind.

Critics have long noted that in the impassioned exchange between Job and his friends, Job says things that do not fit the phrase "the steadfastness [patience] of Job." In response, the word is better translated "perseverance," which has the idea of endurance or dogged perseverance.[6] But even with this understanding, some still maintain that Job's conduct falls short. In further answer, it must be admitted that it is true Job resorts to passionate outbursts, as for example when he cursed the day of his birth (cf. Job 3:1, 11–19) or when he lambasted his friends—"'miserable comforters are you all. Shall windy words have an end? Or what provokes you that you answer?'" (Job 16:2, 3). It is also true that he protested to God, "'I cry to you for help and you do not answer me; I stand, and you only look at me. You have turned cruel to me; with the might of your hand you persecute me. You lift me up on the wind; you make me ride on it, and you toss me about in the roar of the storm. For I know that you will bring me to death and to the house appointed for all living'" (Job 30:20–23). And, "Therefore I will not restrain my mouth; I will speak in the anguish of my spirit; I will complain in the bitterness of my soul. Am I the sea, or a sea monster, that you set a guard over me?" (Job 7:11, 12; cf. 10:18; 23:2).

But though Job cried and complained, he refused to renounce God. Rather he said, "'I know that my Redeemer lives, and at the last he will stand upon the earth. And after my skin has been thus destroyed, yet in my flesh

I shall see God, whom I shall see for myself, and my eyes shall behold, and not another. My heart faints within me!'" (Job 19:25–27). Job refused to surrender his integrity as his wife had urged him to do. He was still blameless and upright. He never ceased believing in God. William Barclay says:

> But the great fact about Job is that in spite of all his torrent of questionings, and in spite of the agonizing questionings which tore at his heart, he never lost his faith in God. "Though he slay me, yet will I hope in him" (Job 13:15). "My witness is in heaven; and my advocate is on high" (Job 16:19). "I know that my Redeemer lives" (Job 19:25). The very greatness of Job lies in the fact that in spite of everything which tore at his heart, he never lost his grip on faith and his grip on God. Job's faith is no groveling, passive, unquestioning submission; Job struggled and questioned and sometimes even defied, but the flame of faith was never extinguished in his heart.[7]

It is true that God straightened him out by reeling off a chain of natural phenomena that Job could not explain (Job 38—41). Then God said in effect, "If you can't understand the physical world that you see, how can you understand the moral world you cannot see?" But in all this Job persevered in his suffering and faith.

What an encouragement to know that God does not expect stoic perseverance in the midst of trials. He knows we are clay. He understands tears. He accepts our questions. But he does demand that we recognize our finiteness and acknowledge there are processes at work beyond our comprehension. A plan far bigger than us is moving toward completion. And God demands that we, like Job, hold on to our faith and hope in God.

Job's perseverance is a real-life example meant to help us persevere in real life. So is the real ending (literally "the end of the Lord," which our text translates as "the purpose of the Lord," v. 11). Job had come to the end of his words in great bitterness. But the end for Job was very different than some might expect, for God loaded Job down with blessings supernal.

His primary blessings were *spiritual*, for Job attained a profound humility.

> Then Job answered the LORD and said:
>
>> "I know that you can do all things,
>>   and that no purpose of yours can be thwarted.
>> 'Who is this that hides counsel without knowledge?'
>> Therefore I have uttered what I did not understand,
>>   things too wonderful for me, which I did not know.

'Hear, and I will speak;
   I will question you, and you make it known to me.'
I had heard of you by the hearing of the ear,
   but now my eye sees you;
therefore I despise myself,
   and repent in dust and ashes." (Job 42:1–6)

Job prostrated himself before God in deep humility because he saw God's greatness and his own finiteness. Job saw his presumptuous speech for what it was and repented. "Blessed are the poor in spirit, for theirs is the kingdom of heaven" (Matthew 5:3).

Along with his humility, Job received spiritual insight. His immortal words in Job 42:5 describe this: "I had heard of you by the hearing of the ear, but now my eye sees you." Annie Dillard has written, "You do not have to sit outside in the dark. If, however, you want to look at the stars, you will find that darkness is required." Many Christian graces are imperceptible until the time of trial, and then they shine forth with great brilliance.

Job was still on a garbage heap. He was still covered with running lesions. Flies still fed on him. His wife still loathed him (cf. 19:17). All his possessions were gone, and his children were dead. But he had been infinitely *blessed*, for Job saw God as he had never seen him before.

Job's secondary blessings were material. In fact, God blessed him with outward prosperity even more than previously, so that all the East could *see* God's pleasure in Job. Some make too much of this. Sure, Job had more than before, and he again had three daughters and seven sons, and he loved these children with all his heart. But he never forgot the loss of the first children. Only in Heaven will everything be perfect.

Our end will even exceed Job's earthly end. We will grow in spiritual insight in both the sunshine and darkness of life until we see his face and receive "an inheritance that is imperishable, undefiled, and unfading, kept in heaven for you" (1 Peter 1:4).

James' concluding phrase ties the bow perfectly: "the Lord is compassionate and merciful." We must not allow ourselves to be persuaded by men or devils to think ill of God—that God is cold. He has a father's heart, even when he allows darkness to come. God cannot be unkind to his children. Says our Father, "Can a woman forget her nursing child, that she should have no compassion on the son of her womb? Even these may forget, yet I will not forget you. Behold, I have engraved you on the palms of my hands" (Isaiah 49:15, 16a).

James coined a new word to say the Lord is "compassionate."[8] Other ways of saying this are, "very, very compassionate," or "full of tender compassion." To this compassion James couples "merciful." God is full of compassion as he cares for us in our misery, and he is full of mercy as he forgives our sins. All of which says to those who are undergoing hardships: God is good.

Are times hard? Are you feeling alienated from God? If so, consider James's examples—the perseverance of the prophets and the perseverance of Job. If we persevere we will be "blessed," for we will draw near to him and we will see him as never before, and our end is sure to be good.

The Lord is good!

But above all, my brothers, do not swear, either by heaven or by earth or by any other oath, but let your "yes" be yes and your "no" be no, so that you may not fall under condemnation.

5:12

25

Straight Talk

JAMES 5:12

SEVERAL YEARS AGO the UPI wire services carried this prayer by Reverend Fred Holloman, chaplain of the Kansas Senate:

> Omniscient Father:
> Help us to know who is telling
> the truth. One side tells us one
> thing, and the other just the opposite.
> And if neither side is telling the
> truth, we would like to know that,
> too.
> And if each side is telling half
> the truth, give us the wisdom to put
> the right halves together.
> In Jesus' name, Amen.

The report didn't indicate the tone with which the chaplain delivered the prayer—whether with a twinkling Mark Twain irony or righteous despair. However it was prayed, it represents a biting cynicism regarding those in public life. And in the wake of our Watergates, Irangates, and Pearlygates—ABSCAMs and savings and loans scams—Senators perjuring themselves, plagiarizing speeches, and lying to their families and constituents about their personal lives—the cynicism is understandable. Recently a *New Yorker* cartoon put it very well as it pictured two clean-shaven middle-aged men sitting together in a jail cell. One is saying to the other: "All along, I thought our level of corruption fell well within community standards."

This cynicism regarding honesty—and truth itself—extends to the literature of our day. Mortimer Adler, philosopher and former editor of *The*

Encyclopedia Britannica and the *Great Books of the Western World Series*, says in his classic *How to Read a Book*:

> The question, Is it true? can be asked of anything we read. It is applicable to every kind of writing. . . . No higher commendation can be given any work of the human mind than to praise it for the measure of truth it has achieved; by the same token, to criticize it adversely for its failure in this respect is to treat it with the seriousness that a serious work deserves. Yet, strangely enough in recent years, for the first time in Western history, there is a dwindling concern with this criterion of excellence. Books win the plaudits of the critics and gain widespread popular attention almost to the extent that they flout the truth—the more outrageously they do so, the better.[1]

There was a time when western culture was distinguished from other cultures by at least a conventional consensus that one ought to be telling the truth. But now there is a pervasive indifference to truth-telling which has not only infected day-to-day conversation but the most solemn pledges of life. Perjury under solemn oath is epidemic, the sacred vows of marriage are broken almost as frequently as they are pledged, and God's name is daily invoked by blatant liars as witness to their truthfulness.

Many reasons can be cited for this. A popular culprit is the relativistic subjectivism of our day. With so many liars defending and excusing themselves with clichés like "What's true for you is not necessarily the same for me," or the specious appeal to the supreme court of self, "My opinion is as good as yours!" truth suffers. One of the rich and famous, Ernest Hemingway was an inveterate liar who lied about everything including his childhood, his athletic prowess, his military exploits, his liaisons, so that he was, as one of his wives called him, "the biggest liar since Munchausen."[2] With this being too typical today, how can we expect our society as a whole to be any different? If our gods be mendacious frauds, how can we be otherwise? But the main reason there is a crisis in truth is that we are, in fact, congenital liars. Right in the middle of the string of depravity in Romans 3 we read, "they use their tongues to deceive" (Romans 3:13). Our untruthfulness reveals our condition. No one had to teach us how to lie.

For all these reasons there is a crisis in truth. And we Christians must not make the mistake of thinking the problem is only "out there." George MacDonald, the great writer and preacher, candidly wrote to his father on December 6, 1878, "I always try—I *think* I do—to be truthful. All the same I tell a great many lies."[3] His candidness says what we all must say in moments of honesty. Our situation is exacerbated by the calculated seas of deception that flood back and forth over our culture through its media, so that we sometimes scarcely know what truth is. Many Christians today traffic in untruth. And some, tragically, do not even know it.

James' teaching is a radical call to radical truthfulness: "But above all, my brothers, do not swear, either by heaven or by earth or by any other oath, but let your 'yes' be yes and your 'no' be no, so that you may not fall under condemnation" (v. 12). If heeded, this call will set us apart from the rest of the world, and even get us in trouble at times. But radical truthfulness will also bring power to our lives and grace to a confused world.

James took this teaching directly from the lips of his elder brother Jesus, who had said virtually the same thing in the Sermon on the Mount when he gave his fourth example of radical kingdom righteousness:

> Again you have heard that it was said to those of old, "You shall not swear falsely, but shall perform to the Lord what you have sworn." But I say to you, Do not take an oath at all, either by heaven, for it is the throne of God, or by the earth, for it is his footstool, or by Jerusalem, for it is the city of the great King. And do not take an oath by your head, for you cannot make one hair white or black. Let what you say be simply "Yes" or "No"; anything more than this comes from evil. (Matthew 5:33–37)

The Old Testament on Truthfulness

From Christ's summary statement and the rest of the Old Testament, we understand two things about the swearing of vows and oaths in Old Testament times.

First, *they were encouraged.* Deuteronomy 10:20 reads, "You shall fear the Lord your God. You shall serve him and hold fast to him, and by his name you shall swear." Not only were godly people encouraged to make vows, they were admonished to do so—in God's name! God even taught through the prophet Jeremiah that swearing in God's name was a sign of spiritual vitality: "And it shall come to pass, if they will diligently learn the ways of my people, to swear by my name, 'As the Lord lives,' even as they taught my people to swear by Baal, then they shall be built up in the midst of my people" (Jeremiah 12:16).

Secondly, *making a vow and not keeping it was discouraged.* Moses' writings repeatedly emphasized this: "You shall not swear by my name falsely, and so profane the name of your God: I am the Lord" (Leviticus 19:12). "If a man vows a vow to the Lord, or swears an oath to bind himself by a pledge, he shall not break his word. He shall do according to all that proceeds out of his mouth" (Numbers 30:2). "If you make a vow to the Lord your God, you shall not delay fulfilling it, for the LORD your God will surely require it of you, and you will be guilty of sin" (Deuteronomy 23:21).

In the Old Testament vows were assumed to be part of a committed life. But once made, they were not to be broken under any circumstances.

The problem was, by New Testament times traditional, Biblical teaching had come under amazing abuse. For example, some rabbis had begun to teach that an oath was not binding if it omitted God's name or did not imply it. Therefore, if you swore by your own life or someone else's life or the life of the king (as Abner did in 1 Samuel 17:55) or by your health (Psalm 15:4) or by some object, but avoided mentioning or alluding to the name of God, you were not bound. The *Mishnah* devotes one whole section called *Shebuoth* ("oaths") to an elaborate discussion of when oaths are binding and when they are not.[4] In effect, the swearing of oaths had degenerated to a system that indicated when a man could lie and when not.

The results were disgraceful. There was an undying epidemic of frivolous swearing. Oaths were continually mingled with everyday speech: "By your life"—"By my beard"—"May I never see the comfort of Israel if . . ." There was a trivialization of everyday language and a devaluation of integrity. Evasive swearing became a fine art. The height of accomplishment was, while lying, to convince another you were telling the truth by bringing some person or eminent object into reference. For instance, one rabbi taught that if one swore *by* Jerusalem one was not bound, but if one swore *toward* Jerusalem it was binding—evidently because that in some way implied the Divine Name.[5] All of this produced a moral schizophrenia: "I'm really not lying, but I'm also not telling the truth." The use of oaths was like children's "I had my fingers crossed!"

James and Jesus on Truthfulness

The situation was utterly fantastic, so James gave them a piece of Jesus' mind: "But above all, my brothers, do not swear, either by heaven or by earth or by any other oath" (v. 12a). The full portion of Jesus' mind was given by his own words in Matthew 5:34–36: "But I say to you, Do not take an oath at all, either by heaven, for it is the throne of God, or by the earth, for it is his footstool, or by Jerusalem, for it is the city of the great King. And do not take an oath by your head, for you cannot make one hair white or black." Jesus and James rule out making vows using any references to people or objects as backup.

The reason for this is, *God stands behind everything.* The entire creation is God's, and you and I cannot call up a part of it without ultimately referring to him. Matthew 23:16–22 records Jesus' frightening woe to anyone who imagines otherwise:

Woe to you, blind guides, who say, "If anyone swears by the temple, it is nothing, but if anyone swears by the gold of the temple, he is bound by his oath." You blind fools! For which is greater, the gold or the temple that has made the gold sacred? And you say, "If anyone swears by the altar, it is nothing, but if anyone swears by the gift that is on the altar, he is bound by his oath." You blind men! For which is greater, the gift or the altar that makes the gift sacred? So whoever swears by the altar swears by it and by everything on it. And whoever swears by the temple swears by it and by him who dwells in it. And whoever swears by heaven swears by the throne of God and by him who sits upon it.

All oath-taking that calls into witness people or items of God's created order actually calls God's name as witness, and it is a grievous sin to do so. If there is anything in our speech that even approaches swearing by something else, we must drop it at once.

James' brief encapsulation of Jesus' words—especially his opening words, "Above all, my brothers, do not swear" and his closing words, "Let your 'yes' be yes and your 'no' be no" (cf. Matthew 5:34a, 37)—categorically tells us that the righteous man or woman must not make a practice of swearing that he or she is telling the truth. Jesus and James ask for a radical truthfulness that supersedes the requirements of the Law—a radical truthfulness that does not need oaths.

Oath-taking is popular because people are liars. It's that simple. Dr. Helmut Thielicke, the scholar and pastor who resisted compromising his integrity during the Hitler era, put it like this:

Whenever I utter the formula "I swear by God," I am really saying, "Now I'm going to mark off an area of absolute truth and put walls around it to cut it off from the muddy floods of untruthfulness and irresponsibility that ordinarily overruns my speech." In fact, I am saying even more than this. I am saying that people are expecting me to lie from the start. And just because they are counting on my lying I have to bring up these big guns of oaths and words of honor.[6]

Jesus and James are telling us we must never use "big guns" like "on my mother's grave" or "as God is my witness." Everyday speech and pulpit speech and courtroom speech are all to be the same—radically true!

Radical Truthfulness

What are the implications of this radical teaching for our lives? Are we never to take personal oaths? What about the public oaths we are asked to take in court? Some—for example, the Reformation's Anabaptists and later the

Moravians and Quakers—have taken this as a prohibition against taking oaths in any circumstance. George Fox, the uncompromising founder of the Quakers, gave this famous rejoinder to the judges at Lancaster who sentenced him to prison for refusing to swear over a Bible that he was telling the truth:

> You have given me a book here to kiss and to swear on, and this book which you have given me to kiss says, "Kiss the Son," and the Son says in this book "Swear not at all." Now I say as the book says, and yet you imprison me; how chance you do not imprison the book for saying so?[7]

Today because of George Fox's courage you do not have to lay your hand on a Bible in a court of law and swear you are telling the truth "so help me God." You may simply affirm that you are telling the truth.

I admire George Fox and his followers, but I do not think they are correct. The contexts of Jesus' original teachings argue against this understanding because Jesus' examples of oath-taking abuses come from everyday common speech. Even more decisive is the fact that Jesus honored the official oath put upon him by Caiaphas before the Sanhedrin by answering, as recorded in Matthew 26:63, 64a: "But Jesus remained silent. And the high priest said to him, 'I adjure you by the living God, tell us if you are the Christ, the Son of God.' Jesus said to him, 'You have said so.'" In addition to Jesus' clear example we have the repeated examples of Paul swearing that he was telling the truth: "But I call God to witness against me—it was to spare you that I refrained from coming again to Corinth" (2 Corinthians 1:23). "For God is my witness, whom I serve with my spirit in the gospel of his Son, that without ceasing I mention you always in my prayers . . ." (Romans 1:9, 10a). Paul would never have called God a witness that he was telling the truth if he thought it was wrong.

How does this translate into life? Oath-taking is permitted, but it is not encouraged. In civil life, as in a courtroom, oath-taking is permitted. And when one is put under oath, he or she is not sinning against Christ's teaching. Also, on rare occasions such a practice may be necessary, as it was for Paul. This said, oaths are not to be a part of everyday conversation. Christians simply should not need such devices. They should be known to be people of truth.

Radical Call

We are called to profound truthfulness in a radically deceptive world—a world that is deceptive in its *radix*, its root. Congenital lying, philosophical relativism, and cultural traditions have spawned a society of Baron Munchausens. We are routinely lied to by the media. Even more telling, rational argument is regularly abandoned to convince us of a product's good. Drink a certain beer and you will become a broad-shouldered hombre who radiates such powerful élan that your "tune" jams the radios in the convertibles of beautiful women as they pass by. We daily drown in a sea of hyperbole, so that words hardly have meaning.

And the truth is, we are all affected! We all find it difficult to be truthful. Listen to George MacDonald's admission in full:

> I always try—I *think* I do—to be truthful. All the same I tell a great many petty lies, *e.g.* things that mean one thing to myself though another to other people. But I do not think lightly of it. Where I am more often wrong is in tacitly pretending I hear things which I do not, especially jokes and good stories, the *point* of which I always miss; but, seeing every one laugh, I laugh too, for the sake of not *looking* a fool. My respect for the world's opinion is my greatest stumbling-block, I fear. . . .[8]

We often embellish the truth, sometimes without even realizing it: profits become greater, one's strengths grow, our humility increases, all in the telling. We sometimes frighten ourselves at how easily we fall to this. But the greatest tragedy is when we shrug our shoulders and go on, for after all, to bend an aphorism, "to lie is human."

It is not easy to be a totally truthful person today, but it is necessary for the church and the world. The story of Ananias and Sapphira shocks us because they suffered death for such a "small" infraction: in giving to the church they misrepresented what percentage they gave of their just profits. "Why death? After all, *they did give*—which is more than many people do!" The answer is, the church cannot prosper with deception among its members. Deception wounds the Body of Christ and is a sin against God. This is why Peter cried to Ananias and Sapphira at the moment of their deaths, "You have not lied to man but to God" (Acts 5:4b). Thus, radical truthfulness is one of the greatest needs of the church today. The church needs people who not only refrain from blatant lying, but represent themselves and others as they really are. Paul says truthfulness is necessary for growth in the church: "Rather, speaking the truth in love, we are to grow up in every way into him who is the head, into Christ" (Ephesians 4:15). We are to be literally *truthing in love*—speaking and doing truth to each other. How the church needs this!

This great need in the church is directly linked to the needs of our lost world, for the world longs for liberation from dishonesty. Sure, it cultivates deception and promotes it, but deep down inside its people long to escape the pretense. People will eagerly embrace believers who model the honesty and integrity for which they long. Thielicke said in his native Germany, "The avoidance of one small fib . . . may be a stronger confession of faith than a whole 'Christian philosophy' championed in lengthy, forceful discussion."[9] A truthful spirit is a great evangelistic tool. I have known people who were drawn to Christ because they saw this quality in a church or individual. Truthfulness will be, for some, as tantalizing as a cool drink in the desert.

What can we do to promote radical truthfulness—a no that is truly a no and a yes that is truly a yes—in our lives?

1) As we have already mentioned, we must be sensitized to the horror of deception in the Body of Christ. Its being a heinous sin is substantiated by the deaths of Ananias and Sapphira. The heart, as well as the mind, must not only accept this truth but welcome it.

2) We must remember that for Jesus words are sacramental—an outward sign of an inward condition. Jesus said, "For out of the abundance of the heart the mouth speaks" (Matthew 12:34; cf. Mark 7:14–23). A continually truthful spirit will produce an increasing veracity of speech.

3) We must understand that we will be judged by the words we say—every word: "I tell you, on the day of judgment people will give account for every careless word they speak, for by your words you will be justified, and by your words you will be condemned" (Matthew 12:36, 37). Our human words are freighted with eternity.

4) By the fullness of the Spirit, we must appropriate the life of Christ in us so that his words become our words, and so we will speak the truth, for Jesus never lied, and "there was no deceit in his mouth" (Isaiah 53:9).

5) We must feed on the Word of God. Jesus' prayer for us is, "Sanctify them in the truth; your word is truth" (John 17:17). When we discipline ourselves to feed on the Word, we will fill ourselves with truth, progressively producing what God desires—"truth in the inward being" (Psalm 51:6a).

6) It is from carelessness as much as intentional lying that so much falsehood abounds. So we must be careful about what we say. If it is not true, we ought to correct ourselves. If we have been giving the wrong impression, straighten it out.

As usual, James has minced no words: "But above all, my brothers, do not swear, either by heaven or by earth or by any other oath, but let your 'yes' be yes and your 'no' be no, so that you may not fall under condemnation."

Lord, help us to be radically truthful!

Is anyone among you suffering? Let him pray. Is anyone cheerful? Let him sing praise. Is anyone among you sick? Let him call for the elders of the church, and let them pray over him, anointing him with oil in the name of the Lord. And the prayer of faith will save the one who is sick, and the Lord will raise him up. And if he has committed sins, he will be forgiven. Therefore, confess your sins to one another and pray for one another, that you may be healed. The prayer of a righteous person has great power as it is working.

5:13–16

26

The Divine Prescription
for Healing

JAMES 5:13–16

AMY CARMICHAEL, the turn-of-the-century missionary to India, described the attempted healing of one of her treasured coworkers, a woman named Ponnammal, who contracted cancer in 1913. Amy was, of course, aware of James' prescription to call for the elders of the church to anoint the ill and offer the prayer of faith, but she and her fellowship were not sure what to do. So they sought a sign asking that, if it was God's will, he would send someone to them who was earnest about James' prescription for healing. The person came—an old friend of hers from Madras. As her biographer Elisabeth Elliot describes it:

> It was a solemn meeting around the sickbed, the women dressed as usual in their handloomed saris, but white ones for this occasion. They laid a palm branch across Ponnammal's bed as a sign of victory and accepted whatever answer God might give, certain that whether it was to be physical healing or not, He would give victory and peace. It sounds like a simple formula. It was an act of faith, but certainly accompanied by the anguish of doubt and desire which had to be brought again and again under the authority of the Master. . . . From that very day Ponnammal grew . . . worse. The pain increased, and her eyes grew dull as she lingered for days in misery until she reached her limit and her "warfare was accomplished."[1]

Prima facie James' directions did not "work" for Ponnammal, the faithful servant of Christ. Honesty demands that we admit that such is often the case when Christians attempt to follow this Scripture. Why is this so? How is it that two believers become ill and both call for the elders of the church, both are anointed, both are prayed over, yet one dies and the other is healed?[2] Are we all to follow James's prescription? How are we to apply this Scripture in the church today? We hope to answer these and similar questions as we consider *The Divine Prescription for Healing* in the church.

As we consider the text we must note that the prescription is in the middle of a thought unit that begins and ends in prayer and in which every turn of thought mentions prayer. James begins by commanding prayer: "Is anyone among you suffering? Let him pray. Is anyone cheerful? Let him sing praise" (v. 13). His commands are a congenial attack on the universal human tendency during trouble to get angry or indulge in self-pity or complain, or on the other hand, when one is untroubled and happy, to forget God. James commands that Christians pray throughout the whole spectrum of emotions. Whether low or high, at the bottom or the top, in the pits or on the pinnacle, either prayer or praise is appropriate.

This was a command that James personally lived out as evidenced by his own body, for the ancient historian Eusebius testified that "his knees grew hard like a camel's because of his constant worship of God, kneeling and asking forgiveness for the people."[3] Just as a laborer's hands testify to his occupation, or a runner's feet to his training, James' callused knees testified to a life of serious prayer. So we ought to listen to what he says, not only because he is the Lord's earthly brother, and not only because his writing is Scripture, but because he "walked his talk"—*on his knees.*

Prescription (v. 14)

What is James' prescription? Very simply, "Is anyone among you sick? Let him call for the elders of the church, and let them pray over him, anointing him with oil in the name of the Lord" (v. 14). This is the divine prescription, the *only one* in all of Scripture! The prescription contains clear direction to the sick first and then to the elders.

To the sick the *explicit* instruction is to "call for the elders of the church." James clearly places the responsibility for initiating the procedure on the sick person, not on the church leadership. This does not exclude pastors or elders from suggesting that the sick person consider calling for the healing ministry, but the request must come from the ill.

This is most important, for the explicit instruction to call for the elders makes two *implicit* personal demands on the ill. The first is that before one calls on the elders *there must be personal confession of all known sins.* This is substantiated by the promise at the end of verse 15 that "If he [the sick] has committed sins, he will be forgiven." James is not saying one's sickness is necessarily a result of sin, for he knew that when the Lord Jesus was asked if a man's blindness was due to sin the Lord answered, "It was not that this man sinned, or his parents" (John 9:3). Similarly, "the steadfastness of Job," mentioned previously in 5:11, was severely tested by his friends who *wrongly* kept insisting he was ill due to his sin.

On the other hand, James is in agreement with other New Testament teaching that sometimes associates illness and even death with one's sin—as, for example, was the case when some in the Corinthian church suffered physical judgment because of unconfessed sin in their lives when they partook of the Lord's Supper (1 Corinthians 11:27–32). Another example comes from Jesus' healing of the paralytic in Capernaum on which occasion he said, "Son, your sins are forgiven" (Mark 2:5), which may indicate the paralysis was linked to personal sin. Similarly, there is an indication in Jesus' words to the paralytic at Bethesda—"See, you are well! Sin no more, that nothing worse may happen to you" (John 5:14). Therefore, before one calls for the healing ministry he must, as best he can, examine his life for any known sin and humbly confess it to God (cf. Psalm 66:18; 139:23, 24; Proverbs 28:13). In this respect the miseries of illness can open avenues of grace as they help clear away the traffic that has stalled its flow.

The second demand implicit in the sick person's calling for the elders is *the subjective sense that this is what the Holy Spirit is directing him to do*. We must realize it is not always God's will for a sick person to call for the elders to pray the prayer of faith and to be healed, for ultimately we will all have a sickness or trauma that will result in death.[4] Our calling for the elders must not be a whim—"Sure, I'll try anything!"—but with a definite sense that it is God's will. This can be difficult because often when we are sick we are too ill to think clearly, much less pray with concentration about God's will. Thus I am not suggesting there must be an iron conviction that it is God's will as a prerequisite for calling the elders, but rather, for want of a better expression, a sense that calling for the elders is "right."

The overall point here is that James is recommending that when one is ill, he or she, having confessed all known sin, should prayerfully consider calling for the elders of the church. Too few Christians even consider this in our secular, mechanistic age.

The *explicit* directions to the elders are equally clear. They are to "pray over him, anointing him with oil in the name of the Lord" (v. 14b). Though oil was used for medical purposes in the ancient world, the use here is not medicinal. Neither is it sacramental. It is not a "vehicle of divine power" that by application promotes healing in the ill—*ex opere operato*. Also, this verse provides no basis for the Roman Catholic Church's sacrament of extreme unction, wherein the dying is anointed with oil with the purpose of removing any remnant of sin and strengthening the soul for dying.[5] A simple reading of the text makes it clear that the anointing with oil is to promote healing, not to ease dying.

Rather than being medicinal or sacramental, the anointing is *symbolical*. Anointing in the Scriptures is usually associated with consecrating or setting apart someone for special service or attention.[6] In this respect oil is also a symbol of the Holy Spirit, who indwells and watches over each believer (cf. 4:5).[7] So the applying of oil to the sick is a rich symbolic act—setting the sick apart to be ministered to in a special way by the Holy Spirit. When applied by the loving hands of the elders, it is a profound vehicle for comfort and encouragement.

It is difficult to determine from the language of this verse whether the anointing is to take place before or during the prayer, but what is clear is that not the anointing but the prayer (the main verb) is by far the most important action. This prayer—"the prayer of faith" (v. 15)—is the heart of it all, as we shall see in a moment. The elders here are described as praying "over him" (v. 14), which seems to suggest a picture of the elders standing by the bed of the sick and extending their hands while praying.[8]

The procedure I have followed in ministry is:

1) The elders assemble at the home of the ill.
2) After greetings, a general prayer is offered.
3) James 5:13–16 is read.
4) The sick person is briefly and gently questioned about the meaning of the passage—as to whether confession has been made, the nature of the illness, and if he or she senses that God is calling for the prayer of faith.
5) The sick person is then anointed with oil in the name of the Father, Son, and Holy Spirit.
6) The elders gently lay hands on the ill and each prays, concluding with the singing of the doxology.

Result (v. 15)

And now as we turn from the prescription for healing to its result, what do we find? Verse 15a says, "And the prayer of faith will save the one who is sick, and the Lord will raise him up." Unqualified healing—pure and simple—and in this lies the "problem." This verse would be so much easier if it read, "And the prayer offered in faith *may* make the sick person well; the Lord *may* raise him up." But that is not what it says. Rather, it presents healing as the guaranteed result of "the prayer offered in faith." It doesn't mention the possibility of failure.

This raises some tension for us because we all know some who have prayed but not been healed. Even the storied spiritual giant Amy Carmichael and her committed band experienced this, as we have seen. More amazing, the Apostle Paul saw his prayers fail to bring healing, for Paul wrote to his disciple Timothy that he had had to leave "Trophimus, who was ill, at Miletus" (2 Timothy 4:20). Similarly, his dearly beloved Epaphroditus was "ill, near to death" (Philippians 2:27). Why was he not healed outright instead of going to death's door as the illness ran its course? And Paul prayed three times for his own healing of his "thorn" (2 Corinthians 12:7–10), but had to go on living with it until he died.

In light of this we must ask, were Trophimus and Epaphroditus and Paul and Amy Carmichael lesser Christians because of their failures in these instances to find healing? No! There are better Christians, with greater character and faith than you and I will ever have, who will not be healed. As in all things, God is sovereign in this matter.

The understanding of verse 15 depends on the definition of "the prayer of faith." What are we to understand about this healing prayer?

First, the prayer of faith comes from a faith in Almighty God who sovereignly carries out his will. Nothing is beyond him. He can heal anyone anytime he wills, and *he does heal today!* He does as he wills in every circumstance, working all things to his glory.

Secondly, the prayer of faith carries a Spirit-given conviction that the Lord will indeed heal the person who is being prayed for. We are truly able to pray the prayer of faith only when we are sure it is God's will. The Apostle John speaks of this saying, "And this is the confidence that we have toward him, that if we ask anything according to his will he hears us" (1 John 5:14). This is also what Jesus repeatedly refers to when he assures us that if we ask *in his name* (that is, according to his will), it will happen:[9] "Again I say to you, if two of you agree on earth about anything they ask, it will be done for them by my Father in heaven. For where two or three are gathered in my name, there am I among them" (Matthew 18:19, 20); "Whatever you ask in my name, this I will do, that the Father may be glorified in the Son" (John 14:13); "You did not choose me, but I chose you and appointed you that you should go and bear fruit and that your fruit should abide, so that whatever you ask the Father in my name, he may give it to you" (John 15:16); "Truly, truly, I say to you, whatever you ask of the Father in my name, he will give it to you" (John 16:23).

And the Apostle John adds, "Beloved, if our heart does not condemn us, we have confidence before God; and whatever we ask we receive from him, because we keep his commandments and do what pleases him" (1 John 3:21, 22).

From this we understand that the prayer of faith is not something we can manufacture by saying "I believe, I believe, I believe, I really believe, I truly believe, I double believe!" *It is a gift from God.* As John Blanchard has said, "the 'prayer offered in faith' is circular in shape; it begins and ends in heaven, in the sovereign will of God."[10]

James is saying that when the elders have the Spirit-wrought conviction that the Lord will heal the one being prayed for, they will pray the prayer of faith, and the sick will be healed. Not only that, but "if he has committed sins, he will be forgiven" (v. 15b). That is, if the illness was due to personal sin, the healing will also signify that his or her sins are forgiven.

James' challenge is a powerful call for the modern church to practice the Biblical ministry of praying for healing. Being ignorant of this teaching in James' epistle, today's church does not see healings like it ought. Another reason for this is that much of its leadership—lay and pastoral—is so fleshly that it cannot hear the Holy Spirit when he is calling for the prayer of faith. Yet another cause is pride. If we become ill, and if we think God is prompting us to call for the elders to pray the prayer of faith, what if it fails? Won't people think we are unspiritual? Remember, greater Christians than we have sought healing and failed. It is better to fail in an attempt to exercise faith than to let it lie dormant and fruitless. God never belittles those who attempt to follow him, but he does chasten those who refuse to attempt anything for him. Also, both faith and "the prayer of faith" are gifts. Who knows when God will choose to give them to us?

In verse 16 James carries his thought a bit further. As Peter Davids says, James "consciously generalizes, making the specific case of 5:14–15 into a general principle of preventative medicine."[11] Prayer for each other brings spiritual and physical healing to the church.

What should the church's attitude be as it attempts to fully minister to its people? In answer I would like to share the guidelines for the healing ministry in the church I serve.

Ministry of Healing

In accordance with Biblical teaching we affirm that God sovereignly heals *some* of his children from disease. We also affirm that God is not limited as to the means or instruments he chooses to use in bringing healing. This said, we believe that the normal Scriptural pattern for healing involves calling for the elders of the church to anoint and pray over the ill for healing as described in James 5:13–16:

> Is anyone among you suffering? Let him pray. Is anyone cheerful? Let him sing praise. Is anyone among you sick? Let him call for the elders of the church, and let them pray over him, anointing him with oil in the name of the Lord. And the prayer of faith will save the one who is sick, and the Lord will raise him up. And if he has committed sins, he will be forgiven. Therefore, confess your sins to one another and pray for one another, that you may be healed. The prayer of a righteous person has great power as it is working.

This teaching, understood in its context, places the human initiative on the ill and presupposes a life in fellowship with Christ, the confession of known sins, and the inner urging of the Holy Spirit (divine initiative) to call for prayer by the elders.

Procedure

In order to carry out the divine ministry of healing as prescribed in James, the following steps are suggested:

1) *Seeking God's will.* In considering whether to call for the elders, one should carefully read James' directives, confess all known sin, and ask God to indicate his will in regard to calling for "the prayer of faith." Here the prayer of godly friends and pastoral counsel are recommended.
2) *Pastoral contact.* If the sick person believes God is leading him or her to call for the elders, a pastor or elder should be contacted. The leaders will prayerfully discuss the matter with the sick in respect to James' directions and will determine a time for anointing and prayer.
3) *Preparation.* The ill will spiritually prepare for the appointed time. And the elders will likewise prepare: confessing all known sins, praying for the ill, and asking God for believing faith both for the ill and themselves.
4) *Congregational support.* If there is time, the congregation will be informed of the anointing, so a broad base of prayer can be established.

Praise God—following his Word is a time of great joy and glory to him!

Therefore, confess your sins to one another and pray for one another, that you may be healed. The prayer of a righteous person has great power as it is working. Elijah was a man with a nature like ours, and he prayed fervently that it might not rain, and for three years and six months it did not rain on the earth. Then he prayed again, and heaven gave rain, and the earth bore its fruit.

5:16–18

27

The Prayer of the Righteous

JAMES 5:16–18

DURING THE FOURTH CENTURY the city of Antioch in Syria produced one of the greatest preachers of the church, John of Antioch. Because of his careful exegesis, unrelenting moral application, and unmatched eloquence he was given a nickname that became his storied title, Chrysostom, "goldenmouthed." This appellation was well-deserved, as is evidenced by his description of the power of prayer, perhaps the most exciting account ever given:

> The potency of prayer has subdued the strength of fire, it has bridled the rage of lions, hushed anarchy to rest, extinguished wars, appeased the elements, expelled demons, burst the chains of death, expanded the fates of heaven, assuaged diseases, dispelled frauds, rescued cities from destruction, stayed the sun in its course, and arrested the progress of the thunderbolt. There is *(in it)* an all-sufficient panoply, a treasure undiminished, a mine which is never exhausted, a sky unobscured by clouds, a heaven unruffled by the storm. It is the root, the fountain, the mother of a thousand blessings!

In this amazing description Chrysostom stacked *some* of the Scriptural evidences of prayer's power atop each other in neatly sculptured phrases until they formed an overwhelming monument to the power of prayer. None of the phrases are exaggerations or hyperboles. This is truth piled upon truth.

James has been telling us that all of life is to be bathed in prayer: prayers when we are down, prayers of song when we are up, prayers for the sick, and now, in verse 16, prayers for each other: "Therefore, confess your sins to one another and pray for one another, that you may be healed. The prayer of a righteous person has great power as it is working." James here encourages a transparency with one another in which we share our sins and shortcomings and bear one another's burdens (cf. Galatians 6:2).

The Prayer of the Righteous—Its Power (v. 16)

The joyous axiom here is: "The prayer of a righteous person has great power as it is working." Notice that he didn't say, "the prayer of the spiritual elite," but rather mentions a righteous Christian who has the imputed righteousness of Christ and lives an ethically righteous life. The prayer of a godly Christian is very powerful in the way it works. May we exercise our power daily!

James also emphasizes the power of mutual confession: "Therefore, confess your sins to one another and pray for one another, that you may be healed. The prayer of a righteous person has great power as it is working" (v. 16). This is generally understood to be a broad directive for enhancing the physical well-being of the congregation because the immediately preceding context gives a prescription for physical healing. It is indeed that—in part. Mutual confession of sin and resulting prayer truly does elevate the health of God's people. But confession and prayer also has a broader application that includes *spiritual* health because the verse under discussion is closely connected with verses 17, 18, which have to do with the general power of prayer in the life of the righteous. In this respect the word "healed" (v. 16) can refer to the figurative healing of diseases of the soul, as it does in several New Testament references (cf. Matthew 13:15; John 12:40; Hebrews 12:13; 1 Peter 2:24).[1] *There is healing power in mutual confession and mutual prayer.*

Regarding confession, the essential, primary, and continual confession of all Christian souls must be to God the Father through our Lord Jesus Christ. "For there is one God, and there is one mediator between God and men, the man Christ Jesus, who gave himself as a ransom for all" (1 Timothy 2:5, 6a). No human being can forgive another's sin. Absolution is in the hands of Christ alone. Thus there is no basis here for the institution of confession to a priest or other religious leader or forgiveness by them. Notice that the confession is *mutual*—"to one another," which also effectively rules out confessing to an elite priesthood.

Having said this, there is a place for Spirit-directed mutual confession between believers. Prior to World War II in Nazi Germany, Pastor Dietrich Bonhoeffer conducted an underground seminary for the training of young pastors in Pomerania, where he shared a common life with about twenty-five students. His experience produced a now famous spiritual classic, *Life Together*, in which he documents the Biblical insights gained from that experience. In the fifth and final chapter of the book, "Communion and Confession," he gives some reasons for the practice of mutual confession. Primary among them is the isolation that sin brings. Sin drives Christians apart and produces a hellish individualism—a deadening autonomy. Says Bonhoeffer, "Sin demands to have a man by himself. It withdraws him from the community. The more isolated a person is, the more destructive will be the power of sin over him."[2] But confession to a fellow brother or sister destroys this deadly autonomy. It pulls down the barrier of hypocrisy and allows the free flow of grace in the community.

The other main benefit of confession is that it brings healthy humiliation. Bonhoeffer goes on:

> Confession in the presence of a brother is the profoundest kind of humiliation. It hurts, it cuts a man down, it is a dreadful blow to pride. To stand there before a brother as a sinner is an ignominy that is almost unbearable. In the confession of concrete sins the old man dies a painful, shameful death before the eyes of a brother.[3]

Thus confession helps promote a poverty of spirit that is acceptable to God: "Blessed are the poor in spirit, for theirs is the kingdom of heaven" (Matthew 5:3).

There are, of course, other reasons for mutual confession, the most obvious being explicitly stated in our text: mutual confession enhances mutual prayer and makes possible the bearing of one another's burdens (Galatians 6:1, 2). We must also mention the value of spiritual accountability, which always follows the confession of one's sins to a mature brother or sister. How much sorrow would be avoided if this were commonly practiced today by both clergy and laity! I am thinking particularly of young men fallen to sensuality who would have been saved from tragedy had they gone to a godly older brother and confessed their sin, thereby obtaining accountability and prayer.

Are there dangers in mutual confession? Yes, and they are substantial. Psychologically needy persons sometimes use confession to get attention for themselves. Through the apparently spiritual medium of "confession" they can handcuff a captive audience as they relate the details of their sin with a deluded or feigned contrition. Confession can also foster spiritual exhibitionism, a perverted moral pleasure in airing one's laundry. The overly morbid can bend confession to become an excuse for unhealthy hyper-introspection. Ostensibly humble confession can also be used as a vehicle for spiritual aggression: "I want to ask your forgiveness for being bitter toward you over the years"—but what follows is not a confession, but an egregious assault. There are other dangers as well, making confession a pious work that becomes, in Bonhoeffer's words, "the final most abominable, vicious, and impure prostitution of the heart."[4] Confession turned into religious routine is deadly!

The real dangers should not keep us from Biblical confession. Here are some guidelines. First, confession should generally be made to an individual. There are exceptions, of course—as, for example when a sin has been against the whole group. But normally confession to all the church is not required to restore one to fellowship with the whole congregation. "I meet the whole congregation in the one brother to whom I confess my sins."[5]

Second, if the sin has been against a fellow Christian, it is to that person that we must make confession. Jesus said, "So if you are offering your gift at the altar and there remember that your brother has something against you, leave your gift there before the altar and go. First be reconciled to your brother, and then come and offer your gift" (Matthew 5:23, 24). The rule of thumb is, the confession should not exceed the range of commission.

Third, if the sin is not against a person, and if it is such that we need to confess it and gain spiritual counsel and support, we must go to a mature Christian. This cannot be stressed enough! An immature Christian should not be expected to carry such burdens. Moreover, confession to the immature may provide a temptation to gossip. Along this line, those whom we would confide in must be people of prayer.

Fourth, the confession must be concrete, not amorphous. This is not to suggest, however, that all the lurid details be shared. One sins in confession if his recounting becomes voyeurism.

Fifth, confessing sins to one another is not a law, but a divinely given help[6] and is to be practiced only as God directs.

There is power in a confessing fellowship, but the power is not in the confessing, as necessary as it is, but in the resulting prayer, as is emphasized by the last half of verse 16: "and pray for one another, that you may be healed. The prayer of a righteous person has great power as it is working."

When the righteous pray for each other, there is power! All Christians are righteous *positionally*, as they have received "the righteousness of God" (Romans 1:17; cf. 1 Corinthians 1:30; Philippians 3:9b). But more than that is meant here, for the emphasis is on *practical* righteousness. Those with righteous lives are powerful in prayer. This principle was expressed in Isaiah's ancient words, "Behold, the LORD's hand is not shortened, that it cannot save, or his ear dull, that it cannot hear; but your iniquities have made a separation between you and your God, and your sins have hidden his face from you so that he does not hear" (Isaiah 59:1, 2). Similarly the psalmist said, "If I had cherished iniquity in my heart, the Lord would not have listened" (Psalm 66:18). And, "The eyes of the LORD are toward the righteous and his ears toward their cry" (Psalm 34:15). Proverbs states positively, "The LORD . . . hears the prayer of the righteous" (Proverbs 15:29).

If you are "confessed up" and walking with Christ, your prayers are spiritual dynamite, especially as they are offered for your needy brothers and sisters in Christ! A *confessing* and *praying* church is packed with spiritual power. Think what could happen if Christians not only confessed their sins to God but, as the Holy Spirit directed, confessed certain sins to each other and then as righteous people prayed for each other! Such confession was at the heart of the small group meetings that fueled the Methodist movement. Indeed confession has been at the heart of the periodic revivals that have graced the American church since New England's Great Awakening. "The prayer of a righteous person has great power as it is working" (v. 16). Is God convicting us to make confession and seek the prayers of the righteous? Then may we do it! Our humble resolve may well mean great blessing for the church.

The Prayer of Righteous Elijah—Its Power (vv. 17, 18)

In order to enhance what he is saying about the power of prayer, James calls up the example of the prophet Elijah. Many feel that Elijah was "the grandest and most romantic character that Israel ever produced."[7] The mention of Elijah especially caught the ear of James' Hebrew audience, who remembered him as fighting a life-and-death battle with idolatrous Ahab and Jezebel, slaying the prophets of Baal, fleeing for his life, exercising more than human power, seeing sights beyond the experience of other men, raising the dead, multiplying the widow's meal and oil, eating from the beaks of ravens, feasting in the wilderness at the hands of angels, foretelling both famine and the coming of rain, outrunning Ahab's chariot to Jezreel, learning the secrets of God's presence in the caves of Horeb, and finally vanishing from the earth in a chariot of fire. Whew!

Elijah's name was even connected with paving the way for the coming Messiah (Malachi 4:5, 6; Mark 9:12; Luke 1:17). Elijah was so highly regarded that some were tempted to think he was superhuman,[8] and some therefore could conceivably wonder how his example of powerful prayer could apply to them. Thus James introduces him by saying, "Elijah was a man with a nature like ours" (v. 17a). He had the same human nature, the same fallible passions as us. He was an ordinary mortal (cf. Acts 14:15, which uses the same word). Therefore Elijah's experience has lessons for all of us.

What do we learn from Elijah? *Passionate prayer*: "He prayed fervently that it might not rain, and for three years and six months it did not rain on the earth. Then he prayed again, and heaven gave rain, and the earth bore its fruit" (vv. 17, 18). Interestingly, the account of this miracle in 1 Kings 17, 18 nowhere mentions that Elijah prayed for the drought to begin, though James here says that "he prayed fervently."

How did James know about this prayer? Possibly because of extra-Biblical literature such as Ecclesiasticus 48:1–3, so that James, under the inspiration of the Holy Spirit, authenticated the historical record. "He prayed fervently that it might not rain" is literally "in prayer he prayed," a Hebrew idiom for intensity or passion.[9] Elijah's prayer was not a laid-back request— "God, it would be nice if it would not rain." Rather, he passionately poured out his heart to Heaven. Apparently (cf. 1 Kings 17:1) God had told him a drought was coming, so he prayed with all he had that God's word would transpire. And it did, with a terrible three and a half years of famine.

And when God revealed to his prophet that it was time for the drought to end, saying, "Go, show yourself to Ahab, and I will send rain upon the earth" (1 Kings 18:1), there was again passionate prayer: "And Elijah went up to the top of Mount Carmel. And he bowed himself down on the earth and put his face between his knees" (1 Kings 18:42). After he had bent in this passionately prayerful posture seven times "the heavens grew black with clouds and wind, and there was a great rain. And Ahab rode and went to Jezreel" (1 Kings 18:45).

God sovereignly delights to answer the passionate prayers of his children. This is not to suggest that he delights in manufactured passion, nor that passion is a meritorious work. Nor are we suggesting that sweaty, frantic prayer is necessarily pleasing to God. But real passion, however it is expressed through the medium of one's personality, is a part of prayer that God is pleased to answer.

Elijah's heart was a whirlwind of passion, and so it has been with all great prayers offered to God. Consider, for example, Jacob, who wrestled with the angel at Jabbok. What a storm of passion broke on God's throne that night! Jacob's passion pulled his body apart, and he, limping, became Israel—which means, "he struggles with God" (Genesis 32:22–32).[10]

When Hannah pled over her barrenness, the priest Eli thought she was drunk, so great was her passion, and "said to her, 'How long will you go on being drunk? Put your wine away from you.' But Hannah answered, 'No, my lord, I am a woman troubled in spirit. I have drunk neither wine nor strong drink, but I have been pouring out my soul before the Lord'" (1 Samuel 1:14, 15). And God granted Hannah's prayer.

Of Ezra, the restorer of Israel, we read, "And at the evening sacrifice I rose from my fasting, with my garment and my cloak torn, and fell upon my knees and spread out my hands to the Lord my God" (Ezra 9:5, 6a). So it was also with his cohort Nehemiah, who prayed and wept over Israel's fallen walls (Nehemiah 1:4ff.). God answered both men's prayers.

Then, in the age of the gospel, came passionate Paul: "I could wish that I myself were accursed and cut off from Christ for the sake of my brothers, my kinsmen according to the flesh" (Romans 9:3). Consider also his disciple Epaphras, of whom Paul told the Colossians, "[He is] always struggling on your behalf in his prayers, that you may stand mature and fully assured in all the will of God" (Colossians 4:12). Or the widow who wore the judge out with her petitions (Luke 18:1–5). But the great and grand example is Christ, who "offered up prayers and supplications, with loud cries and tears, to him who was able to save him from death" (Hebrews 5:7).

The message is clear to all of us: "The prayer of a righteous person has great power as it is working" (v. 16)—or as some scholars think it is better translated, "The prayer of a righteous man is of great power when energized," the energizer being the Holy Spirit.[11] As the Holy Spirit energizes the prayer, the one praying is energized so that he passionately throws his energy into it—which is precisely what Elijah's example illustrates. Therefore, if one is "righteous," having confessed all known sin, being energized by the Holy Spirit to pray passionately, there will be great power.

Today's church needs to live out the two grand duties of this passage. *It needs to be a confessing church.* Is the Holy Spirit prodding us to confess our sin to a brother or sister against whom we have sinned? If so, let us do it before we worship again. Are there sins in our lives that need to be confessed to a mature Christian, perhaps an elder or a pastor, so they can pray for us and hold us accountable? If so, may we not put it off. Martin Luther felt the Christian life was unthinkable without mutual confession. In his *Large Catechism* he wrote: "Therefore when I admonish you to confession I am admonishing you to be a Christian."[12] Confession is humbling, but good for the soul.

The second great duty of the church is to engage in powerful prayer, which comes through *purity* and *passion*. The prayer of a pure, righteous man or woman of God is powerful, and when it is prayed with passion from God it is Elijah-powerful!

Be earnest, earnest, earnest—
Mad if thou wilt;
Do what thou dost as if the
stake were Heaven.

Charles Kingsley[13]

The prayer of a righteous man or woman is a great force when energized by God.

My brothers, if anyone among you wanders from the truth and someone brings him back, let him know that whoever brings back a sinner from his wandering will save his soul from death and will cover a multitude of sins.

5:19, 20

28

Spiritual Reclamation

JAMES 5:19, 20

THOSE OF US who were in youth ministry in the 1960s can testify that though those years were difficult because of cultural and political turmoil, they were banner years for evangelism. This was due in part to the self-conscious "openness" of that decade. It was "in" to be open to anything and everything—from free love to monasticism, LSD to alfalfa sprouts, Hinduism to Christianity. "Do your own thing" . . . "Peace, brother!" Virtually everyone was open to discussing Christianity. And *many* came to Christ! I remember a year in which almost every week at least one, and sometimes several, professed Christ in a Bible study I conducted.

One of these was a remarkable young man in his early twenties who was the quintessence of hippie chic—tie-dyed shirts, bell-bottoms, long red hair, olympian beard, steel-rimmed John Lennon glasses. He was "cool," to say the least! And he was intelligent, winsomely direct, and magnetic. We all loved him.

I'll never forget one Sunday night, about a month after his profession of faith, when he stood unprompted before our large congregation and gave testimony to his finding Christ, saying something to the effect that he would have become a Christian sooner if only someone had told him. He ended with a challenge to get on with the job of spreading the good news. Here was an "Exhibit A" testifying to the effectiveness of our youth ministry. I was so proud!

You can imagine then the hurt and chagrin I felt a few weeks later when, after injuring his knee in a picnic softball game, he slapped us with a lawsuit! Even worse, he declared his religious experience an aberration and became a foe of the gospel. And as far as I know he has continued in his apostasy.

This gave me great cause for sorrow and reflection. His "conversion" was so real. He understood . . . I know he did by the way he dialogued regarding Christ. There had been a change in his life, and he had such joy.

During that time the deep mystery of true faith and of the church itself came home to me as never before. And it was here that Jesus' teaching about the four soils in the so-called Mystery Parables took on fresh meaning to me (cf. Luke 8 and Matthew 13). The mystery unfolds when we understand that the gospel is sown on four kinds of hearts.

First, there is the *hard heart* (Luke 8:5, 12). The farm fields in Palestine were long narrow strips divided by footpaths that became hard as rock from the combination of occasional moisture, the constant pounding of feet, and the kiln-like effect of the blazing sun. When the *farmer* (God the Holy Spirit) sows the *seed* (God's Word, living and pregnant with life) on the *path* (hard human hearts), it is trampled on, and the birds eat it up, which means, as Jesus explained, "the devil comes and takes away the word from their hearts, so that they may not believe and be saved" (Luke 8:12). These are impenetrable hearts, minds that are shrouded in a materialistic fog. Satan's vulturous beak snatches the precious seed of the gospel from hardened hearts before it germinates.

Second, there is the *shallow heart* (Luke 8:6, 13). Palestine is covered with bedrock and a thin coating of soil, which enhances the sprouting of new seed because the bedrock is quickly warmed by the sun and brings speedy germination. But the fresh sprouts also quickly die because the shallow soil does not allow an adequate root system. This is like the grass that briefly sprouts in spring in the cracks on an expressway. I once saw a similar phenomenon when I spotted a moving patch of green in the desert in Mexico—it was a turtle greened with the temporary grass of a previous summer's seeds!

Jesus makes the application so clear: "And the ones on the rock are those who, when they hear the word, receive it with joy. But these have no root; they believe for a while, and in time of testing fall away" (Luke 8:13). This, I believe, explains my painful experience with the young man who sprouted so beautifully but faded overnight. He received the word "with joy." His effervescence and smiling excitement was a reproach to the lukewarm. Nothing is greener than a new sprout. In fact, it may even appear more healthy than the other seed. (This in no way depreciates emotion, for conversion ought to result in joy that cannot be contained.)

The problem with shallowness is that "these have no root," so "in time of testing [they] fall away." This is especially common today because so much theology is man-centered. Christ is preached with the emphasis on what he can do for us, and receiving him is viewed as doing him a favor. This shallow theology airbrushes the doctrine of sin and minimizes the holiness of God, producing bogus converts.

Jesus' exposition of the shallow heart is a warning to all of us to honestly reflect on the reality of our conversion. Has the Word truly taken root? Are we growing? Or was there a brief spurt and then nothing? We must also guard against the disillusionment that may come when we see "converts" sprout up and wither.

The third kind of heart is the *infested heart* (Luke 8:7, 14). Some of the seed of God's Word falls on thorn-infested soil that strangles the promising beginnings of new life. Christ says, "And as for what fell among the thorns, they are those who hear, but as they go on their way they are choked by the cares and riches and pleasures of life, and their fruit does not mature" (Luke 8:14). The trio of murderers—"cares . . . riches . . . pleasures"—all strangle by the clutch of *materialism*. Today we call it "keeping up with the Joneses"—buying things we don't need with money we don't have to impress people we don't even like. A man can sit in church for years and never hear the Word because all he does in those moments is worry about his riches and pleasures. The telltale sign is that they, in Jesus' words, do "not mature" (Luke 8:14b). And in failing to mature, they produce no fruit. If there is no fruit in our lives, and if our focus is on material possessions, we are probably not Christians. We have fooled others and, even more tragically, have fooled ourselves.

Finally, there is the *fertile heart* (Luke 8:8, 15). Our Lord says of it, "And some fell into good soil and grew and yielded a hundredfold" (v. 8), and then explains, "As for that in the good soil, they are those who, hearing the word, hold it fast in an honest and good heart, and bear fruit with patience" (v. 15). *True believers bear fruit!* Our Lord adds in Matthew's account that the yield is "a hundredfold, in another sixty, and in another thirty" (Matthew 13:23). This is first of all *inward* fruit—the fruit of the Spirit: "love, joy, peace, patience, kindness, goodness, faithfulness, gentleness, self-control" (Galatians 5:22, 23). These inner fruits come into full bloom, then produce the *outward* fruit that James emphasizes.

The panoramic significance of the four hearts is that all of them exist in the mystery of the *visible* church! The visible church has three kinds of unregenerate hearts within it—the *hard* heart, the *shallow* heart, and the *infested* heart. Those with regenerate hearts, true Christians, are the *fertile*, fruitful hearts. To be sure, there are degrees of fruitfulness, and all believing hearts at times wrestle with hardness and shallowness and infestation, but God's Word is rooted deeply, and there is ongoing fruit.

We must bring Christ's perspective to his half-brother James' exhortation about the danger of apostasy with which he closes his letter. From the beginning James has been concerned that people within the visible confessing church have true faith.[1] Faith, according to James, produces works that affect how one spends his money, how he relates to the poor and to the world, and so much more. Faith shows itself in the use of the whole body, especially the tongue. Aberrations in any of these areas may indicate a bogus faith and the danger of apostasy. His call to keep our brothers and sisters on track is a fitting conclusion to his great letter.

The Possibility of Apostasy (v. 19a)

James graphically presents apostasy as a very real possibility in the opening phrase of verse 19: "My brothers, if anyone among you wanders from the truth . . ." The Greek word for "wanders" is *planao*, from which we derive the word "planet," a heavenly wanderer.[2] James sees some believers as potentially cut loose from the church and wandering alone across a desolation. But he does not see this wandering as unconscious or absent-minded. Moreover, this is not simply a doctrinal wandering from the truth, but a wandering in lifestyle. The Hebrew mind, and especially that of James, never separated the *intellectual* from the *behavioral*, or the *doctrinal* from the *moral*, as the Greeks did. Truth was something people *did* (John 3:21, NASB).

Thus apostasy could be discerned in two ways: doctrinal aberration or moral deviation. In fact, the Bible teaches that a moral deviation can, and often does, affect one's doctrine. Thousands today change what they believe to accommodate their moral behavior. On the other hand, thousands more take up false doctrine, then apostatize in their actions. In the New Testament we read of Demas forsaking Paul for moral reasons: he was "in love with this present world" (2 Timothy 4:10). On the other hand, Alexander the metalworker did Paul great harm because he objected to his doctrine—"he strongly opposed our message" (2 Timothy 4:15). Both had distinct reasons for apostasy but would join hands doctrinally and morally as time went on.

As Christians who care for the church, we ought to be sensitive to moral changes in our own behavior and (while avoiding judgmentalism) be sensitive to changes in our brothers and sisters. In our day moral wandering may be as sure an indication of apostasy as mental theological wandering. As Billy Graham has said:

No man can be said to be truly converted to Christ who has not bent his will to Christ. He may give intellectual assent to the claims of Christ and may have had emotional religious experiences; however, he is not truly converted until he has surrendered his will to Christ as Lord, Savior, and Master.[3]

The Blessing of Reclamation (vv. 19b, 20)

James' great concern is not just that we are able to discern apostasy, but that we do something about it: "My brothers, if anyone among you wanders from the truth and someone brings him back, let him know that whoever brings back a sinner from his wandering will save his soul from death and will cover a multitude of sins" (vv. 19, 20). This is *spiritual reclamation.*

Restoration *covers over a multitude of sins.* "Covering" sins signifies forgiveness, and "a multitude of sins" indicates the extent of forgiveness. It is always a multitude of sins that is covered! When I was brought to Christ, millions of sins were covered over, and it was the same with you. This is viewed in the Bible as supreme blessedness. "Blessed is the one," sings the psalmist, "whose transgression is forgiven, whose sin is covered" (Psalm 32:1; cf. 85:2). What a blessed feat is accomplished when a sinner is turned away from his error. God alone does this. But he does use human instruments who love him and who love people, for "love covers all sins" (Proverbs 10:12, NKJV).

This covering of sins flows from the ultimate fact that turning a sinner back *saves him from death.* The act of saving someone from death has regularly invoked a lifetime of gratitude by the one saved. Not a few ex-soldiers carry photos of someone who put it all on the line for them. But the saving act here is even greater, for it is a saving from *spiritual* death, saving a man or woman or boy or girl from an existence of body and soul in eternal separation from God. This is salvation from a horrifying existence that Scripture describes in various ways, all terrible: "the unquenchable fire" (Mark 9:43), "their worm does not die" (Mark 9:48), "the smoke of their torment goes up forever and ever" (Revelation 14:11), "the bottomless pit" (Revelation 20:1).

To be part of saving one from spiritual death is the greatest thing one human can ever do for another! If we were super-rich and were able to give another the deeds to our lands, our stock portfolios, our seat on the New York Stock Exchange, and our prestige, that would not come close to the marvels of saving that person from spiritual death. Recently F. F. Bruce, the greatest evangelical Biblical scholar of our time, passed away. His commentaries have sold millions, and he has influenced thousands and thousands of students and pastors. Bruce said at the end of his career:

> For many years now the greater part of my time has been devoted to the study and interpretation of the Bible, in academic and nonacademic settings alike. I regard this as a most worthwhile and rewarding occupation. There is only one form of ministry which I should rate more highly; that is the work of an evangelist, to which I have not been called.[4]

To save another from spiritual death is indeed the greatest thing one human can do for another!

These are stupendous matters. "Whoever brings back a sinner from his wandering will save his soul from death and will cover a multitude of sins" (v. 20). It is this motivation that has impelled James in writing his letter from beginning to end. This is why he has been so hard-hitting—"in your face," so to speak.

This is a warning to the *hard* hearts, *shallow* hearts, and *infested* hearts that populate the church visible. I do not know who they are, but I know they are well-represented throughout the church. *Newsweek* (December 17, 1990) mentioned those who consider their "private lives off limits" to the church.[5] For such folk, wandering is both *theological* and *moral.* And to such our text is a tender pastoral warning, for James gently says, "My brothers, if anyone among you wanders from the truth . . ."

But this is also a call for the church to consciously practice a ministry of reclamation, a ministry that has five steps:

1) *Love.* The church must engage in love instead of rejecting the wandering soul. The preacher of a century ago, Charles Spurgeon, wrote:

> I have known a person who has erred hunted down like a wolf. He was wrong to some degree, but that wrong has been aggravated and dwelt upon till the man has been worried into defiance; the fault has been exaggerated into a double wrong by ferocious attacks upon it. The manhood of the man has taken sides with his error because he has been so severely handled. The man has been compelled, sinfully I admit, to take up an extreme position, and to go further into mischief, because he could not brook to be denounced instead of being reasoned with. And when a man has been blameworthy in his life it will often happen that his fault has been blazed abroad, retailed from mouth to mouth, and magnified, until the poor erring one has felt degraded, and having lost all self-respect, has given way to far more dreadful sins. The object of some professors seems to be to amputate the limb rather than to heal it.[6]

Again, "love covers all sins" (Proverbs 10:12, NKJV), not because our love can atone for them, but because love cares and maintains a relationship through which the grace of God is pleased to move. Have we written a wanderer off lately?

2) *Integrity.* If we are to be used to help reclaim another we must possess what we wish them to have. Paul said exactly this: "Brothers, if anyone is caught in any transgression, you who are spiritual should restore him in a spirit of gentleness. Keep watch on yourself, lest you too be tempted" (Galatians 6:1). Integrity of heart, the authenticity of one's soul, is seen in the eyes and heard in the tone of voice. Restorers must be truly spiritual people.

3) *Prayer.* The Apostle John, near the end of his first pastoral letter, says, "If anyone sees his brother committing a sin not leading to death, he shall ask, and God will give him life" (1 John 5:16). We must pray for the erring. Sadly, so often instead of our words going up to God, they go out in gossip. Our prayers ought to be specific, detailed, regular, and passionate. As James has just reminded us, "The prayer of a righteous person has great power as it is working" (5:16b).

4) *Confrontation.* The call to confront the sinner is firmly expressed in Scripture. God's word through Ezekiel was, "If I say to the wicked, 'You shall surely die,' and you give him no warning, nor speak to warn the wicked from his wicked way, in order to save his life, that wicked person shall die for his iniquity, but his blood I will require at your hand" (Ezekiel 3:18). Paul told the Thessalonian church regarding a disobedient Christian to "warn him as a brother" (2 Thessalonians 3:15), and to the Ephesians he gave his own personal example: "Remember that for three years I did not cease night or day to admonish every one with tears" (Acts 20:31; cf. Colossians 1:28). There are times when we must prayerfully undertake confrontation.

I especially remember a situation in which my wife was called to confront another. A friend of hers, a wife with several children, had taken a secretarial position, and her boss had made advances toward her. The woman was flattered and had decided to toss everything for the affair. Few people like to confront, and my wife would have welcomed an out, but there was none. She prayed, I prayed, and we prayed together. She went to confront her friend, and I prayed more! When Barbara returned four hours later, she was exhausted. She explained that it had been a battle—she actually felt she was fighting with the devil for the woman's soul. It was as if the devil had hold of one arm and my wife the other. Every rationalization imaginable was argued—and with considerable heat! But God be praised, the woman repented. And it was a true repentance, for she went on to serve Christ and the church in the following years. When we are called to confront, we must do so, relying on the wisdom and love of God.

5) *Discipline*. This is always a last resort. Jesus himself instructs us in the process in Matthew 18:15–17. There are times we must do this for the sake of the wanderer's soul and the life of the church (cf. 1 Corinthians 5:1–5).

Commitment to the process of spiritual reclamation as *love* plus *integrity* plus *prayer* plus *confrontation* plus *discipline* says one thing: we love the church and believe with James that "Whoever brings back a sinner from his wandering will save his soul from death and will cover a multitude of sins" (v. 20). May we live redemptive lives, reclaiming wandering souls for Christ!

Soli Deo gloria!

Notes

Chapter One: Count It All Joy

1. Simon J. Kistemaker, *Exposition of the Epistle of James and the Epistles of John* (Grand Rapids, MI: Baker, 1986), pp. 18, 19, 27.

2. Ibid.

3. D. Edmond Hiebert, *The Epistle of James* (Chicago: Moody Press, 1979), p. 42, who quotes Edgar J. Goodspeed, *An Introduction to the New Testament*, p. 290.

4. Kistemaker, *Exposition of the Epistle of James and the Epistles of John*, p. 5, says in note 6,

> I have counted only true imperatives and not the participles that take the place of the imperative. Expanding the use of the imperative, C. Leslie Mitton in *The Epistle of James* (Grand Rapids, MI: Eerdmans, 1966), p. 235, mentions sixty occurrences.

5. Eusebius, *Ecclesiastical History*, vol. 1, trans. Kirsopp Lake, The Loeb Classical Library (Cambridge, MA: Harvard University Press, 1965), p. 171 (II. 23.3–9).

6. Lloyd John Ogilvie, *Drumbeat of Love* (Waco, TX: Word, 1978), pp. 176, 177.

7. James Hardy Ropes, *A Critical and Exegetical Commentary on the Epistle of St. James*, in *The International Critical Commentary* (Edinburgh: T. & T. Clark, 1968), p. 135 says the word means "'steadfastness,' 'staying-power,' not 'patience.'"

8. Martin Dibelius, *A Commentary on the Epistle of James*, trans. Michael A. Williams (Philadelphia: Fortress Press, 1975), p. 73, says, "One can see that there is more heroism in this word than the translation 'patience' would suggest. Paul, also, has this heroic endurance in mind in Romans 5:3 and 1 Corinthians 12:16."

9. Peter H. Davids, *The Epistle of James*, in *The New International Greek Testament Commentary* (Grand Rapids, MI: Eerdmans, 1982), p. 70.

10. Lehman Strauss, *James, Your Brother* (Neptune, NJ: Loizeaux, 1972), p. 12.

11. Oswald Sanders, *Spiritual Leadership* (Chicago: Moody Press, 1978), p. 141.

Chapter Two: If Any of You Lacks Wisdom

1. Ralph Martin, *Word Biblical Commentary, Volume 8, James* (Waco, TX: Word, 1988), p. 17, writes:

> The catchword is the verb "to lack," picked up from the preceding verse. The situation of the readers who are facing trial is such that they need to know how to cope with these experiences. Hence there is the need of "wisdom." . . . The conditional clause . . . does not imply doubt or suggest a contingency. Rather it presupposes "a standing fact" (Hiebert, 79). The readers are facing some real problems arising from persecution, and it is

the gift and application of wisdom to see these trials in their proper light and respond accordingly.

Similarly, Peter Davids, *The Epistle of James*, p. 71.

2. Lehman Strauss, *James, Your Brother* (Neptune, NJ: Loizeaux, 1972), p. 19.

3. Allan Bloom, *The Closing of the American Mind* (New York: Simon & Schuster, 1987), p. 60.

4. A. T. Robertson, *Word Pictures in the New Testament*, vol. 6 (Nashville: Broadman, 1933), p. 13.

5. F. J. A. Hort, *The Epistle of St. James* (London: Macmillan, 1903), p. 7.

6. James Hardy Ropes, *A Critical and Exegetical Commentary on the Epistle of St. James* (Edinburgh: T. & T. Clark, 1968), p. 39.

7. Martin, *Word Biblical Commentary*, Volume 8, James, p. 17.

8. Strauss, *James, Your Brother*, p. 20.

9. D. Edmond Hiebert, *The Epistle of James* (Chicago: Moody Press, 1979), p. 81:

But more probably the article relates directly to God, and the participle between them, as attributive, stresses that "giving" is the inherent nature of God. The present tense of the participle sets forth God's generous nature as continually giving. He has revealed Himself as a God who is continually giving to men.

10. Ibid., p. 85.

11. Ropes, *A Critical and Exegetical Commentary on the Epistle of St. James*, p. 143.

Chapter Three: Wisdom for the Humble and the High

1. G. Abbott-Smith, *A Manual Lexicon of the New Testament* (New York: Charles Scribner's Sons, n.d.), p. 439 says "*low-lying*; metaph. a) *lowly, of low degree, brought low.*"

2. Manford George Gutzke, *Plain Talk on James* (Grand Rapids, MI: Zondervan, 1969), p. 35.

3. Paul Hendrikson, *Seminary: A Search* (New York: Summit Books, 1983), p. 313.

4. John Calvin, *A Harmony of the Gospels Matthew, Mark and Luke; and James and Jude*, trans. A. W. Morrison, Calvin's New Testament Commentaries, vol. 3 (Grand Rapids, MI: Eerdmans, 1972), p. 266.

5. Rudolf Stier, *The Epistle of St. James*, trans. William B. Pope (Minneapolis: Klock & Klock, 1982), p. 242, eloquently remarks regarding the necessity of lowliness:

Let the brother that is rich rejoice that he is made low! Mark that well! Rejoice in *this*, that thou knowest the Lord, who dealeth in mercy upon earth, and giveth grace to the humble; that thou hast seen the danger, and escaped the snare of riches, and art no longer a camel too large for the needle's eye; that thou hast found security against destruction, and a better hope than fleeting riches can afford. It is the curse of all whom the old serpent deceives to go upon the earth like him, and like him to eat the dust.

Rejoice that thou hast learned this; rejoice in thy *lowliness* before God as a spiritually poor man, who is not wanting in His spiritual gifts; so that, as a brother of the poor, thou art also an inheritor of the kingdom, and *rich in God!*

6. Simon J. Kistemaker, *Exposition of the Epistle of James and the Epistle of John* (Grand Rapids, MI: Baker, 1986), p. 44.

Chapter Four: The Source and Course of Temptation

1. Ralph Martin, *Word Biblical Commentary, Volume 8, James* (Waco, TX: Word, 1988), p. 41, says:

We may infer these from the cautionary word in v 16a: "Don't be led astray, my dear brothers." Unless this is an otiose remark, thrown in as an aside, we should take it seriously and find it to register the presence of some alien teaching the readers were being subjected to and were in danger of embracing. At the heart of that error was an aspersion cast on the divine character. The testing referred to in v 12 lay exactly in the threat of unbelief that was brought to the surface by their hardship and which, in turn, compelled them to raise some tough questions about the sovereign control and lordship of God in the face of the trials they were called on to endure. The obvious "easy answer" offered to explain their present miseries was evidently that God had lost patience with them and as a mark of disfavor had abandoned them to their fate. Or else the proposal was that he was deliberately testing them with malevolent designs in view.

2. Jesus the son of Sirach argues against this tendency among the Jews:

Do not say, "Because of the Lord I left the right way"; for he will not do what he hates. Do not say, "It was he who led me astray"; for he has no need of a sinful man. The Lord hates all abominations and they are not loved by those who fear him. It was he who created man in the beginning, and he left him in the power of his own inclination. If you will, you can keep the commandments, and to act faithfully is a matter of your own choice (Ecclesiasticus 15:11–13).

3. John Calvin, *A Harmony of the Gospels Matthew, Mark and Luke; and James and Jude*, trans. A. W. Morrison, Calvin's New Testament Commentaries, vol. 3 (Grand Rapids, MI: Eerdmans, 1972), p. 218, defends against those who would blame God for their sin, saying:

There are two points to be noted. When Scripture assigns blinding or hardening of hearts to God (Exod. 9. 12), it does not name Him as the first Mover, nor does it make Him the Author of the evil and so liable for the blame. James insists just on these two points. Does Scripture say that God gave men up to their vile passions (Rom. 1. 26), or was it that God depraved and corrupted their hearts? No, their hearts were made subject to vile lusts, for they were already corrupt and vicious. And is it the case that, when God makes a man blind or hard, He is the instigator or accomplice of sin? No indeed, this is His vengeance upon sin, and the fair retribution

He takes upon the evil-doers, who have spurned the direction of His Spirit. Consequently, neither is the origin of sin to be found in God, nor is its blame to be imputed to Him, as though He sought pleasure in wrong. We conclude that it is a vain manoeuvre for man to attempt to throw the blame of his errors upon God, for whatever the evil, it comes from no other source than from the perverse affections of man himself.

4. Robert Johnstone, *Lectures Exegetical and Practical on the Epistle of James* (Minneapolis: Klock & Klock, 1978), p. 104.

5. Paul Johnson, *Intellectuals* (New York: Harper and Row, 1988), pp. 138–72.

6. Douglas J. Moo, *The Letters of James* (Grand Rapids, MI: Eerdmans, 1988), p. 72.

7. James Hardy Ropes, *A Critical and Exegetical Commentary on the Epistle of St. James* (Edinburgh: T. & T. Clark, 1968), p. 155.

8. D. Edmond Hiebert, *The Epistle of James* (Chicago: Moody Press, 1979), p. 104.

9. James S. Hewitt, *Illustrations Unlimited* (Wheaton, IL: Tyndale House, 1988), p. 52.

10. A. T. Robertson, *Studies in the Epistle of James* (Nashville: Broadman, n. d.), p. 52. See also Joseph B. Mayor, *The Epistle of St. James* (Minneapolis: Klock & Klock, 1977), p. 54, who writes, "In like manner the first effect . . . is to draw the man out of his original repose, the second to allure him to a definite bait."

11. Dietrich Bonhoeffer, *Temptation* (London: SCM Press Ltd, 1961), p. 33.

12. Spiros Zodhiates, *The Work of Faith: An Exposition of James 1:1–2:13* (Grand Rapids, MI: Eerdmans, 1960), p. 72.

13. Hiebert, *The Epistle of James*, p. 109.

Chapter Five: The Goodness of God

1. Kent and Barbara Hughes, *Liberating Ministry from the Success Syndrome* (Wheaton, IL: Tyndale House, 1987), p. 23.

2. Thomas Hardy, *Tess of the D'Urberviles* (London: Zodiac Press, 1980), chap. 59.

3. Joseph Katz, ed., *The Complete Poems of Stephen Crane* (Ithaca, NY: Cornell University Press, 1966), p. 125. Crane's use of the refrain continues through five stanzas, the first of which reads:

A man adrift on a slim spar
A horizon smaller than the rim of a bottle
Tented waves rearing lashy dark points
The near whine of froth in circles.
God is cold.

4. D. Edmond Hiebert, *The Epistle of James* (Chicago: Moody Press, 1979), p. 111, notes that "'perfect' (*telion*) marks the gift as 'complete,' lacking nothing to meet the demands of the recipient."

5. Alfred Edersheim, *Sketches of Jewish Social Life in the Days of Christ* (Grand Rapids, MI: Eerdmans, 1964), p. 268.

6. John Murray, *The Epistle to the Romans* (Grand Rapids, MI: Eerdmans, 1971), pp. 39, 40, where he writes of the "divine nature":

> "Divinity" is generic as distinguished from power which is specific. This term reflects on the perfections of God and denotes to use Meyer's words, "the totality of that which God is as a being possessed of divine attributes" (*ad loc.*). Hence divinity does not specify one invisible attribute but the sum of the invisible perfections which characterize God. So, after all, the statement "eternal power and divinity" is inclusive of a great many invisible attributes and reflects on the richness of the manifestation given in the visible creation of the being, majesty, and glory of God. We must not tone down the teaching of the apostle in this passage. It is a clear declaration to the effect that the visible creation as God's handiwork makes manifest the invisible perfections of God as its Creator, that from the things which are perceptible to the senses cognition of these invisible perfections is derived, and that thus a clear apprehension of God's perfections may be gained from his observable handiwork. Phenomena disclose the noumena of God's transcendent perfection and specific divinity.

7. Gary Vanderet, *Discovery Papers*, "The Skill of Resisting Temptation," Catalogue no. 3986, James 1:13–18, May 4, 1986.

8. Joseph Bayly, "The Severity and Goodness of God," *Eternity* (September 1986), p. 80.

9. Peter Davids, *The Epistle of James* (Grand Rapids, MI: Eerdmans, 1982), p. 90.

Chapter Six: Accepting the Word

1. Paul Tournier, *To Understand Each Other* (Richmond, VA: John Knox Press, 1970).

2. Simon J. Kistemaker, *Exposition of the Epistle of James and the Epistles of John* (Grand Rapids, MI: Baker, 1986), p. 57.

3. John Blanchard, *Truth for Life* (West Sussex, UK: H. E. Walter Ltd, 1982), p. 73.

4. Paul Johnson, *Intellectuals* (New York: Harper and Row, 1988), p. 91.

5. Joseph Katz, ed., *The Complete Poems of Stephen Crane* (Ithaca, NY: Cornell University Press, 1972), p. 5.

6. D. Edmond Hiebert, *The Epistle of James* (Chicago: Moody Press, 1979), p. 130, says:

> It is an inner disposition, a spirit of gentleness and considerateness, the opposite of self-assertiveness. Instead of brashly asserting themselves in anger, they need to be humble and teachable in order to "receive" rightly the divine message.

Chapter Seven: Doing the Word

1. Charles R. Swindoll, *Improving Your Serve* (Waco, TX: Word, 1983), pp. 170, 171.

2. James Hardy Ropes, *A Critical and Exegetical Commentary on the Epistle of St. James* (Edinburgh: T. & T. Clark, 1968), p. 176.

3. John Calvin, *A Harmony of the Gospels Matthew, Mark and Luke; and James and Jude*, trans. A. W. Morrison, Calvin's New Testament Commentaries, vol. 3 (Grand Rapids, MI: Eerdmans, 1972), p. 273.

4. J. I. Packer, *Knowing God* (Downers Grove, IL: InterVarsity, 1973), p. 34, says:

> John Owen and John Calvin knew more theology than John Bunyan or Billy Bray, but who would deny that the latter pair knew their God every bit as well as the former? (All four, of course, were beavers for the Bible, which counts for far more anyway than a formal theological training.)

5. Ralph Martin, *Word Biblical Commentary, Volume 8, James* (Waco, TX: Word, 1988), p. 50.

6. D. Edmond Hiebert, *The Epistle of St. James* (London: Macmillan, 1903), pp. 135, 136, explains:

> "He that looketh" (*ho parakupsas*) pictures the man as bending over the mirror on the table in order to examine more minutely what is revealed therein. "Into" (*eis*) suggests a penetrating look. The verb may denote a cursory look, but that meaning is excluded here by the following participle, "and continueth" (*parameinas*), which is closely connected with the first participle as being under the government of one article. Both are compound forms with the preposition *para*, "beside, alongside of," suggesting proximity. He bent over the mirror, and gripped by what he saw, he continued looking and obeying its precepts. This feature marks his crucial difference to the first man.

7. Douglas J. Moo, *The Letters of James* (Grand Rapids, MI: Eerdmans, 1988), p. 84, gives an unusually clear explanation of what "the perfect law, the law of liberty" means:

> This law was frequently called "perfect" (*cf.* Ps. 19:7) and to it was sometimes ascribed the power to give true freedom (*cf.* Mishnah, *Abot.* 6:2). But the context makes us pause before accepting the identification of "law of liberty" with the Old Testament law. Because of the flow of the text, the "perfect law" of verse 25 must be the same as the "word" of verse 22; and the "word," in turn, is identified as "the word of truth" that mediates spiritual birth (v. 18) and whose reception leads to salvation (v. 21). In light of this, it is necessary to associate "the perfect law of liberty" closely with the gospel. The pervasive influence of the teaching of Jesus on James' ethics suggests that this "law" may particularly involve Jesus' ethical demands. James wants to stress to his hearers that the "good news" of salvation brings with it an unavoidable, searching demand for complete obedience. The use of the word "law" to describe this commanding aspect of the Christ "Word" is entirely natural for someone in James' position (and anticipates in some ways the "law/gospel" distinction in later theology). This "law" includes Old Testament commandments, as 2:8–11 makes clear, but James' characterization of the Law as *perfect* suggests that these commandments must be seen in

the light of Jesus' fulfillment of the Old Testament law (Mt. 5:17). And, while still a "law," this summons to obedience is nevertheless "liberating" because, in accordance with Jeremiah's new covenant prophecy (31:31–34), it has been written on the heart (*cf.* "implanted" in v. 21). With the searching, radical demand of the gospel comes the enabling grace of God. When Jesus called people to "come" to him and to take his "yoke" upon them, he promised that "my yoke is easy, and my burden is light" (Mt. 11:28–30).

Chapter Eight: Acceptable Religion

1. James Hardy Ropes, *A Critical and Exegetical Commentary on the Epistle of St. James* (Edinburgh: T. & T. Clark, 1968), p. 181, writes:

> This adjective is not found elsewhere excepting in lexicons, but derivatives are common, notably *threskeia* (vv. 26, 27), which means "religious worship, especially, but not exclusively, external, that which consists in ceremonies" (*Lex.*). *Threskos* means "given to religious observances." . . . In the present verse *threskos* doubtless refers to attendance on the exercises of public worship, but also to other observances of religion, such as almsgiving, prayer, fasting (*cf.* Mt. 6:1–18, 2 Clem., Rom. 16:4). . . . The English words "religion," "religious," used here and in v. 27 for *threskeia, threskos*, are to be understood in the external sense of "worship," "religious rite," etc., in which formerly they were more used than at present.

2. Ralph Martin, *Word Biblical Commentary, Volume 8, James* (Waco, TX: Word, 1988), p. 52.

3. Lehman Strauss, *James, Your Brother* (Neptune, NJ: Loizeaux, 1972), p. 64.

4. John Calvin, *A Harmony of the Gospels Matthew, Mark and Luke; and James and Jude*, trans. A. W. Morrison, Calvin's New Testament Commentaries, vol. 3 (Grand Rapids, MI: Eerdmans, 1972), p. 274.

5. James S. Hewett, ed., *Illustrations Unlimited* (Wheaton, IL: Tyndale House, 1988), p. 475.

6. Robert K. Johnstone, *Lectures Exegetical and Practical on the Epistle of James* (Minneapolis: Klock & Klock, 1978), p. 166, says:

> And persons who can take time for much recreation of various kinds, and who, in the midst of a day which they would declare to be quite full of business, could yet certainly *make* time to consider some new remunerative piece of business which unexpectedly presented itself, and accomplish all the rest besides,—such persons cannot at the bar of conscience plead want of time for the discharge of Christian duty.

7. Charles Colson, *Who Speaks for God?* (Wheaton, IL: Crossway Books, 1985), pp. 67, 68.

8. Frank E. Gaebelein, *The Practical Epistle of James* (Great Neck, NY: Channel Press, 1955), pp. 55, 56.

Chapter Nine: The Folly of Favoritism

1. D. Edmond Hiebert, *The Epistle of James* (Chicago: Moody Press, 1979), p. 52.

2. Ralph Martin, *Word Biblical Commentary, Volume 8, James* (Waco, TX: Word, 1988), p. 61, says:

> But the wearing of fine garments and rings was generally a mark of opulence and ostentation (Epictetus, *Diss.* 1. 22. 18; cf. Seneca, *Nat. Quaest.* 7. 31–32: *exornamus anulis digitos in omni articulo gemma disponitur*, "we adorn our fingers with rings; a gem is fitted to every joint").

3. Hiebert, *The Epistle of James*, p. 154, says:

> The man's "fine clothing" was further evidence of his wealth. "Fine" (*lampra*) means "bright" or "shining" and refers either to the glittering color of his clothes or his sparkling ornaments, probably the former. Luke used the adjective of the "gorgeous apparel" in which Herod Antipas and his soldiers mockingly arrayed Jesus (Luke 23:11), and also of the "bright apparel" of the angel who appeared to Cornelius the centurion (Acts 10:30). The reference probably is to the shining white garments often worn by wealthy Jews.

4. Martin, *Word Biblical Commentary, Volume 8, James*, pp. 60, 61.

5. Richard Collier, *The General Next to God* (New York: E. P. Dutton, 1965), pp. 31, 32.

6. Harold L. Fickett Jr., *James* (Glendale, CA: Regal, 1973), p. 52.

7. Charles Colson, *Kingdoms in Conflict* (New York/Grand Rapids, MI: William Morrow/Zondervan, 1987), p. 307.

8. Martin, *Word Biblical Commentary, Volume 8, James*, p. 65, writes, "He uses the definite article . . . which suggests that he did not mean to imply that God had chosen all the poor because they were poor, but simply that God chose poor people (Bammel, TDNT, 6:911)."

9. John Calvin, *A Harmony of the Gospels Matthew, Mark and Luke; and James and Jude*, trans. A. W. Morrison, Calvin's New Testament Commentaries, vol. 3 (Grand Rapids, MI: Eerdmans, 1972), p. 278.

Chapter Ten: The Perils of Favoritism

1. John Blanchard, *Truth for Life* (West Sussex, UK: H. E. Walter Ltd., 1982), p. 130, tells the story recorded in Ernest Gordon, *Through the Valley of the Kwai* (New York: Harper and Row, 1975).

2. Peter Davids, *The Epistle of James* (Grand Rapids, MI: Eerdmans, 1982), p. 115.

3. Ibid., p. 117, says:

> That this unitary conception of the law was held by Jews is clear, for it first occurs in the LXX of Dt. 27:26 and then in a variety of later Jewish writings (Philo *Leg All.* 3:214; 4 Macc. 5:20; Test. Ash. 2:5;b. Shab. 70b; *Sipre* on Dt. 187; *Pesig. R.* 50:1; *Nu. Rab.* 9:12 on Nu. 5:14; cf. Str-B III. 755). More important is the fact that the Jesus tradition contains the same idea (Mt. 5:18–19; 23:23) and so does Paul (Gal. 5:3), which means this unitary concept of the law was current in Christian circles as well.

4. Robert K. Johnstone, *Lectures Exegetical and Practical on the Epistle of James* (Minneapolis: Klock & Klock, 1978), p. 191.

5. Davids, *The Epistle of James*, p. 117.

6. Elisabeth Elliot, *A Chance to Die: The Life and Legacy of Amy Carmichael* (Old Tappan, NJ: Revell, 1987), p. 31.

7. Davids, *The Epistle of James*, p. 119 says, "Certainly the connection must be that in humiliating the poor (whom God honors) and in transgressing the law of love (thus breaking the law) they are also failing to show mercy. As such they could expect no mercy in the final judgment."

Chapter Eleven: Real Faith, Part 1

1. *Leadership*, vol. 4, no. 3 (Summer 1983), p. 81.

2. D. Edmond Hiebert, *The Epistle of James* (Chicago: Moody Press, 1979), p. 177, says, "The negative *me* at the head of the question implies that the answer must be a resounding no."

3. Ibid., p. 174, says in note 1:

Martin Luther, Preface to his 1522 edition of the New Testament. The reference to James as "a right strawy epistle" appeared only in the 1522 edition. See John Dillenberger, ed., *Martin Luther, Selections from His Writings*, pp. 18, 19. Later Luther recognized James's contribution.

4. Douglas J. Moo, *The Letters of James* (Grand Rapids, MI: Eerdmans, 1988), p. 102.

5. James Hardy Ropes, *A Critical and Exegetical Commentary on the Epistle of St. James* (Edinburgh: T. & T. Clark, 1968), p. 208.

6. Paul Johnson, *Intellectuals* (New York: Harper and Row, 1988), pp. 10, 18.

7. Ibid., p. 16.

8. Ibid., p. 21.

9. John Blanchard, *Truth for Life* (West Sussex, UK: H. E. Walter Ltd., 1982), p. 147.

10. Douglas Moo, *The Letters of James*, p. 106, writes:

James, then, uses the device of the imaginary objector to further his argument for the inseparability of faith and works. Any division between the two is unthinkable, indeed impossible. Genuine faith cannot exist without works. When James says to the objector, *Show me your faith apart from your works*, he is not simply challenging him to give evidence for his faith—he is suggesting that the faith the objector claims to have is not faith at all.

11. A. T. Robertson, *A Grammar of the Greek New Testament in the Light of Historical Research* (Nashville: Broadman, 1934), p. 453, renders the phrase "repose one's trust" and, p. 601, says, "The accusative suggests more than an initial act of faith (intrust)." See *Moulten Prolegomena*, p. 68. See also H. E. Dana and Julius R. Mantey, *A Manual Grammar of the Greek New Testament* (New York: Macmillan, 1963), p. 106, which says that *epi* with the accusative case emphasizes motion or direction.

12. William Barclay, *The Letters to the Corinthians* (Philadelphia: Westminster, 1956), p. 289.

Chapter Twelve: Real Faith, Part 2

1. Gary Vanderet, *Discovery Papers*, Number 3989 (May 25, 1986), "The Skill of a Genuine Faith."

2. H. C. Leupold, *Exposition of Genesis* (Grand Rapids, MI: Baker, 1975), pp. 476, 477, writes:

> The biggest word in the chapter, one of the greatest in the Old Testament! Here is the first instance of the use of the word "believe" in the Scriptures. *He'emin*, Hifil of *'aman*, "to confirm" and "support," means "trust," "believe" implying *fiducia* rather than *assensus*. It is construed with *be* as here, or with *le*. The form is unusual, perfect with *waw*, not as one would expect, imperfect with *waw* conversive. Apparently, by this device the author would indicate that the permanence of this attitude is to be stressed: not only: Abram believed just this once, but: Abram proved constant in his faith. . . .

3. Donald Grey Barnhouse, *Let Me Illustrate* (Old Tappan, NJ: Revell, 1967), pp. 105, 106.

4. Abraham Kuyper, *Women of the Old Testament* (Grand Rapids, MI: Zondervan, 1961), p. 69.

5. Martin Luther, *Commentary on the Epistle to the Romans* (Grand Rapids, MI: Kregel, 1954), p. xvii.

Chapter Thirteen: The Peril of Teaching

1. Ethel May Baldwin and David V. Benson, *Henrietta Mears and How She Did It!* (Glendale, CA: Gospel Light, 1970), pp. 176, 177.

2. Ibid., pp. 279, 280.

3. William Barclay, *The Letters of James and Peter* (Philadelphia: Westminster, 1960), p. 84.

4. Allan Bloom, *The Closing of the American Mind* (New York: Simon & Schuster, 1987), p. 20, writes:

> These are the reasons that help to explain the perversity of an adult who prefers the company of youths to that of grownups. He prefers the promising "might be" to the defective "is." Such an adult is subject to many temptations—particularly vanity and the desire to propagandize rather than teach—and the very activity brings with it the danger of preferring teaching to knowing, of adapting oneself to what the students can or want to learn, of knowing oneself only by one's students.

5. Ralph Martin, *Word Biblical Commentary, Volume 8, James* (Waco, TX: Word, 1988), p. 108: "the serious nature of assuming teaching responsibility was a widely known matter (cf. Matthew 23:1–33; Luke 20:47)."

6. Paul Johnson, *Intellectuals* (New York: Harper and Row, 1988), p. 107, note 2:

> "I have not yet met a single man who was morally as good as I, and who believed that I do not remember an instance in my life when I was not attracted to what is good and was not ready to sacrifice anything to it." He felt in his own soul "immeasurable grandeur." He was baffled by the failure of other

men to recognize his qualities: "Why does nobody love me? I am not a fool, not deformed, not a bad man, not an ignoramus. It is incomprehensible."

7. Martin, *Word Biblical Commentary, Volume 8, James*, p. 109.

8. Quotation taken from a recorded message given by Dr. Howard Hendricks at College Church in Wheaton, Illinois, June 1984.

Chapter Fourteen: The Mighty Tongue

1. Ralph Martin, *Word Biblical Commentary, Volume 8, James* (Waco, TX: Word, 1988), p. 113, says:

> With the setting of a hillside covered with dry brush or wood, such an environment is literally a tinderbox just waiting to explode at the slightest spark. The readers of the letter would have no trouble understanding this imagery and appreciating the risk of such a spark's leading to a rapidly spreading fire that would destroy everything in its path (see Elliott-Binns, "The Meaning," 48–50; Mussner, 162; Dibelius, 192; Cantinat, 172).

2. Ibid., p. 113:

> Jewish tradition is a wellspring of sayings that warn that the tongue is a flame or a fire (v 6; see Pss 10:7; 39:1–3; 83:14; 120:2–4; Prov 16:27; 26:21; Isa 30:27; Sir 28:13–26 [esp. v 22: "it (the tongue) will not be master over the godly, and they will not be burned in its flame"]; Pss Sol 12:2–3).

3. Douglas J. Moo, *The Letters of James* (Grand Rapids, MI: Eerdmans, 1988), p. 124, explains:

> The most natural translation of the phrase, which gives *kosmos* the same meaning it has in three of its other occurrences in James (1:27; 4:4), is "the unrighteous world." The phrase is then parallel to Luke 16:9, *mamona tes adikias* (= "unrighteous mammon"), and uses "world" in its well-attested New Testament sense—the fallen, rebellious, sinful world-system.

4. Ibid., p. 125, explains: ". . . the meaning of the verb *kathistatai* while it could be passive ('is appointed'), James uses the same verb in 4:4 with a reflexive, middle meaning: 'makes itself.' i. e., the tongue places itself, as the world of evil, among the parts of the body."

5. Ibid., p. 125; cf. Martin, *Word Biblical Commentary, Volume 8, James*, p. 115.

6. D. Edmond Hiebert, *The Epistle of James* (Chicago: Moody Press, 1979), p. 218, gives an excellent brief summary of the derivation and meaning of Gehenna.

7. John Calvin, *A Harmony of the Gospels Matthew, Mark and Luke; and James and Jude*, trans. A. W. Morrison, Calvin's New Testament Commentaries, vol. 3 (Grand Rapids, MI: Eerdmans, 1972), p. 291.

8. Peter Marshall, "Robe, Ring and Fatted Calf," in Clyde E. Fant Jr. and William M. Pinson Jr., eds., *20 Centuries of Great Preaching* (Waco, TX: Word, 1976), p. 23.

9. John Blanchard, *Truth for Life* (West Sussex, UK: H. E. Walter Ltd., 1982), p. 108.

10. Frederick W. Robertson, *Sermons Preached at Brighton* (New York: Harper and Brothers, n.d.), p. 444.

11. Douglas J. Moo, *The Letters of James* (Grand Rapids, MI: Eerdmans, 1988), p. 127.

Chapter Fifteen: Wisdom from Below

1. J. I. Packer, *Knowing God* (Downers Grove, IL: InterVarsity Press, 1973), p. 92. Note: the book contains two helpful chapters on wisdom—Chapter 9 ("God Only Wise," pp. 80–88) and Chapter 10 ("God's Wisdom and Ours," pp. 89–97).

2. Ibid., p. 93.

3. Ibid., p. 91.

4. Colin Brown, *The New International Dictionary of New Testament Theology,* vol. 2 (Grand Rapids, MI: Zondervan, 1979), pp. 256–67.

5. William Barclay, *A New Testament Wordbook* (New York: Harper and Brothers, n.d.), p. 103.

6. M. R. Vincent, *Word Studies in the New Testament* (Wilmington, DE: Associated Publishers and Authors, 1972), p. 30.

7. James Hardy Ropes, *A Critical and Exegetical Commentary on the Epistle of St. James* (Edinburgh: T. & T. Clark, 1968), p. 245.

8. John Blanchard, *Truth for Life* (West Sussex, UK: H. E. Walter Ltd., 1982), p. 187.

9. Ibid.

10. Ropes, *A Critical and Exegetical Commentary on the Epistle of St. James,* p. 266, says that *erithia* "really means the vice of a leader of a party created for his own pride: it is party ambition, party rivalry."

11. Peter Davids, *The Epistle of James* (Grand Rapids, MI: Eerdmans, 1982), p. 151.

12. Ralph Martin, *Word Biblical Commentary, Volume 8, James* (Waco, TX: Word, 1988), p. 134, says:

> But something more radical is being suggested. The behavior of those in question is thought to be instigated by the demons themselves (so Moo, 134; Davids, 153; Adamson, 152–53). Demonic forces are viewed in the NT as responsible for thoughts and actions in opposition to God (2 Thess 2:9; 1 Tim 4:1; Rev 6:13–14; cf. Foerster, *TDNT* 2:19; see also Ropes, 148–49). The tongue, according to 3:6, is an unruly member that originated from a demonic region. Moo (134) catches the meaning of James' thoughts here when he writes that the wisdom of those in 3:14 is "characterized by 'the world, the flesh, and the devil.'"

Chapter Sixteen: Wisdom from Above

1. Annie Dillard, *Teaching a Stone to Talk*, Chapter 1, "An Expedition to the Pole" (New York: Harper & Row, 1988), p. 24.

2. Ibid., pp. 24–27. See also Day Otis Kellogg, ed., *The Encyclopedia Britannica*, vol. 9, Ninth Edition (New York: The Werner Company, 1898), pp. 719–22 for a detailed account.

3. James Hardy Ropes, *A Critical and Exegetical Commentary on the Epistle of St. James* (Edinburgh: T. & T. Clark, 1968), p. 249.

4. James Adamson, *The Epistle of James* (Grand Rapids, MI: Eerdmans, 1989), p. 154.

5. Douglas J. Moo, *The Letter of James* (Grand Rapids, MI: Eerdmans, 1988), p. 135.

6. Ibid.

7. Richard Chenevix Trench, *Synonyms of the New Testament* (London: Kegan Paul, Trench, Trubner & Co., 1901), pp. 144, 147, says:

> "Gentle" and "gentleness," on the whole, commend themselves as the best; but the fact remains, which also in a great measure excuses so much vacillation here, namely, that we have no words in English which are full equivalents of the Greek.

8. Ibid., pp. 144, 145.

9. Adamson, *The Epistle of James*, p. 155.

10. Moo, *The Letter of James*, p. 136.

11. Ropes, *A Critical and Exegetical Commentary on the Epistle of St. James*, p. 250.

12. D. Edmond Hiebert, *The Epistle of James* (London: Hodder and Stoughton, 1985), p. 236.

13. Moo, *The Letter of James*, p. 137.

Chapter Seventeen: Troubles' Source

1. Annie Dillard, *Teaching a Stone to Talk*, Chapter 1, "An Expedition to the Pole" (New York: Harper and Row, 1988), p. 23.

2. Robert K. Johnstone, *Lectures Exegetical and Practical on the Epistle of James* (Minneapolis: Klock & Klock, 1978), p. 296.

3. Leslie B. Flynn, *Great Church Fights* (Wheaton, IL: Victor Books, 1976), p. 7.

4. Ralph Martin, *Word Biblical Commentary, Volume 8, James* (Waco, TX: Word, 1988), p. 144, writes:

> Since James and his community were situated in a Zealot-infested society and since it is quite conceivable that (at least) some of the Jewish Christians were former Zealots (cf. Luke 6:15; Acts 1:13), the taking of another's life is not out of the realm of possibility for the church members as a response to disagreement (in fact such action may have already taken place . . .).

5. D. Edmond Hiebert, *The Epistle of James* (Chicago: Moody Press, 1979), p. 242; cf. Martin, *Word Biblical Commentary, Volume 8, James*, p. 144.

6. *BAG*, p. 344. See also Sophie Laws, *A Commentary on the Epistle of James* (San Francisco: Harper and Row, 1980), p. 168, who supports the English rendering of the desire or pursuit of pleasures, saying

> It is unnecessary to take pleasure, *hedone*, here as equivalent to "desire," *epithumia*, as Dibelius does, comparing i, 13; it is obviously desire for an object that leads to striving for it, but it is the object desired that is the

focus of the striving, and James in v. 3 considers the nature of this object in relation to the satisfaction or frustration of desire. Desire and its object each presumes the other, and the object here is *hedone*, a word used often, though not always, of sensual pleasure, and frequently with overtones of unworthy or evil enjoyment, as here and in Lk. viii. 14; Tit. iii. 3.

7. James Hardy Ropes, *A Critical and Exegetical Commentary on the Epistle of St. James* (Edinburgh: T. & T. Clark, 1968), p. 253, and William Barclay, *The Letters of James and Peter* (Philadelphia: Westminster, 1960), p. 115.

8. Peter Davids, *The Epistle of James* (Grand Rapids, MI: Eerdmans, 1982), p. 157, urges convincingly that "the fight is within the body of the individual Christian."

9. Neil Postman, *Amusing Ourselves to Death* (New York: Penguin Books, 1986), from the Foreword.

10. Laws, *A Commentary on the Epistle of James*, p. 170, writes:

However there is no evidence that "murder" would be commonly understood in such a non-specific sense. The extension of its meaning is clearly stated in the Matthean and Johannine passages, and it is unlikely that even a Christian author who has absorbed much of the teaching of Jesus, as James has, would simply assume it (if the author of 1 Jn is dependent on that teaching, he still finds it necessary to tell Christian readers that hatred is to be seen as murder, he does not simply use "murder" to mean "hatred").

11. Douglas J. Moo, *The Letters of James* (Grand Rapids, MI: Eerdmans, 1988), p. 140, gives the reasons for supporting placing a full stop after "kill." Similar views are given by Ropes, Martin, and Hiebert *en loc.*

12. Annie Dillard, *The Writing Life* (New York: Harper and Row, 1989), pp. 17, 18.

13. John Blanchard, *Truth for Life* (West Sussex, UK: H. E. Walter Ltd., 1982), p. 217.

14. Ibid.

15. Ibid., pp. 222, 223.

16. C. S. Lewis, *The Screwtape Letters and Screwtape Proposes a Toast* (London: Geoffrey Bles, 1961), p. 50.

17. John Piper, *Desiring God* (Portland: Multnomah, 1986), p. 15.

18. Ibid., p. 14.

Chapter Eighteen: He Gives Us More Grace

1. Douglas J. Moo, *The Letters of James* (Grand Rapids, MI: Eerdmans, 1988), p. 146.

2. Ralph Martin, *Word Biblical Commentary, Volume 8, James* (Waco, TX: Word, 1988, p. 150, argues:

But there is another argument that speaks against construing "the human spirit" as the subject. . . . To take 4:5b as a scriptural confirmation of human jealousy would require that the author has returned to his description of human nature in vv 1–3, but in v 4 James has issued a call to repentance, warning his readers that friendship with the world means enmity with God. Thus, more than likely, v 5 is set down to highlight God's displeasure with the behavior reported in vv 1–4. To conclude, therefore, that the subject . . . is the human spirit is fraught with much difficulty.

3. James Hardy Ropes, *A Critical and Exegetical Commentary on the Epistle of St. James* (Edinburgh: T. & T. Clark, 1968), p. 264, says, "'yearn,' 'yearns over' . . . the longing affection of the lover."

4. Moo, *The Letters of James*, p. 147.

5. John Blanchard, *Truth for Life* (West Sussex, UK: H. E. Walter Ltd., 1982), p. 239.

6. Ibid.

7. Charles H. Spurgeon, *The Metropolitan Tabernacle Pulpit*, vol. 30 (Pasadena, TX: Pilgrim Publications, 1973), p. 141.

Chapter Nineteen: The Gravity of Grace

1. Carl F. H. Henry, *Confessions of a Theologian, An Autobiography* (Waco, TX: Word, 1986), p. 388, says:

History has reserved for renegade humanity in our century an eager embrace of what ancient, medieval and early modern sages fled like a dread disease—the illusion that the human species is the sole crown of the cosmos, generator of the good, touchstone of truth, fashioner of the future and designer of destiny.

2. Clarence Macartney, *The Making of a Minister* (Great Neck, NY: Channel Press, 1961), p. 123, writes:

In that same conversation with Wilson at the Friars Club I heard him say of Henry Van Dyke, quoting, I think, what someone else had said, that Van Dyke was the only man he had ever known who could "strut sitting down."

3. Peter Davids, *The Epistle of James* (Grand Rapids, MI: Eerdmans, 1982), p. 165. Also see Martin and Moo *en loc.*

4. John Blanchard, *Truth for Life* (West Sussex, UK: H. E. Walter Ltd., 1982), p. 254.

5. Charles Colson, *Who Speaks for God?* (Wheaton, IL: Crossway Books, 1985), p. 153.

6. J. Oswald Sanders, *Spiritual Leadership* (Chicago: Moody Press, 1967), p. 60.

7. C. H. Spurgeon, *Lectures to My Students* (Grand Rapids, MI: Zondervan, 1969), pp. 166, 167.

8. Ralph Martin, *Word Biblical Commentary, Volume 8, James* (Waco, TX: Word, 1988), p. 154.

Chapter Twenty: Watch What You Say

1. Walter Wangerin Jr., *Ragman and Other Cries of Faith* (San Francisco: Harper and Row, 1984), p. 26.

2. D. Edmond Hiebert, *The Epistle of James* (Chicago: Moody Press, 1979), p. 266, writes, "The compound verb literally means to 'speak down on' (compare the common expression 'running each other down')."

3. Gerhard Kittle, ed., *Theological Dictionary of the New Testament*, vol. 4 (Grand Rapids, MI: Eerdmans, 1968), p. 5, writes that "It violates the early Christian commandment because of its uncharitableness rather than its falsity."

4. Sophie Laws, *A Commentary on the Epistle of James* (San Francisco: Harper and Row, 1980), p. 187.

5. Douglas J. Moo, *The Letters of James* (Grand Rapids, MI: Eerdmans, 1988), p. 164.

6. Peter Davids, *The Epistle of James* (Chicago: Moody Press, 1982), p. 170, writes:

> His sole right to judge forms a theme in John and Paul (John 5; Rom. 14:4). This is because only God has authority over life and death (Gn. 18:25; Dt. 33:39; 1 Sa. 2:6; 2 Ki. 5:7; Ps. 75:7; Is. 33:22; Mt. 10:28; Heb. 5:7; 2 Tim. 4:8; IQS 10:18; m. Ab. 4:8; Hermas *Man.* 12.6.3; Sim. 9.23.4; *Mek. Amalek* 1 on Ex. 17:9; 1 Clem. 59:3); thus usurping his judging authority by judging a person is really a blaspheming of God (so also Test. Gad 4:1–2).

7. Wangerin, *Ragman and Other Cries of Faith*, p. 27.

Chapter Twenty-One: *Deo Volente*

1. Charles Colson, *Kingdoms in Conflict* (New York/Grand Rapids, MI: William Morrow/Zondervan, 1987), pp. 182, 183.

2. Walker Percy, *The Moviegoer* (New York: Ivy Books, 1960), pp. 199, 200.

3. Mike Mason, *The Mystery of Marriage* (Portland: Multnomah, 1985), p. 71.

4. Ralph Martin, *Word Biblical Commentary, Volume 8, James* (Waco, TX: Word, 1988), pp. 167, 168, writes:

> Some translations understand ἀλαζονεία (pretensions) as modifying the verb "to boast" (NIV, "boast and brag"'; RSV, "you boast in your arrogance"). But to take the noun (which in the text is plural) as describing the manner of the boasting is not the only possibility. The preposition ("about"), when following καυχᾶσαι (sixteen times in the NT; e.g., Rom 2:17; 2:23) always points to the object of the boast. . . . The essence of ἀλαζονεία is rooted firmly in the worldly mindset (see 1 John 2:16 ἀλαζονεία τοῦβίου "the pride of life"). The final estimate is that the merchants of 4:13–16, though probably acting "piously enough" (Davids, 123) at church, actually brag (to other merchants?) that they—not God—control everything in life. They not only omit God from their plan-making (4:13) but they boast about their presumed independence as well.

> Gerhard Delling, *TDNT* 1, p. 27, expresses a similar understanding writing:

> In 1 Jn. 2:16 this denotes the attitude of the cosmic man who does not ask concerning the will of the Father but tries to make out that he himself may sovereignly decide concerning the shape of his life, whereas in actuality the decision lies with God, as is seen in the passing away of the world (v. 17). This is worked out with an example in Jm. 4:16, where ἀλαζονεῖαι are expressions of the ἀλαζονεία which acts as if it could dispose of the future, whereas this is really under the control of the will of God (v. 15).

The Williams translation reads, "But, as it is, you boast of your proud pretensions. All such boasting is wicked." Similarly, Moffatt, "but here you are, boasting
of your proud pretensions. All such boasting is wicked."

5. Douglas J. Moo, *The Letters of James* (Grand Rapids, MI: Eerdmans, 1988),
p. 158, writes:

> More probable is the supposition that James adds the saying as an en-
> couragement to do what he has just commanded. He has told his read-
> ers *what is right*; if they now *fail to do it*, they are sinning. They cannot
> take refuge in the plea that they have done nothing positively wrong; as
> Scripture makes abundantly clear, sins of *omission* are as real and serious
> as sins of *commission*. The servant in Jesus' parable who fails to use the
> money he was entrusted with (Lk. 19:11–27); the "goats" who failed to
> care for the outcasts of society (Mt. 25:31–46)—they are condemned for
> what they failed to do. Another teaching of Jesus reminds us very forcibly
> of James' words here: "that servant who knew his master's will, but did
> not make ready or act according to his will, shall receive a severe beating"
> (Lk. 12:47).

6. James Hastings, ed., *The Speaker's Bible, James* (Grand Rapids, MI: Baker,
1971), p. 177.

Chapter Twenty-Two: Riches That Corrode

1. George Arthur Buttrick, ed., *The Interpreter's Bible*, vol. 12 (New York:
Abingdon, 1957), pp. 62, 63.

2. Douglas J. Moo, *The Letters of James* (Grand Rapids, MI: Eerdmans, 1988),
p. 159.

3. Jack Mabley, "Their Riches Grow, but the Veggies Get Smaller," *The Daily
Herald*, October 24, 1988, Section 1, p. 8.

4. Paul Wachtel, *The Poverty of Affluence* (New York: Free Press, 1983), p. 5;
William Manchester, *The Last Lion, William Spencer Churchill* (Boston: Little,
Brown and Company, 1983), p. 79.

5. Cecil F. Alexander, "All Things Bright and Beautiful," 1848.

6. James Hardy Ropes, *A Critical and Exegetical Commentary on the Epistle of
St. James* (Edinburgh: T. & T. Clark, 1968), p. 283.

7. D. Edmond Hiebert, *The Epistle of James* (Chicago: Moody Press, 1979),
p. 290.

8. Ropes, *A Critical and Exegetical Commentary on the Epistle of St. James*,
p. 285.

9. Ralph Martin, *Word Biblical Commentary, Volume 8, James* (Waco, TX:
Word, 1988), p. 178.

10. Irving Stone, *Lust for Life* (New York: Pocket Books, 1963), pp. 23–79,
esp. pp. 76–79.

11. Hiebert, *The Epistle of James*, p. 290.

12. Lance Morrow, *The Chief, A Memoir of Fathers and Sons* (New York: Macmillan, 1984), p. 225.

13. Ropes, *A Critical and Exegetical Commentary on the Epistle of St. James*,
p. 289.

14. Martin, *Word Biblical Commentary, Volume 8, James*, p. 180.

15. John Calvin, *A Harmony of the Gospels Matthew, Mark and Luke; and James and Jude*, trans. A. W. Morrison, Calvin's New Testament Commentaries, vol. 3 (Grand Rapids, MI: Eerdmans, 1972), p. 307.

16. Moo, *The Letters of James*, p. 166, writes:

> . . . but it is far better to take the reference generically, as a way of describing the kind of man whom the rich persecute. This "righteous man" is one who is "poor and needy" and who trusts in God for his deliverance. He is often pictured as being persecuted by the wicked rich. In Wisdom 2:6–20, for instance, the desire of the wicked who live luxuriously in this life, with no thought for tomorrow, is to "oppress the righteous poor man" (v. 10) and to "condemn him to a shameful death" (v. 20). It is this widespread Jewish tradition (*cf.* also Pss. 10:8–9; 37:32) that James utilizes here to describe the excesses of the rich (*cf.* also Jas. 2:5–7).

17. John Oxenham, *The King's High Way* (London: Methuen, 1916), p. 16.

Chapter Twenty-Three: Patient Till He Comes

1. Ellen Thompson, retired Wheaton College professor of music, personal correspondence with the author, June 3, 1990.

2. William Barclay, *The Letters of James and Peter* (Philadelphia: Westminster, 1960), pp. 143, 144.

3. D. Edmond Hiebert, *The Epistle of James* (Chicago: Moody Press, 1979), p. 296. It is found in Matthew 24:3, 27, 37, 39; Mark 14:62; 1 Corinthians 15:23; 1 Thessalonians 2:19; 3:13; 4:15; 2 Thessalonians 2:1, 8; 2 Peter 1:16; 3:4; 1 John 2:28.

4. Douglas J. Moo, *The Letters of James* (Grand Rapids, MI: Eerdmans, 1988), p. 168.

5. John Piper, *Desiring God* (Portland: Multnomah, 1986), p. 104.

6. Stephen Jay Gould, *The Panda's Thumb, More Reflections in Natural History* (New York: W.W. Norton, 1980), p. 253.

7. Robert K. Johnstone, *Lectures Exegetical and Practical on the Epistle of James* (Minneapolis: Klock & Klock, 1978), pp. 372, 373.

8. John Calvin, *A Harmony of the Gospels Matthew, Mark and Luke, Volume III and The Epistles of James and Jude*, trans. A. W. Morrison (Grand Rapids, MI: Eerdmans, 1972), p. 310.

9. Piper, *Desiring God*, p. 84.

Chapter Twenty-Four: The Perseverance of Job

1. Joseph Katz, ed., *The Complete Poems of Stephen Crane* (Ithaca, NY: Cornell University Press, 1972), p. 125.

2. D. Edmond Hiebert, *The Epistle of James* (Chicago: Moody Press, 1979), p. 302, writes:

> The former noun, which occurs only here in the New Testament, is a compound form meaning "to suffer what is base or evil, to suffer misfortune." The term may have a passive sense denoting the suffering or miseries that

come upon a person, but here it probably has an active force to denote the strenuous efforts made to endure the difficult situation. The second noun (see the verbal form in v. 7) points to their brave endurance without succumbing to the afflictions.

3. Don Richardson, *Lords of the Earth* (Glendale, CA: Regal, 1977), pp. 304, 305.

4. Douglas J. Moo, *The Letters of James* (Grand Rapids, MI: Eerdmans, 1988), p. 171.

5. Malcolm Muggeridge, *Jesus Rediscovered* (Garden City, NY: Doubleday, 1979), pp. 158, 159.

6. Ralph Martin, *Word Biblical Commentary, Volume 8, James* (Waco, TX: Word, 1988), p. 175.

7. William Barclay, *The Letters of James and Peter* (Philadelphia: Westminster, 1960), pp.147, 148.

8. Peter Davids, *The Epistle of James* (Grand Rapids, MI: Eerdmans, 1982), p. 188.

Chapter Twenty-Five: Straight Talk

1. Mortimer J. Adler and Charles Van Doren, *How to Read a Book* (New York: Simon & Schuster, 1972), p. 165.

2. Paul Johnson, *Intellectuals* (New York: Harper and Row, 1988), pp. 154, 155.

3. Greville Macdonald, *Reminiscences of a Specialist* (London: George Allen & Unwin Ltd., 1932), p. 64.

4. Herbert Danby, trans., *The Mishnah* (London: The Oxford University Press, 1974), pp. 408–21.

5. D. A. Carson, *The Sermon on the Mount* (Grand Rapids, MI: Baker, 1978), p. 47.

6. Helmut Thielicke, *Life Can Begin Again* (Philadelphia: Westminster, 1980), p. 55.

7. James Hastings, *The Speaker's Bible, James* (Grand Rapids, MI: Baker, 1971), p. 128.

8. Ibid., p. 130.

9. Thielicke, *Life Can Begin Again*, p. 59.

Chapter Twenty-Six: The Divine Prescription for Healing

1. Elisabeth Elliot, *A Chance to Die: The Life and Legacy of Amy Carmichael* (Old Tappan, NJ: Revell, 1987), pp. 233, 234.

2. John Blanchard, *Truth for Life* (West Sussex, UK: H. E. Walter Ltd., 1982), pp. 330, 331, gives the idea eloquent expression:

Two Christians fall ill, and both call for the elders of the church. They are prayed over, and anointed with oil. One dies, and the other is healed. Why? Hold their cases alongside James's words, and see if there can be any scriptural explanation. In both cases, there are certain *visible* factors that can be checked off as identical in each case. Both are sick, both call for the elders, in both cases the elders come, in both cases the sufferer is prayed over and anointed with oil.

3. Kirsopp Lake, trans., *Eusebius, The Ecclesiastical History*, vol. 1, 2.23 (Cambridge, MA: Harvard University Press, 1965), pp. 170, 171.

4. Ralph Martin, *Word Biblical Commentary, Volume 8, James* (Waco, TX: Word, 1988), p. 215, says:

> Yet believers are still mortal men and women, and no person can be so self-deluded as to imagine that v. 15 guarantees immunity from a final illness that leads to the terminus of one's earthly pilgrimage, which comes to all and to some sooner than they desire.

5. Douglas J. Moo, *The Letters of James* (Grand Rapids, MI: Eerdmans, 1988), p. 178.

6. Ibid., pp. 179, 180.

7. D. Edmond Hiebert, *The Epistle of James* (Chicago: Moody Press, 1979), p. 321.

8. Moo, *The Letters of James*, p. 177, says:

> Only here in Biblical Greek is *proseychomai* (pray) followed by *epi*: it may simply indicate physical position, but could possibly imply that hands were also laid *on* the sick person (see Mt. 19:13). This prayer is to be accompanied by *anointing with oil*—probably at the same time as the praying (viewing the aorist participle, with most commentators, as contemporaneous), but also possibly as a preliminary to the prayer.

9. Ibid., p. 186, writes:

> What we are suggesting, then is that the faith with which we pray is always faith in the God whose will is supreme and best; only sometimes does this faith include assurance that a particular request is within that will. This is exactly the qualification that is needed to understand Jesus' own promise: "if you ask anything in my name, I will do it" (Jn. 14:14). To ask "in Jesus' name" means not simply to utter his name, but to take into account his will. Only those requests offered "in that will" are granted. Prayer for healing offered in the confidence that God will answer that prayer *does* bring healing; but only when it is God's will to heal will that faith, itself a gift of God, be present. Such faith cannot be "manufactured," however gifted, insistent, or righteous we are.

10. Blanchard, *Truth for Life*, p. 334.

11. Peter Davids, *The Epistle of James* (Grand Rapids, MI: Eerdmans, 1982), p. 195.

Chapter Twenty-Seven: The Prayer of the Righteous

1. D. Edmond Hiebert, *The Epistle of James* (Chicago: Moody Press, 1979), p. 325.

2. Dietrich Bonhoeffer, *Life Together* (New York: Harper and Row, 1954), p. 112.

3. Ibid., p. 114.

4. Ibid., p. 120.

5. Ibid., p. 113.

6. Ibid., pp. 117, 118, where Bonhoeffer says:

Does all this mean that confession to a brother is a divine law? No, confession is not a law, it is an offer of divine help for the sinner. It is possible that a person may by God's grace break through to certainty, new life, the Cross, and fellowship without benefit of confession to a brother. It is possible that a person may never know what it is to doubt his own forgiveness and despair of his own confession of sin, that he may be given everything in his own private confession to God. We have spoken here for those who cannot make this assertion. Luther himself was one of those for whom the Christian life was unthinkable without mutual, brotherly confession. In the *Large Catechism* he said: "Therefore when I admonish you to confession I am admonishing you to be a Christian." Those who, despite all their seeking and trying cannot find the great joy of fellowship, the Cross, the new life, and certainty should be shown the blessing that God offers us in mutual confession. Confession is within the liberty of the Christian. Who can refuse, without suffering loss, a help that God has deemed it necessary to offer?

7. Hiebert, *The Epistle of James*, p. 328.

8. Gerhard Kittle, ed., *Theological Dictionary of the New Testament*, vol. 2 (Grand Rapids, MI: Eerdmans, 1968), p. 930.

9. Douglas J. Moo, *The Letters of James* (Grand Rapids, MI: Eerdmans, 1988), p. 188.

10. James Hastings, ed., *The Speakers Bible*, vol. 18 (Grand Rapids, MI: Baker, 1971), p. 2211.

11. Joseph B. Mayor, *The Epistle of St. James* (Minneapolis: Klock & Klock, 1977), pp. 177–79; James Hardy Ropes, *A Critical and Exegetical Commentary on the Epistle of St. James* (Edinburgh: T. & T. Clark, 1968), p. 309; Peter Davids, *The Epistle of James* (Grand Rapids, MI: Eerdmans, 1982), p. 197.

12. Bonhoeffer, *Life Together*, pp. 117, 118.

13. Elisabeth Elliot, *A Chance to Die: The Life and Legacy of Amy Carmichael* (Old Tappan, NJ: Revell, 1987), p. 13.

Chapter Twenty-Eight: Spiritual Reclamation

1. Peter Davids, *The Epistle of James* (Grand Rapids, MI: Eerdmans, 1982), p. 198, explains:

James concludes with a final exhortation which on the one hand flows out of the theme of confession and forgiveness of the preceding section (5:13–18) and on the other gives what must have been the author's purpose in publishing the epistle, i.e. turning or preserving people from error (cf. the similarity in 1 John 5:21). The address indicates that these verses are a separate unit, but one cannot look at the formal separation and juxtaposition of traditional themes beside one another without remembering that there is often an internal thematic connection, a reason why the segments are placed where they are, whatever the source, as is apparent in this case.

2. Douglas J. Moo, *The Letters of James* (Grand Rapids, MI: Eerdmans, 1988), p. 189.

3. Billy Graham, *The Annals of America*, vol. 17, p. 395.

4. F. F. Bruce, "In Conclusion," *The Reformed Journal* (October 1990), p. 15.

5. Kenneth L. Woodward, "A Time to Seek," *Newsweek* (December 17, 1990), p. 54.

6. C. H. Spurgeon, *The Metropolitan Tabernacle Pulpit*, vol. 19 (Pasadena, TX: Pilgrim Publications, 1971), p. 580.

Scripture Index

Genesis
1:18   50
3:6   42
3:12   40
4:10   194
14   106
15:1   106
15:4   106
15:5   106
15:6   106, 107, 109, 111, 112
15:17   107
17   106
18:25   268n6
22   107, 108
22:2   107
22:3   107
22:4   108
22:5   108
22:16–18   108
32:22–32   242

Exodus
17:9   268n6
20:1–17   90
20:5   157
34:14   157

Leviticus
19:12   221
19:13   193
19:15   82
19:18   90, 174

Numbers
12:3   120, 134
30:2   221

Deuteronomy
6:4   90, 100
6:5   90, 100
10:20   221
23:21   222
24:14   193
24:15   193

32:39   175
33:39   268n6

Joshua
2:9–11   111

Judges
7:20   173
12:4–6   71

1 Samuel
1:14   242
1:15   242
2:6   175
3:10   58
17:45   194
17:46   194
17:55   222
25:32   143
25:33   143

1 Kings
3:9   28
3:11   28
3:12   28
17   241
17:1   242
18   241
18:1   242
18:42   242
18:45   242
22:24–27   208

2 Kings
5:7   268n6

Ezra
9:5   242
9:6   242

Nehemiah
1:4ff.   242

Job
1:1   211

1:4	211	16:11	152
1:5	211	18:30	50
1:7	212	19:7	50, 258n7
1:8	120, 212	32:1	249
1:9–11	212	34:8	152
1:12	212	34:15	240
1:15	212	37:4	152
1:16	212	37:32	270n16
1:17	212	39:1–3	263n2
1:18	212	39:5	182
1:19	212	42:1	152
1:20	212	42:2	152
1:21	212	46:10	58
2:4–6	213	51:6	226
2:9	213	63:1	152
2:10	213	66:18	231, 240
3:1	213	75:7	268n6
3:11–19	213	83:14	263n2
7:6	182	85:2	249
7:9	182	90:12	183
7:11	213	102:3	182
7:12	213	102:11	182
9:25	182	103:15	182
9:26	182	106:33	120
10:18	213	111:10	25, 132, 133
13:15	214	119	133
16:2	213	119:97–100	133
16:3	213	120:2–4	263n1
16:19	214	139:23	231
19:17	215	139:24	231
19:25	214		
19:25–27	214	*Proverbs*	
23:2	213	1:7	25, 132
28:12	25	1:20–23	36
28:15	25	3:27	193
28:18	25	3:28	193
28:23	25	3:34	160, 163
28:24	25	4:7–9	36
28:28	25, 132	9:1–6	29
30:20–23	213	9:10	25, 132
38–41	214	10:12	249, 250
40:4	120	10:19	59
40:7–14	175	11:2	132
42:1–6	215	11:9	123
42:5	215	12:6	123
		15:29	240
Psalms		15:33	132
10:7	263n2	16:27	263n2
10:8	270n16	16:32	60
10:9	270n16	17:22	168
14:1	26	18:8	123
15:4	222	18:21	123

22:2	83	4:5	241
25:15	123	4:6	241
26:21	263n2		
28:13	231	*Matthew*	
28:21	82	5:3	33, 84, 215, 239
29:11	60	5:4	168
		5:5	137
Isaiah		5:7	94
1:11–17	74, 75	5:8	167
5:20	76	5:10	211
6:5	128	5:12	211
6:5–7	120	5:17	66, 258n7
6:6	128	5:18	92, 260n3 (ch. 10)
6:7	128	5:19	92, 260n3 (ch. 10)
6:8	128	5:21	150, 208
30:27	263	5:22	61, 150
33:22	268n6	5:23	240
40:6–8	35	5:24	240
49:15	215	5:33–37	221
49:16	215	5:34–36	222
53:9	226	5:34	223
59:1	240	5:37	223
59:2	240	6:1–18	259n1 (ch. 8)
61:1	33, 84	6:13	42
61:2	84	6:19–21	193
		6:24	34, 191
Jeremiah		7:1	174
2:13	152	7:15	174
7:6	92	7:16	174
12:16	221	7:16–21	100
22:3	92	10:28	175, 268n6
22:13	193	11:28–30	258n7
31:31–34	258n7	11:29	134, 137
38:4–13	208	11:30	137
		12:31	127
Ezekiel		12:32	127
3:18	251	12:33	72
		12:34	72, 226
Daniel		12:35	120
4:30	185	12:36	93, 226
4:34	185	12:37	93, 227
4:35	185	13	67, 246
		13:11–13	67
Jonah		13:15	238
4:9	164	13:22	34
		13:23	100, 247
Zechariah		13:55	16
8:2	157	17:27	83
		18:15–17	252
Malachi		18:19	233
2:9	83	18:20	233
3:5	193	18:21–35	94

18:32–35	94	4:19	84
19:13	272n8	6:15	265n4 (ch. 17)
21:35	208	6:20	33, 85
21:36	208	6:24	85
22:6	208	6:24–26	160
22:37–40	90	8	246
23:1–33	262n5 (ch. 13)	8:5	246
23:5–7	117	8:6	246
23:12	169	8:7	247
23:16–22	222	8:8	247
23:23	92, 260n3 (ch. 10)	8:12	246
23:29–37	208	8:13	246
24:3	270n3	8:14	149, 247, 265n6 (ch. 17)
24:27	199, 270n3	8:15	247
24:36	199, 202	9:58	83
24:36–44	205	10:25–37	90
24:37	270n3	10:29	90
24:37–39	199	10:36	90
24:39	270n3	12:15	191
25	67	12:34	191
25:28	67	12:47	269n5 (ch. 21)
25:29	67	12:48	118
25:31–46	269n5 (ch. 21)	13:33	208
26:33	120	14:11	169
26:63	224	15:20	166
26:64	224	16:9	263n3
26:69–75	120	18:1–5	243
		18:11	173
Mark		18:14	169
2:5	231	19:11–27	269n5 (ch. 21)
4:19	191	20:47	262n5 (ch. 13)
6:3	16	23:11	260n3 (ch. 9)
7:14–23	226		
9:12	241	*John*	
9:24	28	1:12	112
9:43	249	1:16	158
9:48	125, 249	3:16	26, 112
10:17	33	3:21	248
10:22	33, 191	5	268n6
10:23–27	191	5:14	231
10:24	33	5:24	36
10:25	33	6:29	102
10:45	16	6:53	177
12:28–31	128	6:54	177
12:41–44	33	7:5	16
13:32	202	7:24	174
14:62	270n3	9:3	231
		12:40	238
Luke		13:17	68
1:17	241	14:13	233
1:48	33	14:14	272n9
4:18	33, 84	14:27	141

14:30	155
15:14	109
15:15	109
15:16	233
16:23	233
17:3	36
17:17	129, 226
20:5	66
20:11	66

Acts

1:9	199
1:11	199
1:13	16, 265n4 (ch. 17)
2:5	17
2:9–11	17
5:4	225
5:40	18
5:41	18
6:1ff.	148
7:51	208
7:52	208, 209
8:1	17
8:13	101
8:21–23	101
10:30	79, 260n3 (ch. 9)
10:34	83
11:19	17
11:20	17
12:17	16
13:39	112
14:15	241
15:13ff.	16
16:25	18
16:30	101
16:31	101, 112
17:25	26
18:21	183
19:21	183
20:9	55
20:10	56
20:11	56
20:12	56
20:31	251
21:18	16
23:3	120
27:37–44	124

Romans

1—11	15
1:9	224
1:10	183, 224
1:17	240
1:20	50
1:26	255n3
2:17	268n4 (ch. 21)
2:23	268n4 (ch. 21)
3	220
3:9–14	119
3:13	220
3:23	119
3:28	98
4:1–5	107
4:5	98, 112
5:2	32
5:3	19, 253n7
5:10	156
5:11	32
5:12	42
5:19	44
5:20	158
7:18	120
7:21–23	149
7:24	67
8:1	93, 118
8:17	32
8:18	211
8:18–22	53
8:32	26
9:3	243
10:9	101
10:10	101
10:14	129
10:15	129
10:17	52
11:3	208
12	172
12—16	15
12:1	76
12:7	16
12:18	142
14:4	268n6
14:12	93, 118
14:19	142
15:28	183
16:4	259n1 (ch. 8)

1 Corinthians

1:11	148
1:26–29	85
1:30	26, 133, 240
2:14	136
3:10–15	203
3:12–15	94, 119

3:15	34
4:5	175
4:19	183
5:1–5	252
10:13	42
11:24	177
11:25	177
11:27–32	231
12:16	253n8
15:7	16
15:23	270n3
16:5	183
16:7	183
16:22	182, 205

2 Corinthians

1:12	144
1:23	224
3:18	167
4:4	155
5:10	93, 118
5:21	177
7:4	18
7:5–7	129
8:9	83
12:7–10	233
12:20	148

Galatians

1:4	155
1:19	16
2:9	16
2:12	16
2:20	44
3:6	107, 111
3:6–14	98
3:7	107, 111
3:10	92
3:13	177
5:3	92, 260n3 (ch. 10)
5:17	149
5:22	137, 247
5:23	137, 247
6:1	239, 251
6:2	237, 239

Ephesians

1–3	15
1:4	52
1:5	52
2:8	28, 112, 118

2:9	122, 118
2:8–10	98
2:13	166
2:14	141
4–6	15
4:3	142
4:15	225
4:25	73
4:29	73
4:31	60
6	165
6:12	165
6:18	166

Philippians

1:17	117, 135
2	169
2:5–8	16
2:9–11	83, 169
2:19	183
2:27	233
3:9	240
3:18	156
3:19	156
4:2	148

Colossians

1:28	241
3:8	60
3:16	133
4:12	243

1 Thessalonians

2:15	208
2:19	270n3
3:13	270n3
4:13–18	205
4:15	270n3

2 Thessalonians

2:1	270n3
2:8	270n3
2:9	264n12
3:15	251

1 Timothy

1:15	35
1:16	34
2:5	238
2:6	238
4:1	264n12

6:9	196	1:9	31–33
6:10	190, 196	1:9, 10	31
6:17	196	1:9–12	31–36 (ch. 3 passim)
		1:10, 11	33–36
2 Timothy		1:12	36, 255n1
3:12	20	1:13	49, 265n5 (ch. 17)
4:8	268n6	1:13–15	39–45 (ch. 4 passim)
4:10	248	1:14	42–44
4:15	248	1:15	44, 45
4:20	233	1:16	49, 225n1
		1:16–18	47–53 (ch. 5 passim), 56
Titus		1:17	49–52, 164
1:7	60	1:18	52, 53, 57, 66, 258n7
2:11–13	205	1:19	57–60
3:3	149, 265n6 (ch. 17)	1:19–21	55–61 (ch. 6 passim)
		1:19–26	148
Hebrews		1:19–27	57
4:12	166	1:20	60, 61
4:16	158	1:21	61, 66, 258n7
5:7	243, 268n6	1:22	64, 65, 66, 258n7
6:3	183	1:22–25	63–68 (ch. 7 passim)
11	108, 112	1:22–27	57
11:4	112	1:23, 24	64–66
11:6	28	1:25	66–68, 258n7
11:7	112	1:26	72–74
11:8	108	1:26, 27	71–77 (ch. 8 passim),
11:9	108		259n1 (ch. 8)
11:17	108, 112	1:27	74–77, 263n3
11:18	108	2:1	82, 83
11:19	108	2:1–7	79–86 (ch. 9 passim)
11:20	112	2:1–11	148
11:22	112	2:2, 3	80
11:24	112	2:2–4	82
11:25	112	2:5–7	84–86
11:29	112	2:8–11	90–92, 258n7
11:31	111	2:8–13	89–95 (ch. 10 passim)
11:32–38	209	2:10	119, 174
11:35–38	209	2:12, 13	92–95
12:11	18	2:14	112
12:13	238	2:14–19	97–102 (ch. 11 passim),
12:22–24	32		105
13:15	129	2:15–17	98, 99
		2:18	100, 112
James		2:19	100–2
1:1	16, 17	2:20	105, 112
1:1–4	15–21 (ch. 1 passim), 23	2:20–26	105–13 (ch. 12 passim)
1:2	17, 18, 24, 26	2:21–24	106–10
1:3, 4	19–21	2:23	111
1:4	24	2:24	98, 112
1:5	24–27, 28, 133, 145	2:25, 26	110–13
1:5–8	23–29 (ch. 2 passim)	2:26	6
1:6–8	27–29	3:1	116–18, 148

3:1, 2	115–21 (ch. 13 passim)	5:7, 8	200
3:2	118–21	5:7–9	199–5 (ch. 23 passim)
3:3–5	123, 24	5:8	201–3
3:3–12	123–29 (ch. 14 passim)	5:9	203–5
3:5, 6	124–27	5:10, 11	207–16 (ch. 24 passim),
3:6	264n12		208–11
3:7, 8	127	5:11	208–16, 231
3:9	148	5:12	219–26 (ch. 25 passim)
3:10	148	5:13–16	229–35 (ch. 26 passim)
3:9–12	127–29	5:13–18	273n1
3:13	134, 140	5:14	230–32
3:13–16	131–37 (ch. 15 passim),	5:15	232–34
	140	5:16	234, 238–41, 243, 251
3:13–18	140	5:16–18	237–43 (ch. 17 passim)
3:14	135, 36, 145, 264n12	5:17, 18	18, 238, 241–43
3:15, 16	140, 144	5:19	248–52, 272n4 (ch. 26)
3:16	136, 37, 148	5:19, 20	245–52 (ch. 18 passim)
3:17	139–44	5:20	249–52
3:17, 18	139–45 (ch. 16 passim)		
3:18	144, 145	*1 Peter*	
4:1	148–50	1:4	215
4:1–3	147–53 (ch. 17 passim),	1:23	52
	266n2	2:9	32
4:1–4	266n2	2:23	177
4:2	150, 151	2:24	238
4:3	151–53, 265n6 (ch. 17)	4:7	205
4:4	155, 156, 263n3, 263n4,		
	266n2	*2 Peter*	
4:4–6	155–60 (ch. 18 passim)	1:16	270n3
4:5	156–58, 232, 266n2	3:3–9	201
4:6	158–60, 163	3:4	270n3
4:7	42	3:10–12	205
4:7, 8	165–67		
4:7–10	163–69 (ch. 19 passim)	*1 John*	
4:8	165–67, 141	Book of	266n10
4:9	168, 169	1:5	50
4:10	169	2:15	268n4 (ch. 21)
4:11	173, 174	2:16	42, 184, 268n4 (ch. 21)
4:11, 12	171–77 (ch. 20 passim)	2:17	268n4 (ch. 21)
4:12	174–77	2:28	270n3
4:13	268n4 (ch. 21)	3:3	140
4:13, 14	180–83	3:15	92
4:13–16	268n4 (ch. 21)	3:17	75, 99
4:13–17	179–86 (ch. 21 passim)	3:18	75, 99
4:14	35, 186	3:21	234
4:15, 16	183–86	3:22	234
5:1–6	189–96 (ch. 22 passim)	4:19	158
5:2, 3	192, 193	4:20	128
5:4	193, 194	4:21	128
5:5	194, 195	5:14	27, 29, 233
5:6	195, 196	5:16	251
5:7	200, 201, 270n2 (ch. 24)		

5:19	155	14:11	249
5:21	273n1	16:6	209
		18:24	209
Revelation		20:1	249
3:17	34	22:7	202
3:20	167	22:12	202
6:13	264n12	22:20	202
6:14	264n12	22:21	202

General Index

1984 (Orwell), 149

Abel, 194
Abigail, 142
Abner, 222
Abraham (Abram), 28, 106–9, 111, 112, 143, 190, 262n2 (ch. 12)
Adam, 40–43
    Second Adam, 44
Adams, Bertha, 192
Adams, Lane, 81
Adamson, James, 141
Adler, Mortimer, 219
Ahab, 208, 241
Alexander the metalworker, 248
"Amazing Grace" (Newton), 158
ambition, selfish, 44, 116, 117, 135, 136, 144, 150, 264n10
Ames, William, 11
Amundsen, 140
Anabaptists, 223
Ananias, 120, 225, 226
Ananias and Sapphira, 225, 226
anger, 60, 61, 175, 257n6 (ch. 6)
Animal Farm, The (Orwell), 149
Asbury, Francis, 102
Augustine, 128, 158, 180

Babcock, Maltbie, 76, 77
Barclay, William, 214
Barnhouse, Donald Grey, 168
Baxter, Richard, 164
Bayly, Joseph, 36, 51, 53
Bereway, 209, 210
Bernard of Clairvaux, 153
Beveridge, William, 176
Bildad, 213
Blanchard, John, 158, 234, 271n2
blessedness, 249

Bloom, Allan, 24, 117
Bonhoeffer, Dietrich, 43, 209, 238, 239, 273n6
Booth, Catherine, 81
Booth, William, 80, 81
Boxer Rebellion, 129
Brave New World (Huxley), 149
Bray, Billy, 258n4
Bright, Bill, 115
Brooks, Phillips, 11
Bruce, F. F., 249
Buckley, William, 144
Bunu, 209
Bunyan, John, 27, 258n4
Burns, Robert, 41
Byron, 126

Caiaphas, 224
Calvin, John, 34, 73, 85, 125, 195, 203, 255n3, 258n3
Carey, William, 19
Carlyle, Thomas, 185
Carmichael, Amy, 93, 229, 233
Carnegie, Dale, 105
Chesterton, G. K., 31
Chicago fire, 124, 125
Childe Harold's Pilgrimage (Byron), 126
Chrysostom (John of Antioch), 237
Churchill, Winston, 124
Closing of the American Mind, The (Bloom), 24, 117
Cohen, Mickey, 167
Collier, Richard, 80
Colson, Charles, 83, 84, 180
confession,
    of Isaiah, 120, 128
    of sin, 45, 128, 230–32, 235, 238–41, 243, 273n6, 273n1
Crane, Stephen, 49, 207, 256n3

Dale, Stan, 209, 210
Daniel, 208
David, 43, 142, 150, 182, 190, 194, 208
Davids, Peter, 20, 91, 234, 253n1, 260n3
    (ch. 10), 261n7, 264n12, 266n8,
    268n6, 268n4 (ch. 21), 273n1
Demas, 43, 248
Dibelius, Martin, 19, 253n8, 265n6 (ch.
    17)
Dickens, Charles, 47, 194
Dillard, Annie, 139, 215
Doll House, The (Ibsen), 60
double-mindedness, 28, 141, 167
Doyle, Sir Arthur Conan, 144
Dunn, Samuel, 80

Ebed-Melech, 208
Einstein, Albert, 26
Eli, 242
Eliezer, 106
Elihu, 213
Elijah, 56, 106, 208, 241–43
Eliphaz, 213
Elisha, 56
Elliot, Elisabeth, 229
Epaphras, 243
Epaphroditus, 233
ethos, 11, 12, 110
Eusebius, 16, 230
Eutychus, 55, 56, 61
Eve, 40, 42, 43
Ezekiel, 251
Ezra, 242

faith, 15, 20, 27, 28, 31–33, 48, 82, 90,
    91, 92, 95, 97–102 (ch. 11 passim),
    105–13 (ch. 12 passim), 142, 156, 165,
    166, 168, 204, 214, 226, 229, 231–35,
    246, 248, 261n10, 261n11, 262n2 (ch.
    12), 272n9
    and works, 15, 97–102 (ch. 11 pas-
        sim), 105–13 (ch. 12 passim),
        261n10
favoritism/partiality, 79–86 (ch. 9 passim),
    89–95 (ch. 10 passim)
Flint, Annie Johnson, 159
Forbes, Malcolm Stevenson Sr., 190

Fox, George, 224
Francis, Saint, 142
Franklin, Lady Jane, 139
Franklin, Sir John/Franklin Expedition,
    139, 140, 145

Gaebelein, Frank, 76
General Next to God, The (Collier), 80
Geraldo, 143
Gideon, 147, 173
"God Is Cold" (Crane), 49, 207, 215,
    256n3
Goldman, Emma, 189
Goliath, 194
Goodspeed, E. J., 15
Gordon, Ernest, 91
grace of God, 18, 20, 21, 27, 51, 52,
    67, 85, 95, 127, 128, 155–60 (ch. 18
    passim), 163–69 (ch. 19 passim), 195,
    221, 231, 239, 251, 254n5 (ch. 3),
    258n7, 273n6
Graham, Billy, 81, 115, 248
Grimes, E. May, 58

Halverson, Richard, 115
Hannah, 175, 242
Hardy, Thomas, 49
healing, 129, 229–35 (ch. 26 passim),
    238, 271n2 (ch. 26), 272n9
Hegesippus, 16
Hell, Gehenna, 101, 125, 126, 129
Hemingway, Ernest, 41, 143, 220
Hendricks, Howard, 121
Henry, Carl, 163
Henson, Matthew, 140
Herod Antipas, 260n3 (ch. 9)
Hitler, Adolf, 124
Holloman, Fred, 219
Hort, F. J. A., 25
How to Read a Book (Adler), 220
Hume, David, 12
humility/the humble, 31–36 (ch. 3 pas-
    sim), 61, 83, 91, 120, 132–34, 137,
    142, 160, 163, 169, 182, 214, 215,
    225, 231, 239, 241, 243, 254n5 (ch. 3),
    257n6 (ch. 6), 261n7
Huxley, Aldous, 149

Ibsen, Henrik, 60
Improving Your Serve (Swindoll), 63
Isaac, 107, 108
Isaiah, 74, 76, 84, 120, 128, 240

Jacob, 242
James (brother of Jesus), 16, 17, 94, 95, 199
Jeremiah, 152, 208, 221, 258n7
Jesus Rediscovered (Muggeridge), 210
Jezebel, 241
Job, 25, 120, 175, 182, 190, 207–16 (ch. 24 passim)
John, the Apostle, 29, 75, 99, 158, 202, 233, 234, 251
Johnson, Paul, 99, 262n6
Johnson, Samuel, 150
Johnstone, James Robert, 147, 259n6
Jonah, 47, 164
Jones, Jim, 116, 121
Joseph of Arimathea, 190
Josiah, 190
joy, 15–21 (ch. 1 passim), 32, 40, 43, 142, 152, 168, 184, 202, 235, 246, 273n6
judgment seat of Christ, 118, 203
justification,
    by faith, 15, 98, 100, 102, 106–13
    by works, 98–100, 102, 109, 112

Kazantzakis, Nikos, 41
Kierkegaard, Søren, 105
Kingdoms in Conflict (Colson), 83
Kingsley, Charles, 243
Kistemaker, Simon, 58, 253n4
Kusaho, 210
Kuyper, Abraham, 110

Large Catechism (Luther), 243, 273n6
law
    of God, 90–93, 106, 127, 173–76, 223, 258n7
    royal, 91, 95, 174
Leupold, H. C., 106, 262n2 (ch. 12)
Lewis, C. S., 151, 152
Liberating Ministry from the Success Syndrome (Hughes), 48
Life Together (Bonhoeffer), 238

Lincoln, Abraham, 143
listening, 57–61, 64–67
"Lite" church, 97–99, 102
logos, 11, 12
Lot, 106
Louis XV, 185
Love
    for God/Christ, 90, 91, 102, 128, 133, 156, 249
    for others, 75, 90–92, 102, 174, 225, 249, 250
    of God, 39, 48, 95, 129, 143, 147, 157–60, 166, 177, 252
Luke, 18, 33, 56, 84, 101, 260n3 (ch. 9)
Luther, Martin, 98, 111, 120, 243, 261n3, 273n6
Lydia, 190

MacDonald, George, 220, 225
MacMurray, John, 151
Martin, Ralph, 25, 79, 253n1 (ch. 2), 255n1, 260n8, 262n5 (ch. 13), 263n1, 264n12, 265n4 (ch. 17), 256n2, 268n4 (ch. 21), 272n4 (ch. 26)
Marx, Groucho, 144
Mary (mother of Jesus), 16, 33
Mary Magdalene, 66
Mason, Mike, 182
Masters, Phil, 209, 210
maturity, 20, 21, 24, 27, 120
Mears, Henrietta, 115, 121
meekness, 132, 134–37, 140
Melbourne, Lord, 180
Methodists, the, 80, 81, 183, 241
Micaiah, 208
Moo, Douglas, 98, 125, 174, 258n7, 261n10, 263n3, 264n12, 266n11, 269n5 (ch. 21), 270n16, 272n8
Moody, D. L., 75
Moravians, the, 224
Morrow, Lance, 194
Moses, 28, 120, 134, 174, 208, 221
Moviegoer, The (Percy), 180
Mozart, 164
Muggeridge, Malcolm, 210
Munchausen, 220, 225
mystery parables, 246

Nabal, 142
Nalimo, 209, 210
Napoleon, 109
Neander, Joachim, 204
Nebuchadnezzar, 185
Nehemiah, 242
Newton, John, 55, 158
Nixon, Richard, 83, 84
Noah, 199

Odyssey, The (Homer), 40
Ogilvie, Lloyd John, 18
Orwell, George, 149
Owen, John, 258n4
Oxenham, John, 196

Packer, J. I., 65, 131, 132, 258n4
parable of the foolish manager, 118
parable of the good Samaritan, 90
parable of the rich fool, 191
parable of the sower, 100
parable of the talents, 67
parable of the unmerciful slave, 94
Pascal, Blaise, 152
pathos, 11, 12
Paul, the Apostle, 15, 18–20, 32, 34, 42, 50, 55, 56, 72, 83, 85, 92, 93, 98, 101, 102, 107, 111, 117, 119, 120, 124, 133, 135, 136, 142, 144, 148, 156, 158, 165, 166, 169, 183, 204, 211, 224, 225, 233, 243, 248, 251, 253n8, 260n3 (ch. 10), 268n6
Peary, Robert, 140
Pensees (Pascal), 152
Percy, Walker, 180
perseverance/patience/endurance, 19–21, 23, 36, 159, 189, 201, 203, 207–16 (ch. 24 passim), 253n7, 255n1, 270n2 (ch. 24)
Peter, 16, 32, 66, 83, 101, 120, 201, 205, 225
Philemon, 190
Philippian jailer, 101
Piper, John, 152, 203
Ponnammal, 229
Poverty of Affluence, The (Wachtel), 190

prayer, 15, 21, 36, 42, 58, 73–75, 119, 128, 133, 134, 137, 142, 160, 164, 166, 175, 184, 185, 203, 205, 211, 219, 226, 229–35 (ch. 26 passim), 237–43 (ch. 27 passim), 251, 252, 259n1 (ch. 8), 272n8, 272n9
    of faith, 229, 231–35
prayerlessness, 151
prodigal son, the, 166, 195
Psalter Hymnal, The, 35
Puritans, the, 183

Quakers, the, 224

Ragman and Other Cries of Faith (Wangerin), 171
Rahab, 106, 110, 111
Rasputin, 40
Red Badge of Courage, The (Crane), 207
Regions Beyond Missionary Union, 209
religion, true, 73, 75, 77
rich, and the poor, 31, 33–36, 79, 81–86, 91, 148, 159, 160, 181, 189–96 (ch. 22 passim), 200, 220, 247, 249, 254n5 (ch. 3), 270n16
Robertson, A. T., 25, 261n11
Rockefeller, John D. Jr., 194
Rogers, Will, 40
Ropes, J. H., 19, 25, 64, 253n7, 259n1 (ch. 8), 267n3 (ch. 18)
Rousseau, Jean-Jacques, 99
Russell, Bertrand, 100

Salieri, Antonio, 164
Salvation Army, 80, 81, 192
Samson, 43
Samuel, 58
Sanders, Oswald, 168
Sarah, 107
Sartre, Jean-Paul, 143
Saul (king), 208
Screwtape Letters (Lewis), 151
second coming of Christ, 199–205 (ch. 23 passim)
Seneca the Younger, 79, 260n2 (ch. 9)
Seume, Dick, 20

Shaftesbury, Lord, 75
Shalom, 141, 145, 165
Silas, 18
Simon the sorcerer, 101
sin, 35, 40–45, 60, 61, 65, 73, 80, 91,
    92, 95, 110, 112, 118–20, 125, 127,
    134, 135, 148, 152, 157, 158, 167–69,
    173–77, 185, 193, 195, 208, 213, 216,
    223–26, 230–32, 234, 235, 237–41,
    243, 247, 249–51, 255n2, 255n3,
    263n3, 269n5 (ch. 21), 273n6
Sinclair, Upton, 189
Sola fide, 98, 110
solidarity, with Adam, 42
    with Christ, 44, 45
Solomon, 28, 59, 60, 168
Spurgeon, Charles, 160, 168, 250
Stanton, Edwin, 143
Stephen, 17, 209
Stevenson, Adlai, 58
Stevenson, Robert Louis, 168
suffering *see* trials
Swindoll, Charles, 63, 124

Table Talks (Luther), 120
temptation, 33, 39–45 (ch. 4 passim), 117,
    160, 195, 240, 241, 262n4 (ch. 13)
Temptation (Bonhoeffer), 43
ten Boom, Corrie, 19, 209
Tess (Hardy), 49
Thielicke, Helmut, 223, 226
Thompson, Ellen, 200
Thoreau, Henry David, 144
Through the Valley of the Kwai (Gordon),
    91
Timothy, 20, 34, 196, 233
Tolstoy, Leo, 119, 174
tongue, 59, 61, 72–74, 77, 119–21,
    123–29 (ch. 14 passim), 134, 172, 248,
    263n1, 263n2, 263n4, 264n12
toughness, 19–21, 24, 36, 203
Tournier, Paul, 57
Trench, Archbishop, 142
trials/suffering, 17–21, 23–28, 31, 34, 36,
    47, 58, 159, 200, 208–11, 214, 215,

230, 231, 253n1 (ch. 2), 255n1, 270n2
    (ch. 24), 271n2 (ch. 26), 273n6
Trophimus, 233
Twain, Mark, 219

Unamuno, Miguel de, 33
Uriah the Hittite, 150

Van Dyke, Henry, 267n2 (ch. 19)
Van Gogh, Vincent, 194
Vincent, Marvin, 27

Wachtel, Paul, 190
Wangerin, Walter, 171, 176
Ward, John, 151
Welsh, Olena Mae, 143
Wesley, John, 35, 73, 74, 80, 102
Westminster Confession, 152
Whitefield, George, 12
Wiesel, Elie, 17
Williams, Gunther Gebal, 127
Wilson, Woodrow, 163
wisdom, 23–29 (ch. 2 passim), 31–36
    (ch. 3 passim), 66, 97, 139–45 (ch. 16
    passim), 183, 184, 192, 196, 200, 219,
    252, 253n1 (ch. 2)
    earthly, false, 25, 131–37 (ch. 15 pas-
    sim), 264n1 (ch.15), 264n12
Word of God, the, 11, 26, 41, 43, 53, 58,
    59, 61, 74, 82, 95, 106, 111, 118, 127,
    129, 133, 142, 164, 166, 173, 174,
    189, 190, 196, 208, 226, 246, 247,
    248, 251
    doing, 63–68 (ch. 7 passim), 74
worldliness, 32, 84, 136, 140, 141, 155,
    156, 157, 167, 191, 196, 203, 225,
    248, 264n12, 266n2, 268n4 (ch. 21)
Wycliffe, John, 134

Yemu, 209, 210

Zeno, 59
Zophar, 213
Zorba the Greek (Kazantzakis), 41

Index of Sermon Illustrations

Action

C. Swindoll's parable of an absent C.E.O. whose messages were read by his employees, even studied, but never acted upon—a parable of how so many treat God's Word, 63, 64

Aging

Our skin bears testimony to our constant changes—pinch the skin on the back of your index finger and if you are six it will snap back in place, but if you're seventy . . . , 51

Agnosticism

Charles Colson's description of searching for the UN's chapel, and finding a "meditation room" with overhead shafts of light focused on a void—"the soul of the brave new world," 179, 180

Anger

Henrik Ibsen's grotesque boast that anger increased his strength, 60

Stephen Crane's poem that pictures a bitter man eating his own heart; the feast of anger is ourselves, 60

Apostasy

The quintessential hippie who "believed in Christ" and rejected him a month later, 245

Arrogance

Nebuchadnezzar's elevation of self and his dramatic fall, 185

Atheism

Charles Colson's description of searching for the UN's chapel, and finding a "meditation room" with overhead shafts of light focused on a void—"the soul of the brave new world," 179, 180

Atonement

W. Wangerin on how a starving spider will release venomous digestive fluids into her own body so her young can feed on her, 171

Belief

Unamuno: those who believe without doubt . . . believe only in the idea of God, not God himself, 33

Bitterness

Henrik Ibsen's grotesque boast that anger increased his strength, 60

Stephen Crane's poem that pictures a bitter man eating his own heart; the feast of anger is ourselves, 60

The New York congregation that fired its priest because they did not want to "pass the peace," 147

Christian who share Communion but scowl and mistreat each other during the week, 147

Quarreling children's response: "Dad, we're playing church!" 148

Blame

The woman who blamed God for her seduction, 39, 40

The typical ancient pagans blamed their gods for their sins, 40

Will Rogers regarding two eras in American history—"the passing of the buffalo and the passing of the buck," 40

The evil monk Rasputin argued it was one's duty to sin because that brought greater forgiveness and joy, 40

Ernest Hemingway's sin was rationalized as "art," 41

Blasphemy

Thomas Hardy—"the President of the Immortals (in Aeschylean phrase) had ended his sport with Tess," 49

Stephen Crane's poem "God Is Cold," 49, 207

Change

Our skin bears testimony to our constant changes—pinch the skin on the back of your index finger and if you are six it will snap back in place, but if you're seventy . . . , 51

Character

George Fox's famous rejoinder and refusal to take oaths: "I say as the book says . . . how chance ye do not imprison the book for saying so," 224

Commitment

"The Lite Church," a parody on worship—the church which accommodated its worship and ministry to the selfish and uncommitted, 97

The origin of DV or *Deo Volente*, "God willing," 183

Compassion

D. L. Moody to man on "mountaintop" who had never won anyone to Christ, 75

How compassion demands action—"I'm sorry five pounds. How much are you sorry?" 99

Letter about a woman who comforted an abused boy who said in retrospect that was "the redeeming factor in his life," 143

Compassionless

Louis XV's rejection by the people because of his sins of *omission*—he did nothing, 185

Confession

D. Bonhoeffer describes confession as the profoundest kind of humiliation, 238, 239

The dangers of mutual confession, 239

Confrontation

The woman who successfully wrestled her friend away from sin, 251, 252

Confusion

The acronym *snafu* replaced by *fubb*, 136

Conscience

Upton Sinclair's ruse in reading James 5:16 to a group of ministers, attributing it to an anarchist, resulting in their declaring she should be deported, 189

Consistency

Correcting Thoreau's misquoted "Consistency is . . ." to "A foolish consistency . . . ," 144

Conversion

Billy Graham: "No man can be said to be truly converted to Christ who has not bent his will to Christ," 248, 249

Conviction

Upton Sinclair's ruse in reading James 5:16 to a group of ministers, attributing it to an anarchist, resulting in the ministers declaring she should be deported, 189

Courage
The gruesome martyrdom of missionaries Stan Dale and Phil Masters in Irian Jaya, 209, 210
George Fox's famous rejoinder and refusal to take oaths: "I say as the book says . . . how chance ye do not imprison the book for saying so," 224

Criticism
The man who waited to hear what the pastor would say when he hit his thumb, 72
John Calvin on the man who destroys the character of others under the pretext of zeal, 73
John Wesley's offer to cut off the tongue of a gossiping, critical lady, 73, 74
Byron's poem emphasizing that those who achieve will be criticized, 126
W. Wangerin on how our words can be like a spider's injection turning the insides of another to warm soup, which we then swill, 171
The young man who rationalized his cutting, critical tongue by saying he had the gift of prophecy—i.e., penetrating insight and an acerbic, confronting demeanor, 172

Deception
Perversion is "gay," abortion is "reproductive choice," etc., 76
Kansas state Senate chaplain's prayer for God's help in knowing which side was telling the truth, 219
New Yorker cartoon picturing jailed businessmen imagining their corruption "fell well within community standards," 219
Mortimer Adler regarding the dwindling concern for truth as a criterion for

contemporary literary excellence, 219, 220
Ernest Hemingway a liar, 220
The practice by *some* rabbis of deceptive oath-taking by avoiding reference to God's name, 222
Helmut Thielicke on how the formula "I swear by God" is an admission that one ordinarily is *not* truthful, 223
George MacDonald describes how, though he tried to be truthful, he still told many petty lies, 225

Delusion
A male butterfly will ignore a living female in favor of a cardboard one, if it is *bigger*, 150
The quintessential hippie who "believed in Christ" and rejected him a month later, 245, 246

Depravity
The evil monk Rasputin argued it was one's duty to sin because that brought greater forgiveness and joy, 40
Ernest Hemingway's sin was rationalized as "art," 41
The young priest who hearing his first confessions responded, "Wow," 42
Puritan William Beveridge's eloquent observations that he could do nothing without sinning, 176

Discrimination
The irony of the British Methodists' exclusion of the poor in 1846, 80
The Lord's "words" to a woman who was not accepted in church: "I've been trying to get into it myself for the last twenty years!," 81
Poem: "The rich man in his castle . . . ," 190

Dishonesty

Kansas state Senate chaplain's prayer for God's help in knowing which side was telling the truth, 219

New Yorker cartoon picturing jailed businessmen imagining their corruption "fell well within community standards," 219

Mortimer Adler regarding the dwindling concern for truth as a criterion for contemporary literary excellence, 219, 220

Ernest Hemingway a liar, 244

The practice by *some* rabbis of deceptive oath-taking by avoiding reference to God's name, 222

Helmut Thielicke on how the formula "I swear by God" is an admission that one ordinarily is *not* truthful, 223

Doubt

Unamuno: those who believe without doubt believe only in the idea of God, not God himself, 33

Earnestness

Charles Kingsley's poem which begins "Be earnest, earnest, earnest . . . ," 243

Ego

Nebuchadnezzar's elevation of self and his dramatic fall, 185

Elitism

The irony of the British Methodists' exclusion of the poor in 1846, 80

The Lord's "words" to a woman who was not accepted in church: "I've been trying to get into it myself for the last twenty years!" 81

How Charles Colson, as presidential aide, influenced his visiting White House guests through giving them the royal treatment, 83, 84

A sumptuous, exclusive Cambridge feast, 89, 90

Poem: "The rich man in his castle . . . ," 190

Envy

The man who asked that one of his eyes be put out, realizing that would mean the man he envied would lose both eyes, 135

Evangelism

F. F. Bruce felt that there was only one ministry higher than his: *evangelist*, 249, 250

Exaltation

Chaplain: "The first thing I would tell you, general, is that in Heaven you will not be a general," 32

Failure

Amy Carmichael's *unsuccessful* attempt to obtain healing for a friend through prayer, 229

Faith

Unamuno: those who believe without doubt believe only in the idea of God, not God himself, 33

How faith and works are like the two wings of a bird, 100

How John Wesley's faith produced amazing works, 102

Kierkegaard's story of ducks who gave verbal assent to their Duck Bible's teaching that they could fly, and then *waddled* home, 105

How true faith acts on God's Word as illustrated by one of Napoleon's corporals taking Napoleon's word that he was now a captain, 109

Martin Luther on how true faith results in good works, 111

How the wings of faith and works lift us from inglorious waddles to the glory of lives on the wing, 112, 113

Amy Carmichael's *unsuccessful* attempt to obtain healing for a friend through prayer, 229

Better to be Amy Carmichael and fall short of "success" than never venture out in faith, 233

Favoritism

How Charles Colson, as presidential aide, influenced his visiting White House guests through giving them the royal treatment, 83, 84

A sumptuous, exclusive Cambridge feast, 89, 90

Flattery

The difference between gossip and flattery, 126

Foolishness

The tragic folly of the ill-prepared Franklin Expedition, 139, 140

Glory

John Piper's realization of the glory of Christ's return as experienced in a jetliner during a nocturnal thunderstorm, 203, 204

God's Goodness

The "benedictions" before the *Shema* celebrate God's goodness, 50

God's immutable goodness illustrated by the fact that a musical A is an A today and will be 10,000 years from now, 51

Joseph Bayly's affirmation of God's goodness in his final article in *Eternity* magazine, 51

God's Immutability

God's immutable goodness illustrated by the fact that a musical A is an A today and will be 10,000 years from now, 51

God's Will

The origin of DV or *Deo Volente*, "God willing," 183

Gossip

John Calvin on the man who destroys the character of others under the pretext of zeal, 73

John Wesley's offer to cut off the tongue of a gossiping, critical lady, 73, 74

The incendiary power of the tongue as illustrated by the Great Chicago Fire, 124

How a gossiper's repentance cannot reclaim the damage done, as seen in the experience of a physician, 126

The "acceptable" civilities with which gossip is often introduced, 126

The difference between gossip and flattery, 126

W. Wangerin on how our words can be like a spider's injection turning the insides of another to warm soup, which we then swill, 171

C. H. Spurgeon regarding how people who have begun to doctrinally err are often driven further away by the unloving conduct of the church, 250

Grace

L. J. Ogilvie's experience of artesian joy in the midst of difficulties, 18

The "gravity of grace"—its ineluctable movement to the lowly and humble, 163

A painting of Niagara Falls captioned "more to follow," a fit emblem of the flood of God's grace, 158

Annie Johnson Flint's poem which begins "He giveth more grace when the burdens grow greater," 159

Guilt

The woman who blamed God for her seduction, 39, 40

The typical ancient pagans blamed their gods for their sins, 40

Will Rogers regarding two eras in American history—"the passing of the buffalo and the passing of the buck," 40

The evil monk Rasputin argued it was one's duty to sin because that brought greater forgiveness and joy, 40

Ernest Hemingway's sin was rationalized as "art," 41

How Conan Doyle's friends left town when he sent them an anonymous message: "Fly at once, all is discovered," 144

Happiness

The ostentatious wealth and extravagance of Malcolm Stevenson Forbes, Sr., 190

Survey reveals that more poor than affluent are "very satisfied with life," 190

Hatred

The New York congregation that fired its priest because they did not want to "pass the peace," 147

Christians who share Communion but scowl and and mistreat each other during the week, 147

Quarreling children's response: "Dad, we're playing church!" 148

Healing

Amy Carmichael's *unsuccessful* attempt to obtain healing for a friend through prayer, 229

Hedonism

Huxley's vision come true: people controlled by "inflicting pleasure," 149

Dr. Samuel Johnson on how no one has ever succeeded in pursuing selfish pleasure, 150, 151

C. S. Lewis' Screwtape admitting that God is the author of all pleasure, 151, 152

Pascal's argument that all men seek their own pleasure, without exception, 152

People controlled like marionettes by a thousand strings of pleasure, 155

Hoarding

Bertha Adams hoarded a million dollars while starving to death, 192

Honesty

Helmut Thielicke regarding how avoidance of a small fib may be a stronger confession of Christianity than a reasoned argument, 226

Humanism

Carl Henry regarding "the illusion that the human species is the sole crown of the cosmos . . . ," 163

Walker Percy's protagonist saying 100 percent are humanists, and 98 percent believe in God, 190

Humiliation

Bonhoeffer describes confession as the profoundest kind of humiliation, 238, 239

Humility

Chaplain: "The first thing I would tell you, general, is that in Heaven you will not be a general," 32

Abraham Lincoln's willingness to change a decision for which the Secretary of War had called him a "fool," 143

The woman who prayed that C. H. Spurgeon would be kept humble, but rejected his similar prayers for her because she was "not tempted to be proud," 160

Donald Grey Barnhouse: "Up is down!" 168, 169

Puritan William Beveridge's eloquent observations that he could do nothing without sinning, 176

Hypocrisy

How Rousseau, a self-proclaimed lover of mankind, mistreated his family and abandoned his children, 99

How Conan Doyle's friends left town when he sent them an anonymous message: "Fly at once, all is discovered," 144

Mickey Cohen's delusion that he could be a "Christian gangster," 167

Singing "How thank we all our God" while underpaying employees, 193

Inconsistency

How Rousseau, a self-proclaimed lover of mankind, mistreated his family and abandoned his children, 99

Influence

How Charles Colson, as presidential aide, influenced his visiting White House guests through giving them the royal treatment, 83, 84

The vast influence of Christian education director Henrietta Mears, 115

Howard Hendricks' account of an 83-year-old woman who taught junior high boys and had great results, 121

Innuendo

"Captain sober today," 126

Integrity

Dr. M. Babcock, a man who refused to compromise his personal ethics, 76

George Fox's famous rejoinder and refusal to take oaths: "I say as the book says . . . how chance ye do not imprison the book for saying so," 224

Helmut Thielicke regarding how avoidance of a small fib may be a stronger confession of Christianity than a reasoned argument, 226

Irreligious

Charles Colson's description of searching for the UN's chapel, and finding a "meditation room" with overhead shafts of light focused on a void— "the soul of the brave new world," 179, 180

Irreverence

Stephen Crane's poem "God Is Cold," 49, 207

Jealousy

The man who asked that one of his eyes be put out, realizing that would mean the man he envied would lose both eyes, 135

Joy

L. J. Ogilvie's experience of artesian joy in the midst of difficulties, 18

Judgment/Motivation

How the knowledge of future judgment energized and directed Amy Carmichael's missionary life, 93

Laughter

Oswald Sanders on laughter being a Christian virtue, 168

Listening

Eutychus' falling asleep in church dramatized, 55, 56

The humorous sights the pastor sees as people fall asleep in church, 56

Paul Tournier regarding most conversations being "dialogues of the deaf," 57

Adlai Stevenson: "I understand I am here to speak and you are to listen. Let's hope we both finish at the same time," 58

Modern man: "Lord, speak to me! You have sixty seconds," 58

The rabbis noted that we have one mouth guarded by a double row of teeth, but two ears that are always open, 59

Love

The power of one man's loving his neighbor as himself to change a prisoner-of-war camp, 91

Lust

A male butterfly will ignore a living female in favor of a cardboard one, if it is *bigger*, 150

Lying

Kansas state Senate chaplain's prayer for God's help in knowing which side was telling the truth, 219

New Yorker cartoon picturing jailed businessmen imagining their corruption "fell well within community standards," 219

Mortimer Adler regarding the dwindling concern for truth as a criterion for contemporary literary excellence, 219, 220

Ernest Hemingway a liar, 220

The practice by *some* rabbis of deceptive oath-taking by avoiding reference to God's name, 222

Helmut Thielicke on how the formula "I swear by God" is an admission that one ordinarily is *not* truthful, 223

George MacDonald describes how, though he tried to be truthful, he still told many petty lies, 225

Martyrdom

The gruesome martyrdom of missionaries Stan Dale and Phil Masters in Irian Jaya, 209, 210

Materialism

The ostentatious wealth and extravagance of Malcolm Stevenson Forbes Sr., 190

Survey reveals that more poor than affluent are "very satisfied with life," 190

Bertha Adams hoarded a million dollars while starving to death, 192

Rockefeller's *private* collection of art, "so much of the world's artistic imagination . . . upon the grass of one man's lawn," 194

Poem which begins "Christ stands at the bar of the world today . . . ," 196

"Keeping up with the Joneses": Buy things you don't need, 247

Maturity

Description of how parents, like God, must not intervene in all their children's problems, for that would retard their growth and maturity, 19, 20

A butterfly must not be aided in its struggle from the chrysalis, for if helped it will not develop the strength to live, 20

An oyster develops its pearls by covering its irritation with the most precious part of its being, 20

Poem which begins "When God wants to drill a man . . ." as it tracks the necessity of trials and testing to spiritual growth, 21

Poem which begins "My life is but a weaving between my Lord and me . . ." as it teaches how God weaves difficulties and joys into the tapestry of our lives, 23

Mercy

Letter about a woman who comforted an abused boy who said in retrospect that was "the redeeming factor in his life," 143

Mortality

The author's brush with death, 181

A chain of Scriptural similes illustrating the brevity of life, 182

Mike Mason's statement "Lives are the curliques of fire . . . ," 182

The emperors of Constantinople chose their tombstones at their coronations, 183

Our mayfly lives see only a miniscule bit of God's calendar, as the time is "near," 202

The relativity of the word "near" as seen in the contrasting viewpoints of a child and a grandmother, 202

Naiveté, Sin, Depravity

The young priest who hearing his first confessions responded, "Wow!" 42

Narcissism
John Ward's prayer asking that God
would protect his property, and do
with others' as he pleased, 151

Obedience
C. Swindoll's parable of an absent C.E.O.
whose messages were read by his employees, even studied, but never acted
upon—a parable of how so many treat
God's Word, 63, 64

Paradox
G. K. Chesterton: "Truth standing on its
head calling for attention," 31

Peace
St. Francis's prayer: "Lord, make me an
instrument . . . ," 142

Persecution
The gruesome martyrdom of missionaries
Stan Dale and Phil Masters in Irian
Jaya, 209
Annie Dillard: "If . . . you want to look
at the stars . . . darkness is required,"
215

Perseverance
How we toughen spiritually through trials,
like a seasoned fighter, 19

Perversion
Perversion is "gay," abortion is "reproductive choice," etc., 76

Pleasure
Huxley's vision come true: people controlled by "inflicting pleasure," 149
A male butterfly will ignore a living
female in favor of a cardboard one, if
it is *bigger*, 150
Dr. Samuel Johnson on how no one has
ever succeeded in pursuing selfish
pleasure, 150, 151

C. S. Lewis' Screwtape admitting that God
is the author of all pleasure, 151, 152
Pascal's argument that all men seek their
own pleasure, without exception, 152
People controlled like marionettes by a
thousand strings of pleasure, 155

Power
The vast influence of Christian education
director Henrietta Mears, 115
Howard Hendricks' account of an
83-year-old woman who taught junior
high boys and had great results, 121

Prayer
Eusebius' testimony that James' "knees
grew hard like a camel's," 16, 230
John Ward's prayer asking that God
would protect his property, and do
with others' what he pleased, 151
St. Chrysostom's driving, eloquent description of the power of prayer, 237
Passionate prayer as illustrated in the
lives of Jacob, Hannah, Ezra, Nehemiah, Paul, Epaphras, the importunate
widow, and Jesus, 242, 243

Pride
The woman who prayed that C. H.
Spurgeon would be kept humble, but
rejected his similar prayers for her
because she was "not tempted to be
proud," 160
Nebuchadnezzar's elevation of self and
his dramatic fall, 185

Purity
Dr. M. Babcock, a man who refused to
compromise his personal ethics, 76

Rationalizing
The young man who rationalized his cutting, critical tongue by saying he had
the gift of prophecy—i.e., penetrating
insight and an acerbic, confronting
demeanor, 172

Reading
Some of us imagine that reading will course virtue through our souls, much as the primitives thought they could imbibe others' powers by drinking their blood, 65

Rejection
Louis XV's rejection by the people because of his sins of *omission*—he did nothing, 185

Repentance
Mickey Cohen's delusion that he could be a "Christian gangster," 167
The penetrating question: "Did she ever get any sorrow?" 168
Billy Graham: "No man can be said to be truly converted to Christ who has not bent his will to Christ . . . ," 249

Return of Christ
John Piper's realization of the glory of Christ's return as experienced in a jetliner during a nocturnal thunderstorm, 203, 204

Sacrifice
W. Wangerin on how a starving spider will release venomous digestive fluids into her own body, so that her young can feed on her, 171

Secularism
Stephen Crane's poem "God Is Cold," 49, 207
Lord Melbourne's objection to religion's invading public life, 180
Walker Percy's protagonist saying 100 percent are humanists, and 98 percent believe in God, 180

Selfishness
Dr. Samuel Johnson on how no one has ever succeeded in pursuing selfish pleasure, 150, 151

John Ward's prayer asking that God would protect his property, and do with others' as he pleased, 151
Bertha Adams hoarded a million dollars while starving to death, 192
Singing "How thank we all our God" while underpaying employees, 193

Sin
The evil monk Rasputin argued it was one's duty to sin because that brought greater forgiveness and joy, 40
Ernest Hemingway's sin was rationalized as "art," 41
The young priest who hearing his first confessions responded, "Wow!" 42
Puritan William Beveridge's eloquent observations that he could do nothing without sinning, 176
Louis XV's rejection by the people because of his sins of *omission*—he did nothing, 185
Bonhoeffer describes how sin isolates believers from one another, 239

Social Conscience
The statue of Eros dedicated to Lord Shaftesbury, lover of the poor and disenfranchised, 75

Spiritual Growth
Annie Dillard: "If . . . you want to look at the stars . . . darkness is required," 215

Submission
The origin of DV or *Deo Volente*, "God willing," 183

Suffering
L. J. Ogilvie's experience of artesian joy in the midst of difficulties, 18
Description of how parents, like God, must not intervene in all their children's problems, for that would retard their growth and maturity, 19, 20

A butterfly must not be aided in its
struggle from the chrysalis, for if
helped it will not develop the strength
to live, 20

An oyster develops its pearls by covering
its irritation with most the precious
part of its being, 20

Poem which begins "When God wants to
drill a man . . ." as it tracks the necessity of trials and testing to spiritual
growth, 21

Poem which begins "My life is but
a weaving between my Lord and
me . . ." as it teaches how God weaves
difficulties and joys into the tapestry of
our lives, 23

The gruesome martyrdom of missionaries
Stan Dale and Phil Masters in Irian
Jaya, 209, 210

M. Muggeridge's argument that if suffering was taken from the world, it would
be a dreadful place, 210

Annie Dillard: "If . . . you want to look at
the stars . . . darkness is required," 215

Teachability

Abraham Lincoln's willingness to change
a decision for which the Secretary of
War had called him a "fool," 143

Teaching

The vast influence of Christian education
director Henrietta Mears, 115

Professor Allan Bloom on the dangers that
come to an adult teacher who spends
his life in the company of undergradu-
ates, 117

Howard Hendricks' account of an
83-year-old woman who taught junior
high boys and had great results, 121

Temporality

Los Angeles' *Santa Ana* wind illustrates
the temporality illustrated by the
Scriptural example of the flower that
passes away, 35

The *Psalter Hymnal's* poem which begins
"Man is like a tender flower . . . ," 35

The mayfly (*ephemeron*) whose life is
only a day, 35

Our mayfly lives see only a miniscule
bit of God's calendar, as the time is
"near," 202

The relativity of the word "near" as seen
in the contrasting viewpoints of a child
and a grandmother, 202

Temptation

How an old smallmouth bass was
"dragged away and enticed" by his
desires, 42, 43

Bonhoeffer on how when we are in the
grip of temptation "God is quite unreal
to us, he loses all reality . . . ," 43

Testing

How we toughen spiritually through trials,
like a seasoned fighter, 19

Description of how parents, like God,
must not intervene in all their children's problems, for that would retard
their growth and maturity, 19

A butterfly must not be aided in its struggle from the chrysalis, for if helped it
will not develop the strength to live, 20

An oyster develops its pearls by covering
its irritation with the most precious
part of its being, 20

Poem which begins "When God wants to
drill a man . . ." as it tracks the necessity of trials and testing to spiritual
growth, 21

Poem which begins "My life is but
a weaving between my Lord and
me . . ." as it teaches how God weaves
difficulties and joys into the tapestry of
our lives, 23

Time

Our mayfly lives see only a miniscule
bit of God's calendar, as the time is
"near," 202

The relativity of the word "near" as seen
in the contrasting viewpoints of a child
and a grandmother, 202

The Tongue
John Calvin on the man who destroys the
character of others under the pretext of
zeal, 73
John Wesley's offer to cut off the tongue
of a gossiping, critical lady, 73, 74
Poem regarding the tongue which ends
"Who keeps the tongue doth keep his
soul," 74
The incendiary power of the tongue as
illustrated by the Great Chicago Fire,
124
How a gossiper's repentance cannot reclaim the damage done, as seen in the
experience of a physician, 126
The "acceptable" civilities with which
gossip is often introduced, 126
How man can tame every animal (whales,
lions, eagles, cobras) but not the
tongue, 127
W. Wangerin on how our words can be
like a spider's injection turning the insides of another to warm soup, which
we then swill, 171
The young man who rationalized his cutting, critical tongue by saying he had
the gift of prophecy—i.e., penetrating
insight and an acerbic, confronting
demeanor, 172
C. H. Spurgeon regarding how people
who have begun to doctrinally err
are often driven further away by the
unloving conduct of the church, 250

Transformation
The power of one man's loving his neighbor as himself to change a prisoner-of-
war camp, 91

Transitoriness
Los Angeles' *Santa Ana* wind illustrates
the temporality illustrated by the

Scriptural example of the flower that
passes away, 35
The *Psalter Hymnal*'s poem which
begins "Man is like a tender flower . . . ," 35
The mayfly (*ephemeron*) whose life is
only a day, 35

Trials
L. J. Ogilvie's experience of artesian joy
in the midst of difficulties, 18
How we toughen spiritually through trials,
like a seasoned fighter, 19
Description of how parents, like God,
must not intervene in all their children's problems, for that would retard
their growth and maturity, 19
A butterfly must not be aided in its
struggle from the chrysalis, for it
helped it will not develop the strength
to live, 20
An oyster develops its pearls by covering
its irritation with the most precious
part of its being, 20
Poem which begins "When God wants to
drill a man . . ." as it tracks the necessity of trials and testing to spiritual
growth, 21
Poem which begins "My life is but
a weaving between my Lord and
me . . ." as it teaches how God weaves
difficulties and joys into the tapestry of
our lives, 23

Truth
George MacDonald describes how,
though he tried to be truthful, he still
told many petty lies, 225
Helmut Thielicke regarding how avoidance of a small fib may be a stronger
confession of Christianity than a
reasoned argument, 226

Truthfulness
George Fox's famous rejoinder and refusal to take oaths: "I say as the book says

. . . how chance ye do not imprison the book for saying so," 224

Unforgiveness
The New York congregation that fired the priest because they did not want to "pass the peace," 147

Unpreparedness
The tragic folly of the ill-prepared Franklin Expedition, 139, 140

Wealth
The ostentatious wealth and extravagance of Malcolm Stevenson Forbes Sr., 190
Some rich are notable saints, 190
Bertha Adams hoarded a million dollars while starving to death, 192
Rockefeller's *private* collection of art, "so much of the world's artistic imagination . . . upon the grass of one man's lawn," 194
Poem which begins "Christ stands at the bar of the world today . . . ," 196

Wisdom
Allan Bloom regarding how his grandparents, who lacked university degrees, had more practical wisdom for living than their Ph.D., M.D. grandchildren, 24, 25
Einstein, brilliant as he was, lacked an essential element of wisdom: *fear of God*, 26
Wisdom is not superior knowledge, but rather the ability to do the right thing,

as illustrated by the workings of a British railway station, 131

Word of God
The witch doctor who destroyed a missionary's mirror because she did not want it to make ugly faces at her anymore! 65

Works
How faith and works are like the two wings of a bird, 100
How John Wesley's faith produced amazing works, 102
Kierkegaard's story of ducks who gave verbal assent to their Duck Bible's teaching that they could fly, and then *waddled* home, 105
How true faith acts on God's Word as illustrated by one of Napoleon's corporals taking Napoleon's word that he was now a captain, 109
Martin Luther on how true faith results in good works, 111
How the wings of faith and works lift us from inglorious waddles to the glory of lives on the wing, 112, 113

Worship
"The Lite Church," a parody on the church which accommodates its worship and ministry to the selfish and uncommitted, 97

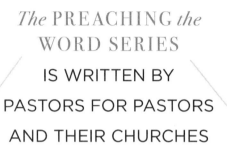

The PREACHING *the*
WORD SERIES

IS WRITTEN BY

PASTORS FOR PASTORS

AND THEIR CHURCHES